POINT ME TO THE SKIES

POINT ME
TO THE SKIES

The amazing story of Joan Wales

Ronald Clements

MONARCH
BOOKS

Oxford, UK & Grand Rapids, Michigan, USA

Sevenoaks, UK

First published in the UK in 2006 by Monarch Books
(a publishing imprint of Lion Hudson plc) and OMF International.

Monarch Books, Mayfield House, 256 Banbury Road, Oxford
OX2 7DH. Tel: +44 (0)1865 302750 Fax: +44 (0)1865 302757
Email: monarch@lionhudson.com. www.lionhudson.com

OMF International, Station Approach, Borough Green, Sevenoaks, Kent
TN15 8BG. Tel: +44 (0)1732 887299 email: omf@omf.org.uk
www.omf.org.uk

ISBN: 978-1-85424-804-6 (UK)
ISBN: 978-0-8254-6157-6 (USA)

Distributed by:
UK: Marston Book Services Ltd, PO Box 269, Abingdon, Oxon OX14 4YN;
USA: Kregel Publications, PO Box 2607, Grand Rapids, Michigan 49501

British Library Cataloguing Data
A catalogue record for this book is available from the British Library.

Printed and bound in Great Britain by Cox & Wyman Ltd, Reading.

OMF International works in most East Asian countries, and among East Asian peoples around the world. It was founded by James Hudson Taylor in 1865 as the China Inland Mission. Our purpose is to glorify God through the urgent evangelisation of East Asia's billions.

In line with this, OMF Publishing seeks to motivate and equip Christians to make disciples of all peoples.

Publications include:

• stories and biographies showing God at work in East Asia
• the biblical basis of mission and mission issues
• the growth and development of the church in Asia
• studies of Asian culture and religion

Books, booklets, articles and free downloads can be found on our website at www.omf.org

Addresses for OMF English-speaking centres can be found on page 6.

English-Speaking OMF Centres

Australia: PO Box 849, Epping, NSW 1710
Tel: 02 9868 4777 email: au@omf.net www.au.omf.org

Canada: 5155 Spectrum Way, Building 21, Mississauga, ONT L4W 5A1
Toll free: 1 888 657 8010 email: omfcanada@omf.ca www.ca.omf.org

Hong Kong: PO Box 70505, Kowloon Central PO, Hong Kong
Tel: 852 2398 1823 email: hk@omf.net www.omf.org.hk

Malaysia: 3A Jalan Nipah, off Jalan Ampang, 55000, Kuala Lumpur
Tel: 603 4257 4263 email: my@omf.net www.my.omf.org

New Zealand: PO Box 10159, Dominion Road, Balmoral, Auckland, 1030
Tel: 09 630 5778 email: omfnz@omf.net www.nz.omf.org

Philippines: QCCPO Box 1997–1159, 1100 Quezon City, M.M.
Tel: 632 951 0782 email: ph-hc@omf.net www.omf.org

Singapore: 2 Cluny Road, Singapore 259570
Tel: 65 6475 4592 email: sno@omf.net www.sg.omf.org

UK: Station Approach, Borough Green, Sevenoaks, Kent TN15 8BG
Tel: 01732 887299 email: omf@omf.org.uk www.omf.org.uk

USA: 10 West Dry Creek Circle, Littleton, CO 80120-4413
Toll free: 1 800 422 5330 email: omfus@omf.org www.us.omf.org

OMF International Headquarters: 2 Cluny Road, Singapore 259570
Tel: 65 6319 4550 email: ihq@omf.net www.omf.org

For Joan

and the Nosu of Daliangshan

'Shine through the gloom, and point me to the skies'

Henry Francis Lyte
Abide with me

Preface

This book both begins and began with a journey. In May 2004 I was travelling to North Wales to speak at a conference. The delegates were predominantly young Christians who were going to East Asia for the summer – contributing to projects for the poor and disadvantaged, getting involved in outreach to students, teaching English, working with churches.

My sole companion, in a red Ford Fiesta which ground out the miles to and from Kent, was the oldest participant at the conference. At eighty-seven, Joan Wales was revisiting China, joining an international team to teach English to 6 to 13 year olds in a remote mountainous region of south Sichuan Province. Joan was no stranger to the area, she had served there as a missionary after the Second World War. Now she was returning each summer to share her skills as a teacher.

If you met Joan in the supermarket adjacent to her home or happened to chat with her at church one Sunday, you would probably part with the impression of a diminutive – she stands no taller than five foot – elderly but active, considerate woman who is unmistakably in love with her Lord. Her natural modesty would leave the reality of an extraordinary life hidden from you.

Knowing something of Joan's story from Jim Broomhall's writings and my own involvement in co-ordinating her recent trips to China, I made the most of our journey together – what had taken her to China in

1945, how had her family reacted, who had been her companions, were there any people she had known in the 1940s who still lived in the mountains?

The story Joan told me had a resonance with issues I now see young Christians struggling with – does God guide, what happens when things don't work out? Joan's story was not one of old-style triumphal missionary endeavour, but had been borne out of family sadness and repeated setbacks. Some may have viewed her departure from China in 1951 as the cheerless conclusion to a misguided vision. God, as we learn, perceived things differently.

'You should write this down, Joan,' I said. 'No-one would be interested in my story,' was her immediate response. I assured her that they would and we left the matter there.

A year later, I had relinquished my position as a China consultant in the belief that God had other purposes for my life. Unexpectedly, the future I envisaged had not materialised. I rang Joan and offered to write her story.

'Please take time to think about it,' I suggested.

'No,' she replied, 'I have already decided. My answer is yes. I would like you to write my story.'

And so I have.

Foreword

"Long obedience in the same direction". There is a generation of China missionaries whose service and testimonies are flesh and bones outworking of Eugene Peterson's evocative phrase. They heard God, pressed through numerous setbacks and challenges, and fulfilled the call of God on their lives. This book is about one such person, Joan Wales. It portrays, in a straight-forward but nonetheless challenging way, her obedience to God's call, first of all to China and then, more specifically, to the people group who in her day were called the Nosu.

Such a testimony raises many questions in the twenty-first century. With the 'pick-a-mix' spirituality of this generation, how many consider that they may have a 'destiny' that is fore-ordained by God? Or more pertinent, that such a destiny might take a lifetime to fulfil and that it might involve a hiatus of several decades in the middle? With our "instant" approach to life, do we lack the stick-ability of former generations? Have we replaced former ways of reaching the un-evangelised world simply through short-term teams and long-range missiles of radio and VCD? And what of the rigours of language study and cultural immersion to gain the tools necessary for heart to heart communication?

Against the backdrop of Communist revolution in China, a small team went to a remote, hostile area seeking to win a despised, opium-besotted people group to Christ. Because of the war, the team had already endured frustrating delay, and post-war China was a dangerous and unpredictable place. Inflation was rampant, communications difficult and the people they were attempting to reach were considered "un-tameable". Yet the team persevered, through medical care won acceptance and through building a clinic acquired a toe-hold in their target community. Yet after all that, barely had the work begun than the new atheistic government shut it down and expelled the missionary team – a story repeated all over China at that time. Was it not all a huge waste of time, money, talent and prayer? Not from God's perspective. He had merely called them to be faithful to His leading and, through prayer and fasting, they had seen a small nucleus of believers won to Christ through their witness. When the fires of persecution came, as they did right across China, it was those who truly knew Christ who continued to stand and who became the backbone of the church in later years. The results proclaim that "God's work done in God's ways never lack His means" - nor His blessing.

This book brings before us other challenges. Though forced to leave China after such a short time, Joan Wales continued to carry the needs of that group in her heart over seven decades, even while taking up other missionary work in the meantime, knowing it was God Himself who had placed the responsibility on her. As soon as the door opened again for foreigners to return to China, Jim Broomhall (her project leader) and Joan returned to the area they had left and were encouraged to see that God had indeed been at work all that time. Prayer had been the means of watering the seed that had been sown.

Today, with many of China's minority groups still unreached or without a body of believers in their midst, not to mention hundreds of other unreached groups across the world, where are those who will accept a similar call to prayer and find their destiny in that?

Many years ago a well known believer in the UK sent me the draft of a book he was writing on the modern house church movement in China. Part of his thesis was that this movement, which numbered even then in the tens of millions, had very little to do with the missionary movement of generations past. Rather, he contended, the missionaries had been a well intentioned but rather ineffectual group. I wrote to him, after reading the draft, to say that such a view was quite untrue to the facts of the church in China. Indeed, frequent evidence makes it clear that God has more often than not built upon the faithful and costly labours of those early pioneers, which has led now to an indigenous church of great size. God's word will not fail. Our labours are never in vain in the Lord.

I fear it would be all too possible for the modern reader to glance with mere passing interest at this book, and then to move on to something that might seem more racy and immediate, more "contemporary". That would be a mistake. There are lessons here in Joan's life for us all, lessons as valuable as they were hard won. If you are one such browser, may I commend this book to you for more than browsing! You will be the richer for it.

The challenge of the unreached today is as great as ever. There could be no greater tribute to Joan's life and witness and obedience than that this book be used to raise up a new generation of those who would go out in costly obedience in Jesus' name and that others would devote themselves to prayer. Consider the book as a baton. Take it in your hand. Run with it.

Ross Paterson, Antioch Missions/Chinese Church Support Ministries

Author's Note

The story presented here comes primarily from Joan Wales' recollections of her life and from her diaries. I have benefited from the reminiscences of Jim and Janet Broomhall's daughters, Pauline, Margie and Joy, and from access to family letters and photographs, in describing events in Leshan and Daliangshan (1947-1951, 1987/8 and 1991). H.W. Oldham's book *Beryl* and the letters of Dorothy Jones and Edith Cork, 1945/1946, provided insights into CIM missionary training and language study in Leshan.

Jim Broomhall contributed several articles for the China Inland Mission publication *China's Millions* while working in Daliangshan and related his story of the work amongst the Nosu in *Strong Man's Prey* (1953). Ruth Dix also depicted events in Zhuhe in *China's Millions*. Ralph Covell's book *Mission Impossible* (1990) describes missionary activity in the Xichang area in the late 1940s. *Emerging from Primitivity – travels in Liangshan Mountains* by Zhong Xiu gives a Chinese perspective on the situation in Daliangshan before and after Liberation. Descriptions of China since the mid 1980s are drawn from my experience of living in China and my journeys to Xichang and Zhaojue. A significant amount of detail has come from CIM/OMF archives and from books on China, of which there now appears to be no end.

All the elements of this story are true incidents and as such present a biography of Joan's life. However, I have chosen to present my research in a story form rather than adopting a strict reporting style. Some events, while based on reported facts, did not, therefore, take place precisely as described. However, the 'additional' material does reflect prevailing attitudes, conversations that did take place and the experiences of others in similar circumstances.

China recognises fifty-five Minority groups. The natives of Daliangshan are part of the Yi Minority, an ethnic group that can be found in Sichuan, Guizhou and Yunnan Provinces. The term 'Nosu' is a traditional name and was the name used by the CIM team. I understand that people in Daliangshan prefer this term and I have therefore retained it here. The term could also be rendered 'Nuosu' but for ease of reading I have used the simpler spelling.

On frequent occasions I have used the term 'Chinese' to refer to the majority Han Chinese (92% of the population), rather than pedantically writing 'Han Chinese' throughout the book. I do recognise, of course, that the term 'Chinese' is applicable to all citizens of China.

Wherever possible I have used Pinyin, the modern Romanisation of Mandarin, for Chinese words. 'Yangtze', which is the spelling usually used in the West, is an exception to this approach. Nosu names and words have been a particular problem and, with no expertise in this area, I have considered it sufficient to represent the words in a way that the reader would have heard them, using or adapting the spellings employed by Jim Broomhall.

It is not possible to accurately present the names of the Chinese and Nosu within the story. There are some people whose surnames I know but have no knowledge of their given names and vice versa. Without the Chinese characters for a name, the Pinyin is not certain. The same spellings in Romanisation systems used in the past can be rendered in alternative ways in Pinyin. My overriding criteria for presenting names has been to simplify or change them to render them more readable. This has also helped to protect people's identity. The reader should be reassured, however, that there are no invented characters in the story.

Acknowledgements

No book is complete without the valuable input of others. I have been extremely fortunate to be able to interview the daughters of Jim and Janet Broomhall, Pauline, Margie and Joy, who appear in this book and provided very helpful insights into the lives of their parents. Dorothy Jones kindly lent me the letters she had written to her parents from China.

I have enjoyed the enthusiastic support of OMF International UK in getting this book published. Rebecca Brooker, Books Publishing Manager, has been a notable source of assistance. Being given ready access to letters, photos and other material from the CIM archives has been of great benefit in my research. The team at Monarch have been encouraging and patient as the first submission of the opening chapters developed into the final manuscript. I am also grateful to Jane and Ian Tandy, Ross and Christine Paterson, David Hails and Faith Cook, who have been generous with their help and comments.

There is a tradition in our home that any serious piece of work needs to go through the family mill of constructive criticism – a refining process that cheers the manufacturers of 'red ink' – all within the context of encouragement to greater things. Bethan has taken particular delight in reducing her father's efforts at literature to a heap of alterations. Emma, Shona, and my wife Anne have proved equally skilled at spotting my literary errors. More importantly, all of them have been the constant support I needed when I doubted my abilities or my decision to write.

I have drawn conclusions from my research and, from these, painted my impressions of the real people who shared Joan's story. Where others, who knew them better, would differ in their descriptions then I can only apologise for the inadequacies of my own attempt. The story presented here remains my responsibility with all its elements of truth, interpretation and imagination.

Finally, my thanks are to Joan herself. Joan graciously and patiently allowed me to record her life history, answered countless questions, and provided her comments on and corrections to the final manuscript. Inevitably, she is at the heart of the story. However, it has long been Joan's desire to point to Jesus, not to herself, and that, ultimately, is the purpose of this book.

Contents

23 January 1951

Chapter 1   25

July 1926

Chapter 2   39

Chapter 3   50

Chapter 4   62

Chapter 5   72

Chapter 6   86

Chapter 7   102

Chapter 8   113

Chapter 9   122

Chapter 10   137

Chapter 11   148

Chapter 12   157

Chapter 13   170

Chapter 14   179

Chapter 15   188

Chapter 16	197
Chapter 17	209
Chapter 18	221
Chapter 19	222
Chapter 20	244
Chapter 21	253

23 January 1951

Chapter 22	259
Chapter 23	268
Chapter 24	279

January 1988

Chapter 25	285
Chapter 26	297
Chapter 27	305
Chapter 28	309
Notes	313
Glossary	316
Name List	318

23 January 1951

Chapter 1

'If they go we may as well die.'

NOSU CHIEF, DECEMBER 1950

The fort parapet was dark with silence. A long line of ill-
clad men and women pulled the poor shelter of their blue-
dyed cloaks around them, shielding themselves against the
harsh, frigid cold, and stared down into our compound.
Only their eyes betrayed their emotions. We, the *Yari*, were
leaving.

The Communist officials milling about me in their
padded jackets ignored the brooding hostility of the Nosu
perched above them. Chinese soldiers stood at the clinic
doors with fixed bayonets prepared to quell trouble.

'Joan...'

I looked up from the bag I was packing.

'...Wang wants to go through the medical inventory
again.'

'Again?' I queried.

'A final check, he says.' Jim shrugged his shoulders.

'Do I unpack it?'

'Not if you can help it. We need to go.' Jim glanced across to the mountain range that barred our path west. The outline barely registered above the wall parapet in the enveloping mists. Swathes of white marked snowfall. Ice-encrusted paths inched their exposed passage around steep inclines. January was a grim time to contemplate such a journey. If dark began to close in before we reached our shelter for the night the mules would be tested as the trails narrowed to mere ledges above 500-foot drops.

The Communist 'liberation' was driving us from China, the land to which God had called us. The advances we had gained through patient prayer and perseverance amongst the Nosu minority people of Xikang Province[1] were being swept away. Our team of four British missionaries partnered by Chinese and Nosu under the leadership of Dr Jim Broomhall, an accomplished surgeon, had been disbanded. Only our interpreter, Zhao, remained with us. Jim had dispensed medicines, performed operations and established a clinic. He had wanted to introduce community health programmes, allowing basic medical aid to be provided by the Nosu for the Nosu. Now none of this could continue; we had to leave.

Hong Kong, our ultimate destination, lay 900 miles away and many more by the route we must take. Our main medical centre had been set up at Zhaojue, an isolated, poverty-stricken location in Daliangshan – the aptly named 'Great Cold Mountains'. It would be four days by mule to get to the nearest Chinese administrative centre, a small walled town called Xichang. How long would it be before we arrived in Hong Kong? Jim reckoned two, perhaps three months. However, his calculations assumed we would not be detained significantly along the route. We had heard of other missionaries under house arrest, unable to get to the border.

We did not believe that we had chosen the wrong course but, as I surveyed our packages strewn around the courtyard, God's purposes seemed as masked in mist as the mountains we must cross.

I hurried into the clinic. 'Wang Comrade?'

'Please check this list.' The official was polite and less hostile than others, if not a little eager. He was barely taller than my petite five foot nothing but wielded more authority than you might expect on first meeting. He, along with a posse of Communist administrators, had arrived from Xichang just before Christmas; part of his task now was to ensure we left the area as soon as was feasible.

He held out the handwritten notes Jim had compiled. I moved to the poor light from the open door and read them carefully, though the contents were more than familiar. 'Smallpox vaccine...' Jim had given his youngest daughter, one-year-old Joy, her inoculation this morning. '...Streptomycin, seventeen bottles...' for the abscess on my arm, which had now healed; the medication had never been used because insufficient doses had arrived from Shanghai. 'Santonin... penicillin... scalpels... syringes... It is correct, Wang Comrade.' The official nodded his thanks, retrieved the papers and moved away to check something else.

My radio stood on the table. And next to it Janet's sewing machine. The radio had been both a luxury and a Godsend. Although we used it no more than a few minutes each day, it brought us news of what was happening in China and at home in Britain. It had been bought in Xichang, our 'base camp', with money sent by Aunt Hilda, my mother's sister.

I reached down and touched it as though it could transmit memories back to England. My mother... what would she have thought of her daughter? Now a 'pioneer missionary' in the wastelands of China, closer to the wilderness of Tibet than the sophistication of Shanghai, so far from the comforts and affluence of the south of England where I grew up. A woman with my own opinion on what I should do and where I should go. Nevertheless she would have been pleased that God had directed my steps to Zhaojue. Of that I was in no doubt. After all, my foremost memories of her were those times spent 'talking with Jesus'.

Would Janet regret leaving the sewing machine, a wedding present from Jim? Later perhaps. The immediate dangers of transporting four daughters under eight years old by mule over the precarious steeps and hazardous descents would be disquieting her and Jim far more. The strain was evident in their gaunt, troubled faces. Both had been shocked by the report of plans to kill us en route and kidnap the girls.

It was the Chinese teenager Baodan, one of the new Christians, who between sobs late on Christmas Day had shaken Jim with the story of an ambush. 'They are going to force you out. But you won't make it to Xichang.'

'What do you mean?' Jim asked, though the implication was plain.

'They will shoot you... on the mountain pass.'

'Who told you this?' Jim had no reason to believe Baodan was making the report up – her tears were more than proof.

'The Communists told my father...' She paused. 'They will sell the children...'

It was unlikely that the authorities would carry out such a plan themselves but the threat was certainly credible. Though we had fostered good relationships with Nosu in the immediate area, there were others in less friendly clans who would be willing to perform the deed for payment or in return for favours. The Nosu were notorious for their violence. Their community was riven by internecine clan warfare and many of the tribes lived in undisguised hostility towards the Han Chinese. We would not be the first foreigners to perish by a bullet from one of the rifles Nosu men always carried.

Slavery was also no myth. Over centuries of hostility, in a savage hierarchy of castes, the superior 'Black' Nosu had coerced their 'White' inferior, a fusion of subjugated Han Chinese and other minorities, into serfdom. Hapless Chinese from the valleys were still being captured and reduced to slavery. We too had lived in uncertainty, never entirely free from the threat of kidnap. There were rumours that American airmen who survived crash landings over the mountains were kept in captivity, though this had never been proved.

We had listened to Jim's account of the conversation and prayed. Our trust had to be in God no matter what happened to us. We accepted God's sovereignty in death as well as in life.

Ruth Dix looked in. 'The mules are being loaded. Have you anything else?' Ruth was the oldest member of the team, certainly an 'old China hand' as far as I, the newest recruit, was concerned. She combined that hallowed status of 'senior missionary' with humility and versatility. Ruth was not one to let seniority keep her from hard work in whatever form it presented itself.

I shook my head. The radio must remain and service new masters. 'Do I take these posters down?' There were still two or three posters pasted around the clinic. Bible texts. In recent months, as restrictions on our movements tightened, we had responded in Communist fashion with a poster campaign. At the centre of the fort the magistrates' building boasted banners proclaiming the promise of religious freedom, 'Zong Jiao Zi You' – a platitude with increasingly little substance, decorating crumbling walls. We had plastered the gospel about our buildings with abandon!

'If we are to be invaded, the intruders may as well have something edifying to read,' contended Ruth. 'Leave them. I doubt they will remain there long but you never can tell what God's Word alone can achieve.'

The Nosu lining the walls followed my movements with their eyes as I emerged from the clinic. Beyond them was Baodan with her sister, Baoli, and a group of three or four other Chinese girls, all new Christians. I waved a hand in the direction of the corner of our compound where the wall had broken away. They picked their way gingerly past the Nosu and down the steps from the rampart. 'Teacher

Wei,' whispered Baoli, 'we don't want you to go. But we will follow Jesus whatever happens. One hundred percent for him!'

I looked into their faces, pausing deliberately over each one, fixing my memory of them. I had wondered how these moments of farewell would feel. It was less than ten days since we had been asked to pack and leave, yet I had imagined our parting untold times. Now it was happening. I needed to live out each moment intentionally, etching appearance and conversation into portraits I would always retain.

I read a Bible passage and we quietly sang choruses, before praying. 'God is able to keep you,' I reassured them. 'I will pray for you. You mustn't be afraid. Talk to Jesus and he will help you.'

Finally the pack animals were ready, our party assembled for departure. Ruth stood with Blackie and Belinda, the mules she and Jim would ride. Janet and I had hired mounts. Zhao, as interpreter, Zitu, one of our leprosy patients, and Mrs Yang, who had cared for the Broomhall children, would come with us the entire journey. Agu, a recognised Nosu leader, accompanied by the son of another chief, had offered to escort us a day's ride. Their servants would then take us to the borders of 'Nosuland' as a guarantee that no Nosu would attack us lightly.

Janet hurried around, checking the children were well protected with their padded jackets over layers of clothing. Jan, aged seven, and Pauline, five years old, were standing motionless together on the edge of the group; passive observers of the activity, their pale faces betrayed inner unspoken apprehension. The toddlers, Margie and Joy, cheeks reddened by the raw cold, were already strapped in wicker panniers to the backs of the men. Jim gave the older girls a hug before lifting them up and setting them down into crude wooden boxes slung either side of one of the mules.

'Ruth, can you just check the hot-water bottles are in place? I think Jan's has slipped too far down. Make sure it's secure.'

Janet reached up to Margie and touched her cheeks. 'Hush, Margie... We're going on a long ride. Don't worry.' Margie was three years old. Old enough to know great changes were taking place, too young to comprehend what was ahead.

Ruth settled Jan again and slipped a small package of food into her hand. 'This one's for you and there's one for Pauline. Don't eat them in a hurry. It will be a good few hours before supper.'

'Ready?' asked Jim. 'Let's walk. At least until we get beyond the fort gates. This may be a bit ignominious but we aren't fleeing our post.' He led the way, guiding Belinda past the guards and onto the track that served as a road between the gates in the fort walls. The fortress was a crude defence built by the rulers of the Qing Dynasty[2] as a haven for the local Chinese whenever trouble erupted with the Nosu, a not infrequent occurrence. Less than ten years ago over 3,000 Chinese had occupied the Zhaojue valley with their troops. Now only a few families and officials remained. Agu and his Ba'chie clan had driven the majority away in a belligerent revolt.

The high stone walls enveloped a square area of rough ground as long and wide as the length of two football pitches. Apart from the relatively prestigious magistrates' halls, the barracks and our compound, there were few other buildings, most of which were in poor repair. In local parlance it was said that a single lamp could light the whole town. People could shout to their neighbours from their homes and expect a response.

The Nosu filtered down from the walls and 200 lined the route as our procession headed for the gate. They were notably distinct from the Han Chinese, with strong aquiline features and swarthy skin. Both sexes wore the dark blue cloaks. The women had headscarves perched high on their heads, some displaying their distinctive, bulky silver earrings. Here and there I saw one or two had donned their better clothes, colourful high-collared tunics over heavy pleated skirts. The men wore turbans, neatly wound around their black hair and coiled into a prominent horn above the brow.

Many of the Nosu had tears in their eyes as we moved slowly through their ranks. Our leaving had not been their choice, nor ours. Whatever suspicions the clans around Zhaojue had of the *Yari* who had taken up residence less than three years before, these had subsided with the knowledge that their medicine was effective. Jim's expert medical care for rich and poor alike, for opium addict and leprosy sufferer, clan chief and serf, Chinese and Nosu, Communist and Nationalist had broken down barriers, not raised them.

Outside the gate Baodan, Baoli and the teenagers I had prayed with were waiting with the other believers. Mrs Qiang, who had given her life to Jesus the previous evening, was there. And Aji, another teenager and one of the very few Nosu to respond. Just half of our thirty recent converts were now left in the area. Hardly any men. The Nationalist soldiers we had shared our faith with had abandoned their post before the Communists arrived, or been marched away as a defeated army.

With the news of our imminent departure had come the same question over and again: 'Who will help us once you have gone?' Even from the nefarious hag, who occupied the hovel by the north gate and was now standing to one side watching and wailing, 'What shall we do now?'

There were no simple answers. 'Help one another. Trust in God.' Were these adequate replies to people who knew so little? Could they be sufficient for eternity? Could we, let alone these new believers, comprehend God's purpose in bringing to an end a work that had been so long in the planning and so short in the implementation?

We paused and prayed with them. Baoli brushed away her tears. 'We must sing!'

They sang the songs we had taught them so recently:

'Joyful, joyful will the meeting be,
When from sin our hearts are pure and free,
And we shall gather, Saviour, with thee,
In our eternal home.'[3]

Unafraid for themselves they walked with us under the scrutiny of the Communist officials across the rice fields and rough treeless terrain of the Zhaojue valley. It was two miles to the Sanwan River that curved away majestically around the base of the mountain we called Great Hen and which now rose above us to over 8,000 feet. Here we would have to say our farewells.

The mules carrying the children moved ahead, kicking through the water and trotting away up the ascending track. Aware that we had stopped, Jan and Pauline, restricted by their bulky clothing, struggled to twist around in their boxes, trying to see their parents. Their cries alerted Janet and Ruth and they pushed on to catch up, leaving Jim and me at the edge of the river.

I surveyed the distraught group, broken now into twos and threes: the fruit of barely three years' labour in meagre soil. The crop that God had chosen to harvest in the land of the wild Nosu. A seedling church that would need to stand in the midst of Nosu lawless violence, drug abuse and drunkenness, hemmed in by animistic superstition. And what pressures would their new atheistic masters bring to bear?

Jim and I sang. 'God be with you till we meet again...' It was clear that this was the final goodbye. 'Till we meet at Jesus' feet ...'[4]

We urged our mounts forward, taking the first slopes at a canter, pointing our whips heavenward beyond the bleak clouds. A declaration of hope in the God we knew to be faithful despite our fears for our friends. And then, a last salute... We glanced back. The believers had regrouped. Faintly we heard them singing their response while they waved. No matter what distance separated us, we would still be under the same sky.

* * *

It was desperately cold on the mountain. Chill numbed the senses in fingers and toes and gnawed through my wadded jackets. To breathe in the frozen air burned our throats and choked our lungs. The climb in single file stifled conversation and as the mists enclosed us I retreated into my own thoughts.

July 1926

Chapter 2

'*A woman is her mother. That's the main thing.*'

Joan swung her legs high. Stretching forward, pointing her toes. Towards the clear unsullied sky. Towards the still rising sun. Down. Over scuffed earth. And up. Past the purples and reds. Full-headed rhododendrons.

Swing higher! Mother is sitting close. Swing higher! In Mother Joan sees God and knows God. And now, God is coming close...

Joan is overwhelmed with joy. Joy in swinging yet closer to the unspoilt sky.

* * *

'Miss Joan...' Nelly's voice was neither command nor rebuke. A stifled plea for obedience without understanding.

Joan looked back from her run up the stairs, eager to be away.

'Your mother is...' A moment's deliberation. 'She is unwell. A headache. Don't trouble her, please.'

'But, I won't...'

'It would be best if she rests. Now, come and help me with the laundry. With your mother not well I'm not as far on as I should be. Can't have Mr Wales finding his clothes still on the washing line when the train pulls in, can we?' Nelly, the companion-helper, held out her hand and enticed Joan away from the stairs that would take her to her mother's room. 'Later maybe.'

But there was no 'later'. Friday evening passed with an air of strained normality for Father and Nelly. Surely Doreen and Eric, Joan's elder siblings, sensed it? Joan would question Doreen when bedtime came. Vivian, at two, was his normal boisterous self and no respecter of uncomfortable undercurrents.

Mother did not emerge from her room over the weekend.

'Mummy is not to be disturbed... I trust you all understand.' Whether they did or they didn't, the tone was sufficient to determine that Father would be obeyed. Quietness was to be maintained. Especially on the stairs and landings. Explanations were not forthcoming and for Joan, at nine years old, there was a simple trust that what was said was to be accepted.

The moratorium was not broken on Monday or Tuesday. Joan retreated to the side of the house adjacent to the vegetable patch. This was her refuge: a place overlooked by few windows. Sharing a bedroom with

Doreen left little space to call her own. She stood, her back pressed hard to the wall. 'I want to see Mummy. Jesus, I must see Mummy.' It was now four days. She counted the days on her fingers. Five days...

Five days without seeing her mother were too much for Joan; her need for intimacy was growing unbearably strong. But Nelly met her at the door each day from school and diverted her in the direction of the kitchen, the dining room, the outhouse or the garden. The first landing almost became off-limits.

By Wednesday Joan was close to breaking point.

'Keep up, Joan!' Doreen shouted over her shoulder. She was several yards ahead and disappearing at the turn in the road where the railway crossed over their route. Diminutive Joan was usually some distance behind. Doreen was 14 after all. Today, however, Joan was determined to express her unhappiness, in dawdling. Any hopes that Nelly would not be barring the way to her mother's bedroom had dwindled to no more than a faint longing.

Joan refused to hurry. Doreen was already out of sight as she reached the bridge. The road curved away sharply to the left and wound up around the gas works. Joan paused. A steam train headed for Hastings was labouring out of the local railway station. Thunder reverberated around her as it traversed the girders supporting the bridge deck high above her.

Joan did not move. She had to make some protest. There were so few ways available to her. Being late home would perhaps bring attention to her despondency. Her wait seemed like an age, though in reality it lasted only a few minutes. A group of older children disturbed her mini-rebellion and she pretended she had dropped something before walking on. There was a lamp post a few yards along opposite the brick wall of the gas works. She slowly swung herself around it three or four times, trying to eke out time. She crossed to the gate beyond the gas works and the path along the edge of the field. The main road winding away under the willow trees was the longer route.

Disobedience, born out of despondency, was forming in her mind. What if? Her natural determination and customary compliance vied for supremacy. What if...? Ten minutes later, determined and decided, she hurried along past Giles' nursery and through the gate to her home, Greenways.

Nelly was waiting for her by the door. 'I was getting worried, Miss Joan. Did school not go well?' Joan shrugged and did not reply. 'I have a little job. Master Vivian needs some attention. Can you do that for me?'

Joan was non-committal. Her plan was now in place.

When Joan was five years old George and Bertha Wales moved south from Seven Kings, Essex, where they had met and married, to Tunbridge Wells in Kent, with Doreen, aged ten, and eight-year-old Eric. As active members of the Methodist Church the couple had been Sunday School teachers. In their new surroundings they readily got involved in the Congregationalist church on Mount Pleasant, a striking building in the town centre fronted by an ancient Greek-style portico. Sunday morning attendance was regular in the Wales' household and for the children it was considered a treat to attend the evening service.

George had progressed from a career in publishing to run a mail order company for surgical appliances in London. Business was good. Greenways, one of only three large houses ranged along a new crescent, was proving an excellent choice. The grounds occupied half an acre enclosing the detached house and ancillary buildings, with a tennis court, a generous garden and a sizeable plot for vegetables to be grown. It was a decent walk to the town centre, the church and to local schools but the fields and beech woods around the house were an immense benefit. Neighbours were few; extensive post-war housing developments were being planned closer to the town. The round towers of the gas works were the one unsightly addition to the landscape, but served their purpose.

A large property had meant the employment of two servants: a maid to aid Bertha's upkeep of the house, and Samson to fill gardener and chauffeur roles. George had taken advantage of the boom in the wake of the First World War to join the rapidly increasing number of private motorists amongst the richer ranks of the middle class.

The arrival of baby Vivian created a further addition to family cares. The maid was released and Miss Nelly Watkins, a companion-helper hailing from Cambridgeshire, was employed to help with the children and free Bertha to provide some secretarial help at home for her husband. But the benefits of this arrangement were to be short-lived. Heart trouble meant Bertha was far from well.

Entirely ignorant of the true state of her mother's health, Joan quietly returned to the hallway. Once she had climbed the first few steps the stairs turned to the left and she would be hidden from Nelly's casual glance down the hall from the kitchen. Her father would not be home before six. An acute sense of guilt threatened to stop her ascent more than once but the determination to see her mother was too strong.

Her parents' room was opposite the top of the stairs. Guardedly Joan approached the closed door. Even in normal circumstances she would not have been allowed in. But today was not to be 'normal'. The heavy handle turned slowly in her hand, rasping out a caution. Joan drew back, glancing towards the stairs. No one came. Inch after inch she pushed open the door and when the gap proved just narrow enough for her she slipped hurriedly inside.

Despite the evening sun, there was little light in the room due to the substantial curtains. Heavy wooden wardrobes kept sentry watch along the walls. The dresser, with its three high mirrors, reflected Joan's image in triplicate. In the centre stood the high-sided bed laden with thick eiderdowns. And cradled against the pillows – it seemed some distance off – her mother, slight and somehow smaller than Joan remembered her.

'Must close the door,' she whispered. She dared not leave it ajar. Almost unaware, Joan held her breath as she advanced across the room. With each step the reflection in the mirrors imitated her progress, broadcasting her presence. It was clear that her mother was very ill. Far worse than Joan had envisaged. Her mother did not stir.

Joan turned away. Tears rolled silently down her cheeks.

'Joan, darling, don't cry...' Mother had seen her face

reflected in the mirror. 'Come here.' Mother lifted her arm a fraction and held it out to Joan. 'Let's talk to Jesus.'

This was Mother's pre-eminent response to all Joan's childish crises. 'We can always talk to Jesus.' Joan loved their intimate times of daily prayers, along with the Bible stories told from before a time Joan could really remember – all founded on her mother's capacity for love that seemed unshaken by failure.

Joan had memories like the day she had helped herself to a lump of loaf sugar from the dining room dresser. Her mother's reprimand had been sharp.

'Mummy, don't you love me any more?'

And Mother had been quick to sweep her up and remind her of God's embrace. 'God doesn't stop loving you, does he? Even when you do wrong and have to say sorry. And neither do I.'

Then there was the day she had swung high in the garden and felt so full of joy. Swinging high. Close to Mother. Close to God.

Joan knelt earnestly by the bed. She said a simple prayer. 'Please make Mummy better.' Then she clambered onto the bed, accepted a gentle kiss and hurried swiftly away.

For Joan the situation was now resolved. Jesus answered prayer. It would not matter if she was forbidden to visit her mother again. Her task was now to wait. Jesus had her anxieties in his hands.

'A little talk with Jesus makes it right, all right', number one in the *Children's Special Service Mission* songbook, had become an immediate favourite with Joan. She had learned the chorus the previous summer at a camp in

Paignton, Devon, and its sentiments readily reinforced her mother's encouragement to pray. She had also been challenged that, while she had known Jesus with her, she had not yet accepted him as Lord and Saviour. One morning at the beach service Joan had understood Jesus was waiting for her, wanting to be invited into her life.

The car journey home was punctuated with Joan's enthusiastic renditions of choruses. She was fit to burst. She wanted to do something for Jesus. After all, she reasoned, look what he had done for her. 'Ask something costly,' she whispered in prayer. 'Something costly, so I can show you how thankful I am.'

Now, almost a year later, that simple prayer was not to go unanswered. At eight o'clock on Saturday evening, Joan was making her way up the second flight of stairs leading to her attic bedroom. Father appeared on the landing and beckoned to her. 'You need to say good night to Mummy.'

Joan brightened and willingly followed her father into the room. 'Is she better?' Perhaps the prayer with her mother was being answered already.

It was clear she was not. Lifted by her father, Joan stretched down and kissed her mother. 'Good night, Mummy.'

'Good night, darling... good night.'

Though sure in her faith in Jesus, Joan was disappointed. He would make it all right, wouldn't he? She fell asleep, still certain that her mother would recover.

Joan awoke to find her grandparents in the house. When they had travelled from Essex she could not be sure. It was strange to think of them travelling in the night. Nana called Doreen, Eric and Joan down to her in turn.

'Joan, my dear... You need to know, Mummy is in heaven.' In that moment Joan's childlike trust was torn apart. She rushed back to her bedroom while the others sombrely gathered for breakfast. 'Leave her,' said Nana. 'So alike, you know. I see so much of Bertha growing up in Joan.'

Tears. Bewilderment. A forlorn loneliness. An inconsolable cry for understanding. Her mother had gone. Had she loved Mummy too much? Why hadn't Jesus answered her prayer?

When the tears had dried, Joan knelt by the bed, hugging the Bible from her bedside table to herself. Finally she opened it at random, looking for consolation. The pages flicked forward through her fingers to John chapter 14.

> *Let not your heart be troubled: ye believe in God, believe also in me. In my Father's house are many mansions: if it were not so, I would have told you. I go to prepare a place for you. And if I go and prepare a place for you, I will come again, and receive you unto myself; that where I am, there ye may be also.*[5]

So pertinent were the words that it felt as though Joan was hearing God speak to her: 'I wanted Mummy to come up to be with me. One day I'm coming back for you. You'll be with Mummy and you'll both be here with me. And in the meantime I want you to share everything with me just as you did with Mummy.'

Had she heard God speak? What other explanation could there be?

A few days later the family gathered in Seven Kings for the funeral. The headstone recorded the bare facts:

BERTHA GRACE
DEARLY BELOVED WIFE OF
GEORGE HENRY WALES
DIED JULY 10TH 1926
AGED 43 YEARS

to which George added the epitaph:

A PERFECT WIFE AND MOTHER

For Joan she had been the perfect mother.

* * *

By the end of July the family was scattered: Father at home in Tunbridge Wells, Doreen and Vivian to Mother's sister Hilda and Uncle Edgar, Eric to the Isle of Wight. Joan was taken by her Sunday School teachers for a holiday to The Mumbles in Wales.

However, the summer's share of upheavals was not yet over. Away for just three weeks Joan could barely contemplate the shock that awaited her at Greenways. On her return Nelly Watkins was no longer companion-helper. She had become Mrs Betty Wales, a new mother for Joan.

Faced with the prospect of raising four children, George, lacking the assets of domestication, had sought the advice of a minister friend. Doreen, now definitely a teenager, was expressing interest in boys and embarking on the transition to womanhood. Vivian, on the other hand, was just finding his feet as a toddler. The hasty solution was to secure immediate care for the children. It would be improper for Nelly to remain in the home without George having a wife. The formalities of marriage were completed without further consideration. In recognition of the social advance to her new status Nelly became Betty to the three older children and 'Mumsi' to Vivian. The children would no longer be 'Miss' and 'Master'.

In a mere matter of two months Joan's world of seemingly unruffled suburban family order, enfolded in the encouragement, love and wisdom of her mother and father, had disappeared. For a while the whirlwinds of the summer settled; Betty was accepted and daily life brought routine back to the household. In the midst of her grief Joan's spirituality had ceased to revolve around her mother. God, for reasons Joan could not fully comprehend, had taken her mother away for a while. Now, graciously and gently, he had taken her place.

Chapter 3

'A good wife and mother is worth a thousand
missionaries in this grief-stricken world.'

GEORGE WALES

Joan was dismayed to find her father striding down the
railway platform at Euston Station towards her. She had
not expected to see him on this particular visit to London.
The events of the weekend were to determine her future
and she knew he did not approve.

Her father leaned down, kissed her cheek and took her
small suitcase. 'The car is parked outside the station,' he
explained. 'I thought it would be better than you getting
across the city in the dark. You haven't much luggage?'

'It's only for the weekend,' replied Joan. 'I go back to
Ireland on Tuesday.'

Joan had graduated from a one-year course at the
Princess Christian Nursery Training College at Windsor in

1934. The following spring she had secured a post with an Irish family, the Martins, in Greystones, a tranquil fishing town just south of Dublin, hemmed between the striking backdrop of Sugar Loaf Mountain and the Irish Sea. Initially there had been two children in her care: Neville and Beryl, both under five. Baby Heather had arrived 18 months later.

As Joan and her father left the station concourse and headed for his car, London was hurrying home. The pavements were overburdened with businessmen jostling their way towards packed platforms in the unpromising hope of finding a seat on their train. Joan followed in her father's wake as he navigated a route through the crowd.

'Where's this place you're going to?' asked her father, sliding onto the car seat beside her.

'120 Aberdeen Park. I have a map.'

'I know it... it's over by Highbury. Won't take long if we can get through this mayhem.' He waited as one of the new trolley-buses, attached by lengthy antennae to a web of electric lines strung above the streets, trundled past. Then he eased the car into the sluggish flow of the Friday evening traffic. 'The roads get more congested every time I drive on them. Do these people have decent accommodation?'

'I don't think it will be plush. Hopefully it will be adequate for a few nights.'

'If you pass the interview, it will need to be more than adequate for a few nights. Isabel and I are concerned for you.'

Isabel and I... Isabel had been an employee at her father's company, where it was her task to measure clients for surgical appliances. Now she was her father's third wife. His marriage to Betty had ended in divorce when Joan was in her mid-teens. The rift had developed while Joan was away from home at boarding school in Devon. At the end of term she had alighted from her train at another London station – Waterloo – to find her father waiting for her. Betty was at his side as expected but Joan sensed immediately that their apparent closeness was feigned merely for her sake. They had sat in the station restaurant eating fish and chips coated in tomato sauce. The tension was tangible.

Ironically it was at Paignton, where Joan had become a Christian, that the marriage had finally broken apart. Father had departed early from their holiday, leaving Betty, Joan, Vivian and Joan's stepbrother, Brian, behind. Betty had been distraught and confined to bed. Joan, now suddenly responsible for a grieving adult and two bewildered children, was thrown into confusion. She had approached a minister – a complete stranger – staying at the hotel and asked him to help Betty. He had turned her down. A request from her father that she get the family back home by train was met with Joan's blank refusal. Father, she had insisted, would have to send Samson with the car. She could not manage the journey with her sick stepmother and cope with Vivian and Brian, a toddler, as well.

Joan had returned to school leaving Father and Isabel to establish their home in Buckinghamshire. The family home in Tunbridge Wells was sold. And with it went photographs and personal treasures, the remaining scraps of her childhood and familiar mementos of her mother.

'Is this right?' enquired her father. Beyond the gate the building stood in dismal darkness. A sign on the gate announced the property belonged to the China Inland Mission.

'The gate says this is it.'

'Doesn't look very welcoming. Are you sure about this?'

'Of course.'

They made their way to the front door and rang the bell. There was a significant delay before lights appeared in the hallway and the door was opened.

'Ah, Miss Wales, we were expecting you. Do come on in. I'm afraid Miss Bond, the warden, is unwell. I am Miss Moody.' In her long skirt and a bodice with a ruffle at the neck Miss Moody could well have emerged from a Victorian novel. Joan winced. Even her name seemed unhelpful. This was not creating a good impression for her father.

They were ushered politely into the sitting room. Joan glanced at her father's expression and sighed inwardly. The worn furniture and sober decoration must have seemed a picture of impoverishment to him. The pictures of the Old Testament Tabernacle set in dry desert scenes which covered the walls looked singularly old-fashioned. It was clear that candidates for CIM training were not to expect luxury.

'Miss Wales will have a medical tomorrow morning. Sunday she is free for church. On Monday morning she will meet the candidates' secretary at CIM headquarters and Mrs Benjamin Broomhall will interview her in the afternoon at her home south of the river. Mrs Broomhall's husband, Dr Broomhall, is the nephew of James Hudson Taylor, our founder...'

'Well, I must say, I do hope they won't accept her,' interrupted Joan's father.

Miss Moody reached for her Christian composure. 'We only want the Lord's will for her, Mr Wales.'

Her reply discomfited Mr Wales sufficiently for him to reassure the lady hastily that he would obviously not want to stand in God's way. To Joan's relief, after eliciting a final assurance that she was able to cope, he excused himself and retreated to the sanctuary of his hotel.

'Miss Wales... you have a telephone call.'

Joan had just settled herself into her room for the night. Bemused that anyone should know how to contact her by phone, she pursued Miss Moody to the training centre office which lay to one side of the main entrance.

'Joan? This is Isabel... Joan?'

'Yes... hello, Isabel. I wasn't expecting you...'

'Joan, are you all right? Your father and I are worried about that place you are staying in. Do you have a bed? You can come to our hotel.'

Joan reassured her stepmother that she was perfectly fine. 'The rooms are a little spartan, but the mattress is more than adequate.'

'Then you must come for lunch tomorrow. George says you only have a medical in the morning.'

Joan acquiesced to the invitation. As with Betty her tacit acceptance of the new arrangements and her natural affection for her father had helped her warmth for Isabel to grow over the last three or four years. The birth of Veronica, her stepsister, had also helped to heal the hurts of the divorce.

'Isabel and Daddy really must stop worrying!' she informed the phone as she replaced the earpiece. She was 20 and had been working independently in Ireland for two years. But the truth was that the roots of their disquiet lay much deeper than mere worry about the accommodation at the women's training centre of the China Inland Mission.

Joan had written to her father from Greystones of her intention to apply to become a missionary. His reply had been full of apprehension. Clearly, he did not want to accept the loss of his daughter to an inaccessible and war-stricken recess of the Far East. China was in part occupied by the Japanese and troubled by civil strife as the Nationalist government engaged in an uneasy stand-off with Communist guerrilla forces. He had other, albeit more commonplace, aspirations for his daughter. Marriage was most certainly high on his list.

A settled occupation was also a desirable objective. After Joan's final term at boarding school, on her arrival at a new home in Torquay, her father had announced he had a surprise for her. He had proudly shown her a small establishment on one of the local shopping streets. To her absolute amazement the shop bore a new sign – 'Joan's Hairdressing Salon'. Joan had been both perplexed and aghast. Where on earth had her father got the idea that she wanted to be a hairdresser? 'Daddy, I want to work with children!'

Quite what had happened to the salon she never asked but she had never been inside it and she had never been back. She had fulfilled her own ambitions, trained as a nanny and obtained the post at Greystones. And now she was sure God wanted her to become a missionary in China.

Joan's memory of receiving her father's response to her plans was as clear as his concern. She had gone to her bedroom in the Martins' home with the letter in her hand and stood by the window looking out onto the garden. 'If your mother was alive she wouldn't want you to go... A good wife and mother is worth a thousand missionaries in this grief-stricken world...' The letter drew on all the persuasions her father could find.

There had been a second letter, written by Isabel: 'You know how fond your father is of you. I think it is very, very unkind to think of going away. It will cost him so much to let you go...'

The sentiments were thrown down as a direct challenge to Joan's sense of God's guidance. She wanted to go wherever God would lead her... but, in the face of such strong opposition from her father, how could she? She felt torn, unable to disappoint her father again, yet clear that God's purposes must come first.

Below her window Joan had watched Beryl tottering about amongst the flower beds. Mr and Mrs Martin would be aggrieved if Joan asked to leave. It would be far easier to stay. Perplexed, Joan had picked up her Bible and opened it at the day's reading, Matthew chapter 4. A story of the disciples, James and John, with Jesus - '...he called them. And they immediately left the ship and their father, and followed him'[6]. So apposite. So unequivocal. She had her answer. Daunting though it might be, the choice was made.

Joan had gone out into the garden to collect Beryl. The

toddler had seen her coming and stumbled excitedly across the lawn in her direction. In a spontaneous gesture she had reached her short arms around Joan's legs as far as she could and hugged Joan.

'God bless you, nurse,' said Beryl. It seemed that God was eager to affirm his pleasure in Joan's decision.

As instructed by the austere Miss Moody, Joan made the twenty-minute walk from Aberdeen Park to the headquarters of the China Inland Mission at Newington Green on the Monday morning. She was feeling nervous, unsure what to expect as she approached the intimidating four-storey brick fortress of an entrance. Passing beneath the imposing curved archway straddled by the newly built Men's Training Home, she made her way to the old office block. High on the parapet was the date of construction – 1894. Adjacent to the side door were two slim white panels displaying Chinese characters – five indecipherable squiggles on each panel. They must mean something. Maybe she would be able to read them some day. The words 'Have Faith in God' had been carved into the stone above the door. That at least was clear.

Joan was welcomed into a building of seemingly interminable, poorly lit corridors punctuated with doorways to a myriad of modest rooms, each with a nameplate indicating the task of the occupant. She was shown into a box-like office, an unpretentious setting for what she presumed was a very important interview with the candidates' secretary.

She emerged an hour later with the address of Mrs Benjamin Broomhall in East Dulwich, instructions on how to get there in time for afternoon tea, and in a perplexed state of mind. Her interview with the candidates' secretary had not progressed as she had anticipated.

'Miss Wales, have you considered reading your New Testament in French?' The question had taken Joan completely by surprise. She had looked back blankly. 'No, I can't say that I have.'

'Has it never occurred to you to do so?'

What did that mean? Joan's puzzlement had affected the rest of the interview and she felt sure that her application would be rejected.

Mrs Broomhall's generous drawing room was a complete contrast to the CIM headquarters. Joan sat in the comfort of fine furniture, contemplating the delights of plates bearing tiny triangular sandwiches and neatly arranged cakes. Her hostess combined her position of influence with a genuine show of warmth.

'You seem disheartened, Joan,' said Mrs Broomhall. 'Did this morning's interview not go well?'

Joan told her of the confusing question she had been asked and Mrs Broomhall seemed amused.

'Reading one's New Testament in French is not a prerequisite for going to China. There are more important things. Perhaps you can tell me why you want to join our mission.'

Paradoxically it had been at the time of her greatest grief, the three-week period in which she had lost her mother and before her shock at discovering she had a new stepmother, that Joan had first encountered the outlandish realm of missionary service. Joan's Sunday School teachers, in an effort to distract her, had found two missionary books for her – the story of Mary Slessor, the 'Queen of Okoyong', in Africa, and the autobiography of Wilfred Grenfell, a real adventure set in the alien world of the Arctic.

'I felt this curious joy as I read these books,' Joan explained to Mrs Broomhall. 'God had a plan for my life. Maybe I could be a missionary. I even wrote to Dr Grenfell telling him. To my amazement he replied. It was a great encouragement. In my teens I wasn't much of a Christian. I went to a Methodist boarding school in Bideford but apart from the daily routines of religion I lapsed badly. I even ceased reading my Bible regularly. It wasn't until I started my nursery college training, when a Christian friend encouraged me, that I began to attend a local Baptist church.

'Then two years ago... that was 1935, at a summer beach mission in Ireland, another girl and I gatecrashed a Girls' Christian Union camp down the road. Our "Sausage Sizzle" had been cancelled because of the rain and we were looking for something else to fill our time. They were all very nice about it and gave us supper. The speaker was a lady – Miss Hilda Steele – a missionary in India. I was sure God had a plan like this for me.' Joan looked a little sheepish. 'I was also sure it couldn't be China... the language would be too difficult.'

'Yet here you are,' replied Mrs Broomhall gently. 'God has a sense of humour, does he not? So how did he come to change your mind?'

'It was at a Keswick Convention in Greystones. God challenged me. Did he mean anything to me? Did he mean more than anything? Did he mean everything to me? I was afraid to answer the third question. If God meant everything to me, couldn't he ask me to do anything he wanted? But then he spoke to me again – "If you can't trust the one who died for you, who can you trust?" That was a turning point in my life.

'About the same time a friend, who knew nothing of this, gave me a book about James Hudson Taylor and the China Inland Mission. As I read the story I understood God wanted me to go to China. I contacted Mr McCarthy, the CIM Ireland representative, and he arranged for me to come for this interview.'

When Joan had finished her story Mrs Broomhall politely poured the tea into delicate china cups. 'Tomorrow you will meet the Candidates' Council. We will tell you our decision once the council has interviewed you. Do help yourself to a sandwich or cake.'

The following morning Joan again made her way from Aberdeen Park to Newington Green. The committee that greeted her was formidable. Ranged along two sides of the lengthy boardroom table, beneath a solemn portrait of the mission's founder, the equally solemn men and women of the Candidates' Council were capable of firing questions at her on any subject with surprising speed. It was a relief finally to escape from their scrutiny while they reached their conclusion.

Mr Rowland Hogben, the candidates' secretary, formally pronounced the council's verdict. 'You will be aware of the scripture, 'Lay hands suddenly on no man'[7], Miss Wales.'

Joan nodded.

'It would seem appropriate to your application. We

consider that you have applied to the mission too soon. There is a need for wider experience in Christian service. And Bible training is necessary; a correspondence course with one of our members is recommended.'

As she boarded her train back to Holyhead and took the ferry to Dun Laoghaire, Joan could only reflect on her disappointment. She wasn't going to China. But the committee members were right. She hadn't even taught in a Sunday School. How could she become a missionary? The pathway ahead had seemed to clear for a while. Now the mists had descended again. Her father had the decision he had requested after all.

Chapter 4

'*...a quarrel in a faraway country between people of whom we know nothing.*'

NEVILLE CHAMBERLAIN, 27 SEPTEMBER 1938

Joan was at breakfast with the children when Mrs Martin brought in the morning newspaper. 'Nurse, there's something here you need to see...' She placed the paper alongside Joan's plate and pointed out an article in the *Irish Times*. 'Isn't this the place you are going to today?'

Shocked, Joan scanned the report and was silent for a few moments.

'It is the house?' asked Mrs Martin.

Joan nodded. 'Yes. How horrific for the Densmores.'

Joan had been due to collect a group of children from the Dublin Children's Rescue Home and escort them to a new orphanage in County Wexford. There she was to take up her new position of nurse-in-charge. The Densmores, house-parents with two children of their own, had already set up the facility in preparation for the young arrivals. The former residence of a Major Butler-Stoney had been made available for the project, and the Quakers and others had generously donated furniture and bedding. Elements within the Roman Catholic community, however, were not so approving of this Protestant initiative. Tensions across the Christian divide were strong.

'It must have been awful,' said Mrs Martin. 'The couple of them forced out of bed like that. At gunpoint! Not to mention the children. And then made to stand on the lawn while the house was burnt down. The shame of it.'

Joan finished her breakfast quickly, the article beside her. She clearly had some thinking and more praying to do. She had given in her notice. Where could she go now? Where was God leading her?

Mrs Martin was not long in reiterating the invitation she had offered a few weeks before when Joan had announced she intended to leave. 'You can stay here in Greystones. You know that.'

'It's very kind of you, Mrs Martin. But I need to get different kinds of work experience. The China Inland Mission won't consider me again without that.'

'The children will miss you,' Mrs Martin persisted. 'You could wait until they are a little older.'

Joan was firm. 'Really, I must move on. I believe God wants me to go to China.'

Shortly afterwards Joan left Greystones and joined the staff at the Dublin Rescue Home. But the standards of care were a far cry from those she had learned at the Princess

Christian Nursery Training College and she quickly felt uncomfortable working there.

'We are expected to feed the children in their playpens,' she told her friends. 'I push the spoon through the bars of their cages. It really is very difficult. And then we leave them sitting on potties half the day. It saves chasing after them but it's heart-wrenching to see them like that.'

It was some relief when she was able to move on again, taking a job at the YWCA[8] in Newcastle, County Down, for the summer, before CIM suggested she engage in a year's training programme as a nurse at Bermondsey Medical Mission Hospital in south London. She could start immediately, in the September of 1938.

The Medical Mission Hospital on Crimscott Street, staffed entirely by women, had been founded by Dr Selina Fox, a medic who had wanted to be a missionary herself but whose health had not been considered strong enough. Keen to be involved in mission, she had become a medical officer at a missionary training school in Bermondsey, before establishing the hospital to treat local disadvantaged women and their children for nominal fees.

Joan had no desire to become a regular nurse but she was familiar enough with aspects of medical practice and terminology through her father's business. The instruction at Bermondsey proved very beneficial, placing her in a Christian environment and widening her range of abilities. She found a month's opportunity to assist in the operating theatre fascinating and was only too glad to volunteer for a second month of training when one of her colleagues dropped out. The rudimentary skills she acquired in these few weeks were to prove invaluable!

Janet Churchill was another of the young women who joined the Mission Hospital training programme at CIM's suggestion, working there for just one month. She had serene blue eyes and neatly combed, long, blonde hair pulled back into a bun, a fashion common amongst missionary women as short hair was frowned on within the mission. Three inches taller than average and three years older than Joan, she combined an extraordinary ability to facilitate the ambitions and dreams of others with her own staunch resolve to serve God wherever he might want her.

To Joan she was intriguing. Janet had been born in Fujian Province on the east coast of China where her father had been a medical missionary for fifteen years with the Church Missionary Society, working at the Union Medical College in the provincial capital, Fuzhou. She had obtained a degree in English from London University before becoming a teacher at a Christian girls' boarding school, Clarendon, in north Wales. Now she was heading back to China, as a missionary with CIM.

Perhaps more fascinatingly, Joan discovered that Janet was engaged to a young doctor and member of the Royal College of Surgeons, James Broomhall. He was the son of Mrs Broomhall, who had interviewed Joan in Dulwich the previous year, and had also been born in China.

'Jim came back to the UK from China for boarding school as a teenager,' explained Janet. 'My parents were his guardians and he stayed with us in the holidays. He fell in love with me when he was thirteen and I was eleven! Of course, he didn't tell me that until I was teaching...'

In an effort to get to China before the anticipated war

in Europe broke out, Jim had already cut short his medical studies and sailed from Britain in October with a group of ten new CIM male missionaries, who had survived on ginger ale and sandwiches across an antagonistic Atlantic Ocean, before travelling on to Shanghai via Canada, Honolulu and Tokyo. He and Janet would marry when she was able to join him in China.

The appeasement policies of the British and French governments in the 1930s had apparently kept the prospect of war for the nations of Western Europe at bay. The British Prime Minister, Neville Chamberlain, remained optimistic that Hitler's ambitions for Germany could be contained, even though the German Chancellor pursued aggressive policies elsewhere on the continent. As Joan completed her work in Bermondsey, events were rapidly unfolding which would compel the British and French governments to confront Hitler. A German invasion of Poland would not be condoned.

In keeping with its assessment of Joan's initial approach to CIM, the Candidates' Council called her for a second set of interviews. Better prepared and less daunted by the prospect, Joan made her case for acceptance. The council approved her application and recommended that she commence their autumn training programme.

On 1 September 1939 Hitler's troops invaded Poland, forcing the British and French governments to declare war with Germany. One of the minor consequences was suspension of CIM training before it had started and, for Joan, any hopes of progressing to China were halted. She must return to live with her father and Isabel and wait.

Twelve months later, Joan found herself in the Kent

village of Bidborough, just a few miles from her childhood home in Tunbridge Wells. The country lane ran past a line of cottages tucked subordinately beneath the hill on which stood the prominent parish church. At the worn wooden lychgate adjacent to the village school the road dipped away down the incline, bringing Joan to the start of a short dirt drive. Here stood a sizeable building of black wooden slats fronted by extensive gardens, commanding an attractive view across the valley. This was 'The Chalet', the temporary location for CIM training.

The warden, Miss Hilda Bond, a 'well-padded' motherly missionary close to retirement, welcomed each of the candidates as they arrived. Joan was pleased to note that a Miss Smyth had replaced the 'Victorian' Miss Moody as the warden's assistant. Both women were at pains to help everyone settle in.

'With ten ladies in a house built for a family of five or six there is not a considerable amount of space in which everyone must exist,' Miss Bond informed the assembled recruits on the first evening. 'Tidiness will be appreciated.' Joan surveyed the living room in which they had gathered for introductions. What was said was true enough but, given that CIM had not provided an abundance of furniture, there was more room available than a family might have expected to occupy. 'You will share rooms, of course,' continued Miss Bond. She read down the list of names. 'Miss Wales. Joan, you will be sharing with Miss Harris. Miss Harris, there is some confusion over your name. Are you Annette or Annetta?'

A slim girl, of similar age to Joan, smiled discreetly across the room. Her face, like her figure, was angular and she had deep-set eyes beneath a crop of dark hair. A serious face, thought Joan, but she detected something in the smile that suggested that Miss Harris was not as severe as she looked. There was a definite hint of mischievousness.

'My name is Annetta, Miss Bond. But I am known by friends as Annette.'

Miss Bond made a note. 'Joan, you will share with Annette.' It was an arrangement that Annette had some cause to regret the next morning.

Joan groped around for her alarm clock. Six thirty. She heaved herself out of bed. Annette was not awake. Should she rouse her? Joan washed and dressed quickly.

'What time is it?' Annette was evidently going to have difficulty starting the day.

'Half six.'

'Are you sure? I simply can't get up. I feel dreadful.'

Joan inspected the clock and grimaced. 'Oh... well, maybe it's midnight...'

Annette needed no further reassurance and settled into her pillow again. 'Just a little too enthusiastic then!'

Joan groaned. 'But I'm dressed!'

Annette offered no advice. After a moment's contemplation of the merits of undressing again, Joan slipped back into her bed and slept fully clothed. In the morning she would have to live with the ignominy as her mistake was revealed over breakfast. Any notions of superiority in the missionary world would be quickly dispelled.

Annette did indeed have a talent for amusement which

teetered on the brink of impropriety, but was never allowed to descend into outright hilarity. When asked to retell the story of Esther, Annette immediately adopted a casual tone, delivered with strait-laced sincerity. "Very well, Haman, my boy,' said King Xerxes, 'just as you please."

The upright members of CIM staff, who had travelled down to The Chalet to provide training, listened in solemnity while Annette's colleagues sitting behind them struggled to suppress their urge to laugh.

Annette and Joan were also assigned to work together in the neighbouring parish of St Peter's Church, Southborough. The church, a striking structure with a slender spire tucked into the oak and beech trees on the edge of the village green, had, until recently, been the responsibility of the assistant home director of CIM. The pitfalls peculiar to door-to-door visiting were explained to them. 'Choose your first words carefully. I suggest a simple introduction of who you are and which church you represent. The example of one of our trainees is not to be advised.'

The unfortunate young female trainee in question had covered herself in confusion as the door was opened. 'Do you have a wife?' she had asked, feeling intimidated at having to engage in conversation with the man who had opened the door.

'No,' he had replied sharply, 'and I don't want one, thank you.'

This, however, was less of an ordeal than outreach in the local pub. While Annette stood by the war memorial on the far side of the road, Joan hesitantly pushed open the door of 'The Hand and Sceptre', an imposing public house dominating the east side of the green. Joan had simply never been inside a pub before. Her reticence combined with her shortness in stature meant she did not command great attention. The evening's evangelistic activity was not an outstanding success.

As Joan, Annette and the others embarked on their missionary training, with the Battle of Britain between the British and German air forces raging above them in the skies over Kent, Janet Churchill was already in China. In the early days of the war she had boarded a boat to Canada and headed to Shanghai. She was now at her first missionary station in central Sichuan Province. Jim Broomhall was working in a town about 30 miles to the northeast of her location, practising medicine. It would be January 1942 before the mission's regulations allowed them to marry.

The war situation in China itself was becoming increasingly bleak. Japanese forces were at the height of their penetration into China. Troops had now made their way as far south as Nanchang[9], Shanghai and Yichang[10], with significant enclaves of power established in the southeast around Hong Kong and Macau and along the coast of Fujian Province. Chongqing[11] in central China, the provisional capital of the Nationalist government, was under threat. Negotiating safe passage to China was hazardous.

In the circumstances, it was inevitable that CIM preparations for service would be halted. A telegram from CIM's general director in China, Bishop Frank Houghton, instructed the mission that training of women recruits was to be suspended. After completing only two of the required six terms of training, the sessions at The Chalet were brought to an end in March 1941, and Joan was once more unsure of her future.

Chapter 5

'...the game of Snakes and Ladders captures, as no other activity can hope to do, the eternal truth that... for every snake, a ladder will compensate.'

SALMAN RUSHDIE

It was Mr Henry Milner Morris, the CIM treasurer, who suggested Joan become the assistant matron at a Fegans Boys' Home. 'You could go up to Yardley Gobion, near Northampton. They have a home there for about 30 boys. Four- to seven-year-olds. Nice place.'

Yardley House, situated on the north edge of the village, was a pleasant and impressive stone Victorian residence built on the brow of a modest rise close to the village green. Two high pillars flanked the gateway to a long drive, lined with shrubs and yew trees. The approach led to the front door, above which was suspended a sizeable, if plain, balcony. Beyond the house lay the stables and gardens measuring 20 acres, an area more than ample for the home's activities. The building was crowned by a distinctive square tower that allowed views over the fields towards the Grand Union Canal.

The Boys' Home had only been open a year when Joan arrived in April 1941. Some of the boys were orphans but others had been abused or were children with parents in prison. Joan joined the matron, Mrs Hayes, a cook and the gardener.

Mr Milner Morris was also the general director of Fegans Homes and had co-opted the Reverend William H. Aldis, home director of CIM, as a member of his council. The evening Mr Aldis and Mr Milner Morris came to tour the premises, Joan was naturally anxious that they would get a good impression of the home. The visit coincided with a measles outbreak and some of the boys were confined to bed. Joan went around rehearsing etiquette with each one.

'You must say 'good evening, sir' and answer their questions politely.'

Tommy was clearly not going to co-operate as the two men approached the dormitory door.

'Tommy... what do you say?' whispered Joan.

'Can't see 'im yet...'

'Tommy!'

'Oh, 'e ain't got no 'air on!'

Joan winced with embarrassment. In a sudden burst of activity she shied away from Mr Aldis, who was the subject of Tommy's outburst, and vigorously tucked in the bed sheets – an action completely unnecessary. To her inestimable relief Mr Aldis moved on without comment.

Mr Aldis, however, had not forgotten. 'How is the little boy who said "e ain't got no 'air on"?' he asked Joan some time later on her visit to the CIM headquarters.

Joan looked suitably embarrassed and muttered, 'He's doing very well, Mr Aldis.' In response he smiled at her and she was thankful that was the end of the matter.

Life at the Fegans Home meant a welcome return to working with small children again, something Joan had not done for three years. The refurbished house and grounds provided an excellent environment for the boys. At age eight they would be transferred to another home a few miles south in Stoney Stratford, the town where Joan attended church each Sunday.

'Isabel?' Joan could hear the anguish in her stepmother's voice on the phone. Isabel was clearly crying. 'Veronica is in hospital,' Isabel sobbed. 'It's nephritis. The prognosis is poor.' Isabel, as a nurse, knew Veronica's true condition. 'I don't know how long she will live...'

There were long pauses as Isabel gathered herself, forcing out the phrases.

'Joan, I need you here. Your father is away... in London with someone else. I'm alone here, having to look after Veronica. With the war on, the hospital just can't spare any staff for her care at night... Oh, Joan, she's only nine years old...'

Father and Isabel had moved with their family to Newnham in Gloucestershire and taken up residence in 'The Manor House' from where Father also ran his business. Veronica was in hospital in Gloucester, an hour away. Their younger child, Heather, was being looked after by her nanny.

Joan paused before replying. She only got one day off a month. 'Isabel,' she said finally, 'I will come to you. I'll take a day's leave and I'll ask for next month's as well so I can be with you overnight.' It was the best she could offer.

'Veronica...' Joan placed her hand over her stepsister's. She had travelled from Yardley Gobion straight to the hospital. Veronica's face was swollen and she complained of pain in her legs. Although memories of her father's divorce from Betty were still painful, Joan's love for Isabel had grown and she was particularly fond of Veronica. It was distressing to see her so sick. 'Veronica, do you know the stories of Jesus?'

Her stepsister responded feebly.

'Then let me tell you about why he died on a cross.' Simply, and in the natural way that she had with children, Joan shared the gospel. 'Do you believe that?' She waited for Veronica to answer. 'Now I'm going to pray with you. Jesus is always with you, Veronica. He never lets you go. You must remember that.' Joan stayed with her a while longer before travelling to Newnham for the night.

Veronica died the next day.

With her father staying in London it fell to Joan to arrange the funeral and help Isabel cope with her grief. She phoned Mr Milner Morris and explained her situation.

'Take all the time you need,' he offered considerately.

The local minister was also full of sympathy but lacking in pastoral propensity. 'I don't envy you your state of affairs Miss Wales,' he told Joan when he came to visit.

'God will help me,' she reassured him, feeling that it was his place to offer her comfort, not the other way round.

When the finalities of the funeral had been completed, Joan was asked to take Isabel and little Heather by train to visit Isabel's sister in Scotland. She was, therefore, absent from her duties at Yardley Gobion far longer than she had anticipated. On her return, however, her time at the boys' home was to be limited.

'Joan, you must leave Fegans!' insisted the CIM office. 'They are stalling. If you are there, they have little incentive to find a replacement for you.' The CIM women's training programme had been re-established in the autumn of 1943 at their headquarters in Newington Green. Joan needed to join the trainees, but having settled herself again at Yardley Gobion she was having some difficulty extricating herself. The home had promised to find an assistant matron if Joan could wait until the newcomer arrived. However, while the war rumbled on, finding a qualified worker would not be easy.

'You must just leave!' The CIM staff wailed like air raid sirens, becoming increasingly more desperate to pull Joan out of Northamptonshire and relocate her in London. 'Leave...' And in the end she did just that.

The recommencement of preparations for China brought Joan back into contact with the supervisory skills of Misses Bond and Smyth. Among the candidates was Annette Harris and a fair-haired Welsh nurse, Dorothy Jones, who was a sharp observer of the foibles of others. To Dorothy 'Little Joan', as she became known, seemed a 'proper little English lady'.

The lectures at Newington Green consisted predominantly of Bible training and a thorough grounding in the history and traditions of the China Inland Mission.

Further tuition was provided at Oakhill College, a good nine-mile bike ride away on the outskirts of London. Joan, having no bicycle of her own, was obliged to borrow Miss Bond's bicycle. Unfortunately the seat was fixed far too high for her short legs. Careful and timely mounting and dismounting was required to maintain the decorum expected of young female missionaries.

The trainees were expected to wear hats while outside the secure confines of the Newington Green centre. 'We'll never get near Oakhill if we have to keep stopping to replace these bonnets,' said Annette as she retrieved her hat for the umpteenth time. 'Goodness knows who makes these rules up.'

'A man probably,' replied Dorothy. She had a healthy view of the inadequacies of the male gender. Compliance quickly gave way to practicality. The hats were speedily dispensed with once the corner of Newington Green had been turned; 'respectability' was restored as the cyclists paused momentarily at the gates of Oakhill.

The instruction at Oakhill covered aspects of missionary life about which Joan had not anticipated having to learn. She was not particularly well acquainted with the anatomy of a cow, and extracting milk from an udder proved more difficult than she had envisaged.

'Miss Wales,' commented her Oakhill instructor in a resigned manner, 'that will barely be enough to whiten a cup of weak tea. We will have to hope that you can entice a little more from the beast when it really matters.'

The least satisfactory aspect of the programme was the language study in the final term before the summer. A member of the editorial department was pressed into guiding the trainees through the opening chapters of Mathews' *Chinese Primer*.

'Have you seen the size of this monster?' Annette dropped the 790-page tome onto the bed. 'It's two and a half inches deep. I've measured it.' She struck a noble pose. 'The esteemed Mr Mathews writes that he trusts it will "do something to lighten the labours of those who are beginning the study of this marvellously expressive language". The weight of the book alone belies his intentions!'

Joan picked it up and turned to the index. There was something daunting about the alphabetical listing of the diverse topics on which they would be required to converse. For the moment some seemed a little superfluous to their prospective mission – when would they engage the Chinese in the mysteries of astronomy, meteorology and solar periods?

'He also writes compellingly in the preface,' finished Annette with a flourish, 'of the delights of 262 lessons, 1,354 characters and 2,030 expressions, all compiled for the convenience of the student. And we, God bless us, don't even know one end of a first tone from the other.'

With no aural help the classes were essentially a cerebral exercise unrelated to the accepted articulation of the five tones of the language[12]. Knowing that the Chinese for 'I' was a 'third' tone, while correct, was of little value if you had never heard one spoken. Added to this were the impossibilities of pronunciation. 'Wade's Romanisation' of Chinese sounds seemed a conundrum contrived to confuse rather than assist.

'Just exactly how do you say h-s-i-o-h?' asked Joan. Nobody really seemed to know. 'Well, why are 'p's pronounced as 'b's?' But no one had much of an idea about that either.

As for the pictographs, which Joan was informed were words not letters, these were to remain a mystery until Joan arrived for formal language training in China. She had, however, learned that the two Chinese scripts displayed by the side door to the Newington Green offices meant 'Ebenezer' and 'Jehovah Jireh' – transliterations of the Hebrew.

At the end of the term Joan managed to convince everyone, including herself, that she had failed her Chinese exam. Her result of 97 percent was the highest mark, and the derision that greeted the announcement was great. 'Little Joan! You'll not be forgiven!' was the general consensus of opinion.

On regular occasions Joan was required to take her turn at fire-watching. CIM headquarters had been badly damaged by a bomb in 1941 but fortunately no one had been injured and the building had not sustained any serious structural damage. The Allied forces were now making gains into France, pushing back the German troops. Germany's response had been the launching of 'vengeance weapons'[13] from France in the direction of London. Joan donned old clothes and took her blankets down to the CIM boardroom where she tried to make herself comfortable beneath the long table. Above her hung the portrait of James Hudson Taylor that had watched over her initial rejection by the mission. As long as the war in Europe continued and the Japanese maintained their belligerent occupation of China, Joan had no prospect of sailing to Asia.

In the spring of 1945 a new member of the group arrived. Beryl Weston had been at Bidborough with Joan and Annette for just one term before a bicycle accident on an ice-covered road had left her in hospital for an extended period. Since parting she had been in the WAAF[14] but was discharged from service early at CIM's request. Beryl had passion, a presence that impacted the whole group. There was a persistent air of purpose about her, whether she was striding along the corridors of the training centre, getting to grips with the pots and pans after a meal, or earnestly engaging others in conversation about the claims of Christ on their lives. She embodied a deep restless desire to get closer to God, her spirituality becoming a serious challenge for the candidates to aspire to. It was clear she had considerable potential for future leadership.

As the last term of training came to its conclusion, the final formal and formidable hurdle for the would-be missionaries had to be faced: the CIM Sailing Council. In the ups and downs of the recent years Joan had learned that God was in control of her life and she had no doubt he would bring his plans to fruition. She needed only to be obedient and patient.

The ordeal passed. Joan emerged from her interview with the information that she would be on the first voyage to China, whenever that may be. The war in Europe was over but Japan was refusing to capitulate to the demands for her surrender. Once again Joan needed to find gainful employment. She had needed to meet the fees for her training while at Newington Green, using what little savings she had, gifts she occasionally received and a legacy of £100 from her grandfather. There would be no funding from CIM until she set sail for China.

During her time at Bermondsey Medical Mission Hospital, Joan had attended and been baptised at Rye Lane Baptist Chapel in Peckham, south London, where the Reverend Theo Bamber, a popular preacher, was the minister. On a Sunday evening the church could be packed with up to a thousand in the congregation. Latecomers would be given seats on the pulpit steps. Despite a bomb destroying the original building, the church crammed into other premises and continued to function throughout the war. Joan had taken up attendance again while at Newington Green, cycling regularly through the hectic traffic-laden streets south of the river on Miss Bond's bicycle.

Mr Bamber suggested that Joan become a deaconess at Rye Lane Baptist. This, he argued, would be helpful in getting to know the members of a large congregation and would give Joan more direct experience in ministry. The church would support her with prayer and finance when she went to China. Joan happily agreed and for a few weeks was busy with the church's activities, visiting the sick and speaking at women's meetings. At a missionary thanksgiving service she found herself uncomfortably seated amongst the 'worthies' who graced the church platform. Required to give her testimony to the full congregation, she spent two days preparing and had her eyes fixed on possible escape routes as she delivered her message.

The 'notice to sail' arrived from CIM on the 23 August 1945, Japan having surrendered on the 15 August. A booking was being arranged for Joan on a cargo ship, the appropriately named *Chinese Prince*, incongruously bound for Bombay[15]. From India, she would fly into Chongqing where the CIM had its wartime headquarters. She must be prepared to leave in September. It was time to say her goodbyes. She might not see family and friends for another seven years.

Would she miss her family? The truth was that they had ceased to be a 'family'. Doreen, Eric and Vivian were living their own lives in different parts of the country. There was Betty in Cambridgeshire, with her son, Brian, now in his late teens. Isabel was with Heather in Scotland. Of course, she cared for them. But the family had become a broken jigsaw, dislocated into fragments that no longer fitted neatly together.

And what of her father? Joan's love for him was clearly reciprocated. She was, she knew, a wistful reminder of her mother to him. Did he still disapprove of her leaving him and sailing to China? He visited her in London. 'I need to buy you a few things,' he said by way of explanation. Together they scoured the shops which were still recovering from the deprivations of the war. Joan came away with cutlery and crockery and various items of bedding as well as a good-sized canvas holdall with leather straps, ideal for her journey.

To Joan's amusement her father had insisted that she purchase a double blanket. The implication was obvious. He was still hopeful that she would marry even though she was now close to 30 years old. How could she explain that her disillusionment with marriage had grown out of his example? She had no desire to find a husband. Much as she would have loved to have children of her own, getting married was not an attractive proposal. But what did he think about her going? That she did not know and could not ask...

At her valedictory service in Newington Green, Joan received a small, printed, buff card signed by the CIM home director and the secretary:

China Inland Mission
Joan Margaret Wales
Received into the Fellowship of the Mission
on September 5th 1945

And handwritten on the reverse:

'I thank Christ Jesus my Lord, who hath enabled me,
putting me into the ministry'

1 TIMOTHY 1. 12[16]

It had been nine years since her call to China. Now she was to be put 'into the ministry'. The path had rarely been straightforward but God had been proved faithful. There had always been a way opened for her. Her financial needs had always been met. She had progressed from the early days of naivety about what was required to a deeper understanding of the ways of God.

Whatever her father's feelings, Joan was gratified to see him at the service. 'You will come to King's Cross Station and see me off?' she asked.

'Of course.'

Under the charge of a senior missionary, Miss Emma Warren, a sailing party of seven congregated at King's Cross. Beryl Weston and Dorothy Jones, now close friends, were there but Annette Harris would sail with a second group in November. They were joined by Edith Cork, a clerk, and May Polhill. May was a nurse and the daughter of one of CIM's celebrated Cambridge Seven, well-educated young men who had caught the imagination of the Christian public in leaving for China in 1885, among them Charles T. Studd, an England cricketer. The Reverend Gordon Harman, the epitome of an earnest Anglican minister, was the only male in the present assembly and would need to maintain his composure as the foil for his female companions' amusement.

Emma Warren was a gaunt, anxious-looking woman, who had served in the Church Army and had 20 years' experience in China. Whatever her qualifications as a missionary it was clear that she was not overjoyed at the prospect of shepherding a bunch of six raw recruits a third of the way around the world. There was little prospect of relief from her responsibility; the company were going to be together for a long while.

The group gathered together towards the rear of their stream train, the 8.55am to Hull, quickly attracting a sizeable crowd of travellers, porters and parties of soldiers returning home. Under the elegant curve of the glass roof and decorated cast-iron arches Mr Aldis solemnly called them to silence and the porters removed their caps as he led in prayer. 'The Lord's my Shepherd'[17], sung vigorously in four parts, sounded across the station forecourt.

Joan said her goodbyes to members of Rye Lane Baptist Chapel who had come to see her leave. There was time for a final few meaningful moments spent with her father and then she boarded the train.

'In pastures green, he leadeth me... Yea, though I walk in death's dark vale...' Familiar words, foreshadowing their futures. The travellers would not forget those final few moments. Moments etched in memories. Moments to reflect on in the good light of day. Moments to treasure in the coming darkness.

At 6.30am Sunday morning on 23 September 1945, the *SS Chinese Prince* eased away from her mooring and headed into the North Sea towards the Channel, the excitement and anticipation of the new missionaries only temporarily disturbed by the explosion of a mine close to the ship early on the Monday morning. It was the final act of war for them in Europe.

Chapter 6

Thursday Sept. 27th.
Rounded Cape St Vincent in the night. Lunch time
saw Africa for the first time. High rocky coastline. A
contrast to the sandy shores of the Spanish coast we
have been following. It is wonderful to see places
that have only existed on maps – the Bay of Trafalgar,
Gibraltar.[18]

Joan looked up from the red 'Egypt series' pocket
notebook that she had designated her diary. Her minute,
neatly formed handwriting matched the concise entries
she had made each day since leaving Hull. Hurrying
footsteps in the corridor brought Beryl bundling
animatedly into the cabin.

'The others are on deck. There are porpoises. Come on!'

Joan pursued her swifter companion eagerly up the
flights of steps to the starboard deck. The group were
leaning on the ship rails, looking out over the dark blue-

grey water that stretched away to the North African coast. As spray splashed up from the cut of the bow, rainbows were refracted in the sunlight. Alongside the boat, pairs of the black-backed mammals were arching up out of the waves, exposing for a moment their white underbellies.

'They're dolphins... You can tell by the snout. Porpoises have blunt noses.' A few yards away two Welsh businessmen were engaged in disagreement.

'No – they're smaller than your dolphin. Dolphins are a couple of feet longer. This close to shore they're more likely to be porpoises.'

'That doesn't mean they *are* porpoises. It's a well-known fact that dolphins follow steamers.'

Dorothy raised her eyebrows in mock scorn of her fellow countrymen and whispered, 'Men! Neither of them will give way. Can't admit to being wrong!'

There were only two other women on the boat: a French secretary heading for Sri Lanka and a British nurse working in Beirut. The rest of the 48 passengers were predominantly businessmen or government officials. The presence of the missionaries had created considerable interest; they were regularly questioned about why they were going to China. In response Joan and her colleagues were only too happy to give their testimonies of God's guidance. One of the Welshmen had taken to giving Dorothy tins of toffee and chocolate in quantities embarrassingly more than sufficient for their needs, reflecting his concern for the deprivations he felt she would be facing.

'I will have to send it back to Wales!' commented Dorothy.

The *Chinese Prince* was a 150-metre-long cargo vessel, just two years old, armed with anti-aircraft guns, which were fired regularly as practice. Her substantial shipment of lorries for the Indian subcontinent meant she lay well in the water, giving them a smooth passage. Amenities for passengers, however, were non-existent and deck space sparse. Forty-eight berths were squeezed into just twelve 'single' cabins. The CIM party were pleased to discover that all the stewards were Chinese but, as the men were Cantonese not Mandarin speakers, they were disappointed that conversation with them was limited to the men's faltering English.

For Joan, the journey was an utter adventure. Apart from a trip to Paris with her school and her work in Ireland she had not ventured any further afield. There always seemed to be new sights to see and Joan never tired of watching the relentless swell of the sea. The ship's sedate progress provided real opportunity for relaxation, while their day-to-day study regime meant there was rarely time for boredom.

Each day started with a cup of tea brought by their cabin boy. His name was 'Johnny', the son of a Chinese father and Filipino mother, and he spoke some English and Spanish. Beryl had befriended him and given him a copy of John's gospel in Chinese characters[19]. Occasionally he and the other stewards would attend their worship services.

Breakfast, after the deprivations of war rationing, was akin to a banquet. Peaches, followed by haddock, followed by poached egg on toast, followed by toast and marmalade with tea. Lunch was a similarly large spread – soup, a choice of curry and rice, beef and pork dishes, cold meats and salad before a generous dessert, all finished off with coffee and cheese and biscuits. The butter available for one meal would have lasted a week in Britain. Dinner was a third feast of the day and it was usually beyond their ability to sample all that was on offer.

The ship sailed on through the throat of the Mediterranean, keeping to the African coast – past Algiers, scenes of small houses dotted on slopes, vines and orange groves perched along hilltops and onto the Bay of Tunis.

Saturday Sept. 29th.
The Dark Continent still in view – a call to prayer

Miss Warren had immediately instigated a daily routine of prayer and study. The team met morning and evening in 'The Sanctuary', the cabin where Miss Warren, Beryl, Dorothy and May slept. While the three younger women took turns in the top bunk to enjoy the view provided by the cabin porthole, their senior missionary had declined the opportunity, saying that she did not like climbing so high.

At other times the group would do 'turret time', settling themselves in one of the high-sided gun turrets at the prow of the ship, sheltered from the wind and hidden neatly away from the noise of crew and passengers.   After breakfast there were lessons in doctrine given by the Reverend Harman. Mandarin lessons with Miss Warren followed afternoon tea. The evenings were spent on an in-depth study of the Sermon on the Mount.

The ship rounded Cape Bon and sailed on to views of

the exotic-sounding islands of Zembra and Pantellaria, before launching out into the deeper waters of the Mediterranean and crossing to the shores of Egypt.

Tuesday Oct. 2nd.
Very hot! Two days without sight of land. Late afternoon saw sand dunes to starboard. 9.30pm the pilot came on board, his boat lit like a Christmas tree. Anchored a mile offshore. Lights of Port Said visible. Watched the police and officials arrive in motorboats. Went to bed late.

Joan rose early and made her way onto deck. In the harbour motor launches had already arrived, crammed with noisy traders selling their wares. Their pidgin English was adequate enough to acclaim the quality of the leather bags, sun helmets and ornaments on sale, barter fiercely with their naïve customers and complete their transaction with a compliment on an excellent choice. Joan withdrew to the gun turret for her 'quiet time'. The prospect of going ashore after a week aboard ship was stimulating, but her times with God would prove more precious.

Tickets to get to the quayside were the equivalent of three shillings: pieces of paper printed with the words 'Motor Lunch Service'.

'You'd think someone would have told them to correct it by now,' Dorothy noted. 'I mean there must have been enough Brits and Yanks through here recently.'

At the top of the gangway was a dishevelled policeman, dressed in a crumpled navy-blue uniform with a tasselled red fez on his head and a rifle slung lazily over one shoulder. He unhurriedly inspected their permits to land and allowed them to proceed.

Port Said abounded with palm and acacia trees sheltering streets of open shopfronts which spilled out onto sandy pavements. There was a surprising number of barbers in business, competing for position amongst the money-changers and teashops. Traders, with barrows hogging space on the roads, and vendors sitting in the gutters, offered the Europeans eggs, fresh dates, ices, lemonade, limes, peanuts and potatoes. And on the agreeable main boulevards they were surprised by their discovery of familiar stores such as Marks and Spencer, and Woolworths.

'Please. You want guide?' An Egyptian approached them and shooed away the few persistent vendors who were following them. He was dressed like a European and wore an armband with the word 'Dragoman' written on it, a status perhaps bestowed officially or possibly self appointed. 'Sixpence.' He waved his hand around the group. 'Sixpence each.'

The party followed their guide through the press of the crowds, picking their way past men in long robes, who seemed to have stepped out of pictures of ancient Palestine, and others in recognisably Western clothes. Joan and her companions were amazed at women swathed in black burkas and fascinated to see men with trays, piled high with rounds of unleavened bread, on their heads. The policemen here, dressed in white uniforms, were much smarter counterparts of their dockland colleagues.

Wherever they went there seemed to be men lounging on benches with apparently little to occupy themselves.

And beggars – mainly children of six to ten years of age. At the quayside they would dive for coins thrown into the water.

'You want?'

Joan turned to find a fair-skinned, curly ginger-haired boy, no older than two, being thrust at her.

'You want to buy? Good boy. Very clever...'

Joan was taken aback. 'Oh, no... No.' She hurried away after the others.

They passed through a residential area with washing hung out to air from upper-storey windows. 'Reminds me of parts of London,' remarked Edith dryly. And then into well-appointed public gardens boasting immaculate lawns with fir trees shaped like tables and chairs. Finally, they were taken to a mosque, a beautiful modern structure complete with electric lights and furnished with mats for the poorer worshippers and carpets for those with higher incomes.

'We are going to be late for the boat.' Miss Warren was getting agitated. 'We can't afford to be late.'

The guide assured her he would get them back in time. 'You first see Greek church.'

Miss Warren pointed to her watch. 'Eleven o'clock. We must be back at the boat. Eleven o'clock.'

The guide refused to be rushed. 'No problem. Greek church also very nice. We have time.'

With an exasperated look Miss Warren followed him, afraid to lose him, worried that without him they might not find their way back.

Thursday Oct. 4th.
Up at 5.45am...

It was Miss Warren who had aroused each of them vigorously to come on deck to see the sunrise as they started down the Suez Canal. Clambering sleepily on to the dark upper decks it was clear that they had risen well before the sun.

'Miss Warren...' groaned Dorothy, 'it's not yet daybreak.' She and Beryl hurried downstairs again to bed until Miss Warren roused them a few minutes later and induced them back with news of cups of tea being brewed by the ship's engineer.

Joan stayed on deck watching the dark gradually thin to translucent grey, seeing the sky washed with the restrained dyes of early dawn. The stillness was barely disturbed by the muted conversations of fellow passengers around her. Beneath her, the black water lapped placidly past the flanks of the ship. Stretching away to the horizon lay the low outlines of sandy hills, amongst which she glimpsed the occasional silhouette of an oasis. Now the sky was imbued with increasing intensity of colour. Above her, overwhelming in beauty, the sky suddenly flushed with orange, then gilded through rapid degrees into resplendent gold. All at once the aureate ball of the sun appeared, launched into orbit above the horizon, captivating them all in awe. The dazzling finale to a breathtaking performance provided by their Creator.

As the ship sailed on, the engrossing cameos of the daily lives of the Bedouin and native Africans were interrupted with sad reminders of the war. Strung out along the canal banks was the mangled rusting wreckage of boats, the decaying steel carcasses of once sea-worthy vessels torn apart by mines. Further along was a vast settlement of tents, home to hundreds of refugees, and then desert acres occupied by internment camps.

They passed an American warship with a dozen wits hanging on the rails shouting, 'You're going the wrong way, buddy! It's all over.' The *Chinese Prince* steamed down the length of the Red Sea, along the Gulf of Aden and out into the isolation of the Arabian Sea.

> *Friday Oct. 12th.*
> *Sighted land for the first time in five days 2.30pm.*
> *We have arrived two days early! Mountains in the*
> *distance. Our 'Gateway to India' – Bombay.*

At dusk the group disembarked. Their early arrival had created difficulties. They had no accommodation. While Miss Warren once again worried, Beryl took the initiative and phoned their host. Beds at the American Methodist Mission Home were secured fairly promptly and an agent from American Express promised to help them make their way there. Dinner could, however, not be provided for such a large group at short notice. Leaving their luggage outside the docks with the obliging man from American Express and with fervent prayers that it would not disappear into the Indian subcontinent, the party clambered into two horse-drawn cabs and headed for the restaurant at the railway station.

India at night was an absorbing contrast to their visit to Egypt. As their cabs, lit with quaint oil lamps, rattled through the incongruous mix of transport – motor vehicles, trams, taxis and buses, all striving for space with rickshaws, ox- and hand-drawn carts – they saw people rolling out straw sleeping mats on the pavement, some of them surprisingly already asleep amidst the cacophony of horns and the shouts of merchants and hawkers still plying their trades. There was the pitiful sight of a beggar scarred with leprosy pleading for alms. And the strange spectacle of sacred white bullocks roaming freely, nosing their way unhindered into shops. The missionaries' destination was impressive: the huge Gothic-style Victoria Terminus[20], reminiscent of London's St Pancras Station, where they ate in the ornate restaurant and waited for the man from American Express to see them to the mission home.

On Sunday they attended a Harvest Festival service conducted in Kannada at the mission church. They were the only Caucasians present amongst a packed church of Indian believers. The Indian pastor preached without notes, both eloquently and enthusiastically, gesticulating passionately at his congregation. The music was provided by the curious combination of a trombone and several violins. Some of the tunes were good 'British' stalwarts. Others they had never encountered before.

'That was quite stirring. I could just feel the spirit of worship,' enthused Edith as they departed.

'Would do congregations back home good to hear that!' declared Dorothy and then added, 'Apparently they auction off the gifts of needlecraft and fruit after the service.'

'Now that would create a stir back home!' laughed Beryl.

The following day the missionaries secured second-class sleeping compartments, refuges of relative seclusion from overcrowded carriages, on the train from Bombay to Calcutta[21]; a 44-hour journey across northern India. Having left Bombay the train climbed into the Western Ghats, giving passengers a magnificent view of the sun setting over rugged black rocks, a backdrop to the golden-green fields through which they were passing.

At mealtimes the train pulled into stations along the route, allowing the passengers to disembark if they wished. British appetites were well established, with a breakfast of porridge, two eggs, sausage, bread and butter provided for them. Here the party again encountered beggars, the children singing songs they had learned from the American forces to solicit sympathy. For the majority of the journey Joan stayed in the compartment, shared with May, Dorothy and Miss Warren, absorbing the view. Wandering along the length of the train was not encouraged. Their senior missionary insisted on keeping the door barred shut so they would not be disturbed.

The rice harvest was being gathered in. Men worked in the fields, carrying sheaves on their heads. The women tramped to and from their wells with large brass pitchers while others scrubbed clothes in pools they shared with their cattle. In the countryside the homes were crude mud-and-rush huts, a contrast to the lofty blocks of flats that dominated the towns. Joan enjoyed the flowers she spotted, particularly the lotus blossoms, but was deeply saddened by the numerous temples and shrines she saw scattered along their route.

In Calcutta there was the same experience of life lived

out on pavements, with all manner of vehicles bent on creating a corridor for themselves down the busiest of streets. Carts carrying idols, accompanied by throngs clapping and dancing to strange rhythms of drums and gongs, trundled heavily through the melee. Typhoon rains created additional havoc, flooding smaller dwellings in torrents of dirty water. It was impossible to travel far without arriving in damp clothes that proved impossible to dry. The city, however, was not unduly perturbed and continued to function in its own unique fashion beneath an abundance of large black umbrellas.

The accommodation in Calcutta was less comfortable than in Bombay; beds were provided in a girls' school and meals supplied at a mission hospital across a city square. The bathroom contained a single tap surrounded by a 'bath' of clay walls, only large enough to stand upright in, and draining out onto the bathroom floor. Hot water was available when the sun shone on their side of the building. It was a week before the CIM agent obtained flights into China for some of the party.

Thursday Oct. 25th.
Had dengue fever. Just wanted to die!

Joan had been unwell briefly in Bombay after a cholera inoculation. Now she had developed a fever, and intense pains aggravated all her joints, down to those of her little fingers. Dengue fever was diagnosed: a short-lived but severe condition that leaves the sufferer earnestly wishing for a similar lifespan!

With only three seats secured on the next available

flight it was decided that Beryl, Dorothy and Edith would fly to Chongqing alone. Gordon Harman and May Polhill would visit 'Chefoo School', a facility established in China in 1881 for the education of the children of CIM missionaries and evacuated to north India due to the war. Joan would wait with Miss Warren in Calcutta until fit to travel.

On the last Sunday in October, following a service at the Methodist church, Joan returned to the girls' school and assiduously donned layer after layer of clothing in the sweltering heat. She and Miss Warren, both stuffed like miniature sumos into thick British winter coats, shuffled self-consciously onto the street and hailed a taxi to the offices of the Chinese Navigation Aviation Corporation.

The luggage allowance for their flight was restricted to a double weight quota of 40 kilogrammes. Books and bedding, crockery and cutlery, all their baggage and belongings needed for seven years' service were to be weighed well in advance of their departure and transported to the airport. Anything that could not be packed into their luggage must be carried one way or another.

'Dorothy says she was 60 pounds over her normal body weight,' reported Miss Warren.

Joan did a quick calculation. That was considerably more than half her own weight. What on earth had Dorothy been wearing?[22] And in this heat?

Alighting from the cab was as difficult as getting in. Joan slid to the edge of her seat as best she could and lowered herself gingerly onto the road, losing her handbag in the ungainly process. There were several minutes of desperate sweaty struggle with her inflated girth before she abandoned her quest to retrieve it and called for help. Both women were relieved once they, along with their luggage, had been weighed and they were allowed to return to the school and divest themselves of their supplementary wardrobe.

'Would you like a piece of chocolate, Miss Warren?' Joan proffered the senior missionary a piece of the soft confectionery as they waited to board the plane very early the following morning. The sultry heat was already causing Joan considerable discomposure in the layers she had donned once more. Miss Warren, for some reason, wanted the fan turned off.

Miss Warren shook her head. 'I think not, Joan. I wouldn't want to put weight on. We were measured quite accurately yesterday. I'm sure it was important.'

Joan gazed at her in incredulity. They had eaten both an evening meal and breakfast and slept since the weighing.

The two women wedged themselves into the basic metal bucket seats of the transport plane, their backs against the ribs of the aircraft. The flight would take them over the jungles of northeast India, across the languid Ganges and into Burma[23] where they would refuel. Beyond that was the hazardous ascent over the infamous 'Hump', the barrier of Himalayan peaks that protected the route into Yunnan Province of southwest China, and the descent to China's 'Spring City', Kunming.

Once they were airborne Joan looked along the plane to the small cloakroom. Some of the male passengers had gathered in the gangway. Despite the discomfort of her attire it would be inappropriate to ask them to make way as she shuffled past, only to emerge minutes later looking considerably slimmer and clutching a large variety of garments, including a range of underwear. Miss Warren was clearly not going to make that particular journey. Joan stayed in her seat.

The final section of the journey carried them north from Yunnan into Sichuan Province. In the late afternoon the extensive terracing of cultivated countryside around the wartime Chinese capital, Chongqing, came into view; a complex collage of fields decorated the landscape, where even the smallest of slopes had been exploited to maximise the harvest. They could see the broad steel grey of the Yangtze River cutting through the steep inclines on which the city had been built.

The plane circled over an island in the river and positioned itself to alight on a short landing strip located there. Within a matter of minutes Joan eased herself from her seat, descended the aeroplane steps and stood on Chinese soil. The first nudging towards missionary service as a child, the growing conviction that God wanted her in China, the uncertainties of proceeding in the face of her family's qualms, the initial rejection and the intermittent timing of her training had all contributed to this moment. There was that acute knowledge that God's plan for her life was being fulfilled.

'*Ni de huzhao.*'

'Your passport, Joan,' prompted Miss Warren.

Joan handed over her distinctly British, midnight-blue passport to the Chinese official. He flicked through the pages, stopping to scrutinise her photograph. Given the rigours of the flight and her recent illness it was to be wondered if the formal portrait of the pretty young woman who had left London bore much resemblance to her current looks, thought Joan. The man turned to the visa she had obtained before sailing, a purple imprint complete with a vivid orange ten-dollar postage stamp and a red-ink chop. Dutifully he added his own date stamp, penning in '29 October 1934'; the year was calculated from the inauguration of the Republic of China, Year Zero – 1911.

'*Ni de zhongwen mingzi?*'

Joan looked blank.

'Your Chinese name,' said Miss Warren, looking increasingly agitated at her pupil.

'I don't have one... yet.' She shook her head. '*Meiyou zhongwen mingzi.*'

The official returned the passport and, with a few instructions incomprehensible to Joan, indicated they were free to go. Beryl, Dorothy and Edith were waiting for them, staggered at the sight of them both still wearing the copious clothing they had left Calcutta in.

A flat-bottomed boat, propelled with an oar at the stern and another on one side, in which they stood not sat, transported the women across the Yangtze. A climb of 400 steps cut into the hillside brought them to the road leading to the CIM headquarters. Due to the restrictions imposed by her clothes, Miss Warren's ascent necessitated the use of a chair carried by coolies, much to the amusement of her young colleagues. No doubt Miss Warren would be relieved to no longer have responsibility for them!

Finally Joan stepped inside the CIM Mission Home. Her journey had taken just over five weeks.

Chapter 7

'Earth and heaven were so commingled that it
seemed as if, like Enoch, she could at such times
have passed from one to the other in a moment.'

H. W. OLDHAM

Joan rose early and walked down to the road beside the
mission home. Beryl, Dorothy and Edith, having arrived in
Chongqing earlier, were going ahead to Chengdu, the
provincial capital. Joan would join them there before they
all started out for language school at Leshan, a sizeable
town located on a major tributary of the Yangtze River.

The missionaries had gathered around a jeep and
trailer parked on the road. At the wheel sat Major Levi
Lovegren, interpreter with the United States Army air
corps and for 18 years affiliated with the American Baptist
Foreign Mission Society in China. He was a married man
in his mid-fifties, slim, with an open honest face, notable

for a tidy clipped moustache. Now, as a leader within a new organisation, the Conservative Baptist Foreign Mission Society, he was exploring the possibilities of setting up a mission station in a remote region of Xikang Province. An area, unfamiliar to Joan, centred around a town by the name of Xichang.

Major Lovegren was on his way to Chengdu and had three spare seats in his jeep. Obligingly he had offered them to CIM. Luggage was heaped into the trailer. There were prayers and then the three women took their places and shouted their farewells.

There had been a remarkable nine days of exploring Chongqing when, free from the restraint of Miss Warren, the four new arrivals were encouraged to find their own way around. Beryl, Dorothy and Edith had suddenly become seasoned experts, in their own eyes at least, showing Joan the things they had already discovered.

They had indulged in silk for wadded gowns, which made them look like 'teddy bears', and cotton overdresses so that their newfound finery would be kept clean; the silk, to their surprise, was as cheap as the cotton. They had climbed and descended 1,250 steps on a trek to a holiday bungalow in the hills across the river. There had been a CIM wedding – innocent fun in preparing an apple-pie bed well in advance of the honeymoon and pangs of regret as they watched the bride, stricken with dengue fever, give her vows sitting on a chair.

Chongqing itself, despite being the wartime capital, was unexpectedly primitive. Most of the houses were roughly built with bamboo and looked vulnerable to the slightest breath of wind. The roads were mostly unmade or cobbled and pitted with holes. In the rain they were simply churned to mire. There were few motor vehicles, though unnumbered policemen patrolled the crossroads; the preferred form of travel was by rickshaw.

The locals were dressed predominantly in a monotony of sombre blues. With very few beggars to pester the missionaries, the population seemed more self-sufficient than the people they had encountered in the Middle East and India. There was a constant fascination with Beryl's feet. Her size eights seemed extraordinarily enormous to the Chinese, used to the bound feet of their women, crushed into slippers barely three or four inches long. Dorothy's fair hair also aroused considerable comment. Joan was thankful for her small stature, brown eyes and dark hair which allowed her to blend in more readily.

On the Sunday they had sat through their first Chinese service, astounded at the distractions of peripheral activity as people came and went. There had been commotion while women dealt with the 'accident' of a small child in split pants. During the collection a significant delay occurred as one lady insisted on getting change before placing her offering in the bag. Afterwards, the pastor had given each of the missionaries a Chinese name. Wales had been transliterated to Wei, the surname preceding Joan's given name, Zhu'an – meaning Bamboo Peace.

Joan returned to her bedroom. She must make her own preparations to travel to Chengdu. Once again she found herself without her friends. It would be good when they were all together at Leshan, Gordon Harman and May Polhill included.

Dorothy Houghton, the wife of the mission's General

Director, came to find Joan that evening. 'We have received a phone call from Chengdu. Major Lovegren's jeep went off the road. Dorothy, Edith and the major were bruised, but they are safe.' She paused. 'Beryl has gone to be with our Lord. She died in the accident.'

Beryl? Beryl, who had seemed the best candidate of them all? Dead? It was not possible... But the news from Chengdu said otherwise.

'You can stay in Chongqing longer if you wish,' said Mrs Houghton gently. 'There is no need for you to depart tomorrow.'

Joan, entwined in her thoughts, looked up. 'No... I would like to be with Dorothy and Edith. They must be devastated. Dorothy and Beryl had become very close.'

Joan sat alone, struck by the strange 'coincidences' of life. It had been Beryl who had requested the singing of Psalm 23 the evening before she, Dorothy and Edith had left Chongqing. There was a deep-rooted memory of partings at King's Cross. And now... a leave-taking they had never anticipated. 'Yea, though I walk in death's dark vale...'

Death was by no means remote. The history of the mission was punctuated with fatality due to disease, accident and hostile forces. Beryl had departed for heaven. This time it was Joan and her friends who had been left behind to grieve.

And it had been Beryl, just days before, who had spoken of being profoundly stirred by a book she had read, *To What Purpose?*[24] – the life of Dr Emil Fischbacher, a CIM missionary from Scotland. Fischbacher and six other young men had crossed the barren terrain of the

Mongolian Gobi in a Ford truck to Urumqi, Xinjiang Province. Within weeks the team had been beleaguered, as in January 1933 a force of 10,000 Kazakhs and Turkis attacked the city. Fischbacher, the only doctor amongst them, was exhausted with treating the injured and dying. Struck down by typhus he had died just fifteen months after his arrival in China. Now Beryl herself had died. But her service, unlike his, had scarcely started.

As the day drew to its heartbreaking close Joan fumbled for answers to her questions. If she had not had dengue, would she have been on the first plane to China? Would she have taken Beryl's place in the jeep? If it was impossible to find purpose in Beryl's death, could there be answers in life? She must embrace the positives - Beryl was alive with Christ. She, Joan, had been given life to live for Christ.

There was added poignancy to the second departure of the week to Chengdu. A hushed gathering listened to earnest prayers for safety in travel. Two senior members of the mission accompanied Joan and her companion, Margery Sykes, to the bus station to ensure they got away without a problem.

'*Tian!* Hang on!'

The bus erupted into a volley of half-strangled cries. The vehicle had suddenly slewed across the road. The driver fought with the steering and thrust his full weight on to the brake pedal. The bus shuddered towards the edge of a paddy field and came to an abrupt stop, tilting alarmingly to one side.

'A wheel's come off. This is going to take a while,' sighed Margery as she rearranged herself again.

Things had not started well with the presence of a crazed individual on the bus. Then the driver had taken the wrong road and needed to retrace the route. It was difficult not to think of Beryl. A tragic accident on a potholed road...

Attempts to repair the bus were rapidly abandoned. The travellers were left squatting at the roadside, surrounded by scattered items of baggage. Alternative transport was needed before night closed in. Their luggage would follow, they were reassured.

'Whatever comes next we get on. Agreed?' said Margery.

Joan nodded. They couldn't wait there forever. Being encircled by inquisitive onlookers was tiring. They prayed for a trustworthy vehicle to get them to the next village. An antiquated cattle truck, the rear already packed out with passengers, rumbled into sight.

'This is it! Scramble in.' Margery gave Joan a push from behind to get her up over the back of the lorry.

'I'm standing on people's ankles!' yelled Joan.

'You can't be genteel getting onto buses, carts or lorries. Otherwise you would be wearing out straw sandals like there were shoe shops on the corner of every street.' Margery swung herself up behind Joan and they squeezed onto crude benches pushed up along wooden stays as the Chinese generously created places for them to press into.

'You get used to it!' shouted Margery as the lorry lurched into motion. 'Oh Joan!'

Joan looked down in horror as the man next to her vomited over her lap. 'Am I to get used to that too...?'

'The Chinese don't travel well,' said Margery, searching desperately for a clean cloth to wipe away the puke. The reply, while factually correct, was no consolation. Sitting with the stench of vomit on her lap, whilst the truck reeled uncertainly onward, was more than enough to make Joan feel sick herself.

Margery negotiated a night at a rather inadequate inn. The two women had been told they would need to be up at 3.30am if they wanted to get another truck. The presence of a battalion of bed bugs, however, denied Joan much rest. 'Don't they wake you?' she enquired drowsily of Margery, who seemed to have slept without trouble.

'Yes,' replied Margery, 'but I give them a nudge and go to sleep again.'

Their luggag, had mysteriously materialised some time during the night and this was loaded with them onto a lorry, which arrived at 5am. Finally, as evening drew in, Margery and Joan took a rickshaw to the high compound walls of the Chengau Mission Home. Tired from a day's travelling, they were thankful there were no further incidents en route, and that there was opportunity for – in Joan's case – a much-needed bath, a luxury normally afforded once a week.

* * *

'We made great progress that first day,' recounted Dorothy. She, Edith and Joan were sitting together around a table, weaving wreaths for the funeral. Dorothy was nursing a swollen mouth. She had lost teeth in the accident. Her glasses had broken too. 'It was going so smoothly. We swapped seats from time to time, taking turns in the front. The major was a real gentleman. A bit traditional. Wouldn't let anyone else drive. 'Too dangerous,' he said. Ironically, he was very right about that.'

'We stopped at the ferry,' added Edith. She too was quite bruised about the face. 'Beryl was talking to the children there. Like you, she's so good... she was... so good with them. Speaking to them in garbled Chinese. Then she found a boy who could speak a few English words. Beryl got some paper and wrote 'Jesus came to save sinners' on it. She gave it to the boy. That was her first real opportunity to share the gospel...' Edith stopped. 'I mean, it's only twelve days since we arrived.'

Just twelve days. Barely time to adjust to daily routines, let alone start an effective ministry. Could one short message, written in a foreign language, for a peasant boy have any eternal significance? It was hard to see beyond the tragedy.

'You'd got to the ferry,' said Joan eventually.

Edith nodded. 'We made it to the inn where we should have stayed the night. The major felt we could carry on to Chengdu. It was after that things started to go awry. We had a puncture. That was sorted out with the spare tyre. Two hours further on – another! The wheel was in poor shape, so the major swapped it for one on the trailer. And that was when the rain started.'

'It sounds abysmal!' Joan said.

'No... we were just having one big adventure. Beryl was in her element. Said this was real missionary territory! The roads were a nightmare. We'd gone no distance at all and another tyre had a flat. It really was dark now. No way to fix it. We just settled as best we could in the jeep and waited for sunrise. First light, the puncture was repaired and off we went again. We were covered in muck, but happy, thinking of the story we could tell when we arrived.

Eventually we found a stream and stopped to wash and breakfast. Beryl got out her *Daily Light* and read to us. "Hope to the end for the grace that is to be brought unto you at the revelation of Jesus Christ"[25] and "He will swallow up death in victory"[26]. Afterwards it seemed sadly significant, but at the time we were just eager to get to Chengdu.

'About eight miles from here, coming through the last range of hills before Chengdu, the road was in a shocking state. The rain had softened up the surface. On a bend we skidded. The jeep just couldn't hold the road. The major hollered, "We're going over". 'Dorothy and I were in the back. We were thrown around like ragdolls. God alone knows how we kept our seats. The trailer flew off at an angle. The jeep rolled over. There were bangs and yells. The horrible scrape of metal on metal. A scream. I thought, 'This is it, I'm going to die'. But in the middle of it all there was an overwhelming sense of peace. It was the strangest experience...

'The jeep slipped rear-end first into a gully. There was a tremendous "thud" as we slammed against a wall of earth. We dropped back onto four wheels. Then stillness.' Edith paused. 'Beryl had been thrown out. She was under the wheels when we righted ourselves... She must have died instantaneously.'

'After that it's hard to comprehend what happened,' said Dorothy. 'The major went off to get help from the next village. Only he didn't come back.'

'What do you mean?' Joan looked astonished.

'He just didn't come back. Edith and I were left sitting on our luggage by the roadside. It was surreal. There we were, surrounded by the beauty of the countryside. I was gazing numbly at these breathtaking "cone" hills with poor Beryl... dead... lying just a few feet away. A few Chinese came. We showed them Beryl and they laughed! I was furious. I could have screamed at them. The people here told us it's cultural, something to do with embarrassment. But... it still makes me angry. I wonder how I can ever learn to love them.

'Then soldiers turned up wanting fuel from the vehicle. They did nothing to help, just went away again. Finally, a man with some English arrived... well, if we wrote down our questions he understood. He said Major Lovegren had gone to Chengdu and would return the next day. He wanted us to go with him to a town about a mile away. I know it's terrible, but we had to leave Beryl lying by the roadside. We paid coolies to carry our luggage and we were taken to the town barracks. The man wanted us to stay in a hotel but we felt had to get to Chengdu. In the end he kindly found a truck for us. On the road into Chengdu we saw the major returning with another jeep, but we couldn't stop. We felt safer where we were anyway!

'In Chengdu we hadn't a clue where to go. The address was on a letter which Beryl had been carrying. We found coolies with rickshaws and they took us to the wrong place twice, before a complete stranger came up with the right street name. I've sent some gospel material to the man who helped us,' Dorothy ended their story. 'I had to do something. I can only pray that some good comes out of Beryl's death.'

By noon the three young women had made seven wreaths from a plentiful bouquet of mixed flowers, bought for 3,000 *yuan*[27], the equivalent of a pound. There was a wreath for each group of bereaved they felt would have wanted to send one, including Beryl's family and her home church; each carried a different Bible verse. For themselves they had chosen 'Death is swallowed up in victory. We will be glad and rejoice in his salvation.'[28] – Beryl's final Bible reading on the day of the accident.

On Sunday 11 November 1945 20 missionaries, most having never met Beryl, gathered for a brief funeral ceremony in the afternoon. Howard Mowll, the archbishop of Sydney and previously bishop of West China, took the service. They sang the hymns, 'For all the saints, who from their labours rest'[29] and 'A mighty fortress is our God'[30].

The archbishop spoke on the text 'To what purpose is this waste?'[31] It was a question the three friends would never truly answer. During their stay in Chengdu their fellow missionaries and Archbishop Mowll comforted and cared for them. They were, as Joan wrote in her diary, 'helped through'. And through it all, as Dorothy confessed later, God held onto them.

The lacquered Chinese coffin, lined with silk and filled with flowers arrayed around Beryl's body, was conveyed to the West China University campus where a small cemetery for foreigners was located. In a simple ceremony of goodbyes Beryl was buried alongside others who, in grateful obedience to God, had given their lives for love of the Chinese.

Chapter 8

'Appreciation turns to love.'

JOAN WALES

Joan, Dorothy and Edith, with their chaperone, Sam Jeffrey, host of the Chengdu Mission Home, had left their boat some distance upstream, stranded on a sandy bank in the middle of the river. Ferried ashore by another vessel, they had watched as their crew strained on ropes wrapped around scantily protected shoulders. Frayed hemp twists grazed their exposed ochre flesh as they bowed their heads close to the water's surface with the effort. The craft, however, was not easily dislodged and in the end the three women and Sam had left the men to their labour and strolled on downstream.

The new missionaries were sailing down the Min River from Chengdu to the language school in Leshan. After the rollercoaster turmoil of the last few days – the exciting initial impressions of China and the wedding in

Chongqing, followed by the accident and sorrow at Beryl's funeral, and then almost immediately having to respond to the joyful announcement of the engagement of two CIM colleagues – it was a time to let the healing of an unhurried boat-ride nurse wounded bodies and begin to unravel a tangle of emotions.

Their vessel was no more than an oversized open rowing boat, about 30 feet long, bulging amidships to eight feet wide. An oval cover of woven bamboo ran two-thirds of the length with room for the six oarsmen at the prow and the steersman to the stern. Their copious baggage, on which they settled themselves as best as they could, was stowed in the boat, along with supplies of food to be cooked on a small oil stove whenever the crew called a halt for meals. This November the weather was dry and warm enough to sleep on deck wrapped in their *pugai*: cotton-filled quilts that they needed to carry wherever they went.

There was something exceptionally pleasant about wandering idly along the shore of the river. They had been blessed with a sunny day to start their three-and-a-half-day journey. There was an unlooked-for harmony in walking together beneath the tall, fern-like bamboo shrubs arched over the rich red earth of their path. They revelled in views of snow-capped mountains beyond the gorges that held the river to its course.

The company came to a cotton factory and watched the workers taking the raw material through stages of cleaning and spinning onto spools before being woven into cloth. 'Like our lives,' commented Edith. 'We're the raw cotton. Someday perhaps God will be able to weave us into something he can use.'

As they walked on towards a village, anticipating the intense scrutiny of the locals, who would be intrigued to know who they were and fascinated with their European jumpers and skirts, the questions over Beryl's death re-emerged. Their challenge, it seemed, was to reconsecrate their lives, which had been spared, to fulfil God's purposes. While Sam Jeffrey preached to the crowds who gathered to see the strange foreigners, the three women handed out tracts. It was the first uncertain endeavour in their fledgling ministries.

Leshan lay at the confluence of the Min and Dadu, both major rivers, meeting almost at a right angle. The town swept across flat terrain in an arc of tiled-roofed brick houses and less engaging ramshackle huts fronting dirt streets, from the west shore of the dominant Min around through 90 degrees to the north shore of its tributary. The CIM mission compound at Leshan was a substantial property situated close to the old city wall, beyond which rose a series of small hills, with the Min River a short distance away. Across the river stood an imposing statue 233 feet high, the largest stone carving of Buddha in the world. Beyond the shorelines were stacked tree-covered hills and, on cloudless days, mountains bordering Xikang Province were visible in the distance.

The seven female language students were housed in the smaller of two large residences with wide balconies supported on brick pillars, sleeping in rooms alongside or above their classrooms. The rooms were furnished with rough wooden desks, chairs and beds – all surplus to the requirements of the American army and rescued before they were destroyed. Each room had been named. Joan and Edith were assigned to 'Praise'. Dorothy was in 'Grace', the bedroom she would share with May Polhill once May arrived from India. The dining room was 'Unity' and the sitting room 'Fellowship'.

There were six members of staff, John and Jean Lockhart and Marvin and Miriam Dunn, together with a language supervisor, Joan Ipgrave, and Joan's companion from Chongqing to Chengdu, Margery Sykes. For Joan this was an occasion to find a family again. The Dunns had a daughter of eight months and the Lockharts a new baby girl, just a few weeks old. Joan was naturally drawn to them. Free time gave her the opportunity to be with the children and help with their care, a role she revelled in.

As the family atmosphere of the compound intensified, every possible occasion for amusement was seized upon, serving as an antidote to the communal afflictions of cultural adjustment, daily living and language acquisition. Joan's birthday in late November was decorated with camellias, ferns and balloons, another item appropriated from the American army. The Chinese cook, who had the look of a scholar rather than a chef, produced a cake complete with icing for her. Other birthdays were celebrated with a meal at the local 'Precious Stream' restaurant. Christmas celebrations were supplemented with stockings, 'secret Santa' presents and 'booby prizes'. Chinese New Year in early February was an opportunity to waken the compound with firecrackers. Banter, teasing and general horseplay were not unusual. The students were also initiated into the enjoyment and exertions of volleyball, a sport new to most of them, played every afternoon.

The China Inland Mission had built a church in the Leshan compound, which now had a congregation of about twenty-five Chinese. Pastor Wu, the young minister and an articulate preacher, looked no older than a teenage boy, but had a wife and four young children. The confused language students, confronted with the demands of services and meetings in Mandarin, were aided by the local believers to find their places in hymn books and encouraged through their first Chinese prayers.

Margery Sykes was allotted the task of taking the students out to the neighbouring mission stations. Joan's turn came at Chinese New Year. At the local Gospel Hall, where Margery was due to preach, Joan waited by the door to greet members of the congregation. One of the first to arrive was an old woman hobbling on bound feet towards the church.

'*Huanying...*' said Joan respectfully, but the woman ignored her completely and headed for the front of the church. Joan watched her get stiffly down on her knees and pray. After a few moments the woman rose, returned to the door and greeted Joan politely.

'*Dui bu qi, Jiaoshi...* I'm sorry, Teacher. I just wanted to wish Jesus a Happy New Year first.'

Despite having limited Chinese the ministries of the new missionaries began to take shape. In April, one by one, they again visited Margery on an outstation, a place altogether less pleasant than the language school, situated adjacent to a gambling den and disturbed throughout the night by rats. Nevertheless their perseverance was to yield fruit, with Margery reporting nine conversions on her return. Joan and Edith's Mandarin teacher also professed a belief in Christ, as did another teacher and the cook. The students also became aware that there was an eagerness to learn English amongst the townsfolk, which enabled them to build relationships and share the gospel.

For their language study, much time was spent lost in the pages of *Mathews' Primer*, mastering the tortuous intonation of Mandarin by endless repetition. Slowly they began to decipher the enigmatic encryption of complex Chinese characters. Milestones were marked by the passing of exams.

As the humidity of the hot summer season began to rise, the school retreated for two months to the cooler heights of Mount Emei, a stunning green curtain of hills, sacred to Buddhists, southwest of Leshan. Seventy pieces of luggage were loaded onto an open truck and most of a party of eighteen clambered up on top. Gordon Harman did not join them. He had already been assigned to a placement in east Sichuan Province. 'If any of you want me to marry you, let me know,' he had told them at his farewell meal. The circle of spinsters had eyed him with some amusement and reassured him that whilst he might officiate they could not accept such a universal proposal.

The truck took the party to the river, and a ferry ride and two buses finally brought them to the lower slopes of the mountains. There they began the steady ascent to the CIM holiday bungalows. Like many other mountains of significance, the route from foot to far summit was cut into a long ascendant staircase of thousands of steps. A journey to the peak could take a day and a half of hiking, climbing the majority of the route in single file. *Huagan*, simple sedan carriages carried by two men, were available to ease the ascent, while coolies carried their luggage on bamboo frames strapped to their backs.

The slopes were studded with Buddhist shrines, surrounded by hillsides dressed in wild beauty. Pilgrims, carrying tiny pots of burning incense, prostrated themselves every few steps. There were new temples under construction and older ones being enlarged. Images of Buddha dominated: rank after rank of mud-and-straw, wooden and stone statues, before which monks chanted and offered their prayers.

While there was much to delight in – familiar and foreign flowers, tea bushes, myrtle trees, rustic bridges over streams spilling into attractive waterfalls, cradled in the magnificence of the landscape, there was a need to be wary. Snakes with the girth of a small tree trunk were not uncommon. One day during their stay, one of the missionaries chanced upon a leopard consuming the remains of a calf.

The CIM bungalows were wooden chalets on stilts, which were to be the students' classrooms and accommodation. Once the group had settled in and routines had been established, they continued their Mandarin studies and completed their exams in the tolerant coolness of the mountain.

The return from Mount Emei in August 1946 signalled the end of formal study. Dorothy would go to Guizhou Province and Edith to Jiangxi. May Polhill would return to work in the town where she had been born, in another region of Sichuan. The women's friendships were to be fragmented, only to be enjoyed at a distance or, occasionally, when their paths crossed. Compounding the sense of loss were the departures of the Dunns, Lockharts and Margery Sykes. The language school was to be closed; new students were already being sent elsewhere. Joan would remain in Leshan with Joan Ipgrave, but the language supervisor would move on when replacement workers arrived in the New Year.

During her first months of study, Joan had needed to come to terms with her feelings for the Chinese if she was to be effective in the full-time ministry she was now starting. In monocultural Britain she had never met a Chinese man, woman or child. Here, she had been confronted daily by, what seemed to her, the strange practices and standards of Chinese society. Initially, there had been so much that seemed peculiar and more that perplexed her.

And there were things that had angered her. How would she get beyond the unresponsive stares that rebuffed her whenever she ventured out of the compound doors? How could she ever reconcile herself to the sight of women's feet broken and pressed into tiny slippers scarcely longer than the length of her fingers? In her mind she still sheltered the vivid image painted by Dorothy of Beryl's body, trapped beneath the jeep. A picture of Chinese peasants laughing. How could they apparently find amusement in such a tragic death? Could they not have helped instead? Did these people have no compassion?

As she had walked to the market Joan had heard hostility in the voices that whispered 'Yang Guizi – Foreign Devil'. The phrase had been like a mantra, repeated over and over, hammering home rejection. It was like the beating of a blacksmith on his anvil. Not shaping a useful tool but devising an ugly twisted implement. A contrivance that Satan could use to drive a rift between Joan and the people she had come to serve.

Joan had swiftly learned that love of the Chinese did not come easily. Time and perseverance were needed. She was encouraged in her outreach by Pastor Wu and the church. As the obscurity of customs and the mysteries of Mandarin had slowly assumed 'normality', Joan had begun to enjoy the challenges of ministry. She saw the needs and had learned compassion. A growing appreciation had taken the place of her antipathy. And finally that appreciation had turned to love.

Chapter 9

'We... counted her for Nosuland but didn't imagine
she could feel so deeply for us.'

JIM BROOMHALL

The arrival of two small children to the CIM compound at
Leshan in the spring of 1947 brought yet another dynamic
to the ever-shifting mosaic of missionary life. Four-year-
old Jan Broomhall was a fair, curly-haired girl with all the
earnest desire of a child to convert anyone who didn't
know Jesus. Her sister, Pauline, at two, had short straight
fair hair, a quieter disposition and an acute determination
not to be dominated by her older sibling. She was also, as
the saying goes, 'as bright as a button'.

Joan knew their mother, Janet, through their nurse
training together at Bermondsey Medical Mission
Hospital. Janet was in the second trimester of another
pregnancy and was no stranger to the risks and rigours of

childbirth and motherhood in a hostile environment. Pauline's birth had been traumatic, coming as the family were fleeing China for India by horse, sedan, truck and plane in the face of the ongoing occupation of China by Japan in December 1944. With Janet close to term, a telegram had arrived at their residence in Guizhou Province by runner from Kunming three days' journey away. The Japanese were advancing on the provincial capital, Guizhou. Getting safe transport to Kunming could be difficult if they delayed their journey.

The family had left their home the next morning and had sought the shelter of a missionary's house at a neighbouring mission station when Janet's contractions started. Jim, her husband, had delivered the baby, while Janet administered her own anaesthetic in the form of an ether pad. The family rested for two days before they were back on the road again, mother and baby bundled into the rough and ready security of a sedan chair hauled along by two Chinese.

Joan had not met Jim Broomhall before. Head and shoulders taller than Joan at six feet one inch, Jim was an attractive and imposing figure as he strode confidently around the town and villages offering aid to the sick. Even in the dreariness and impoverishment of the post-war years he maintained a smart appearance. He had strong, well-defined features beneath neatly cropped, blonde-brown hair. In both his eyes and his stance an observer could visibly sense the depth of his character.

It was also readily apparent that Jim was accomplished in more than just his practice of medicine. He had a love of nature, a keen interest in architecture, and was something of an artist, magician, musician and photographer. He was also a prolific writer of letters and articles. A book he had composed from memories of a minority people's church in Guizhou Province, where the family had worked for four and a half months before their evacuation, was being published in Britain[32].

'It's about a pastor of the Nosu people, by the surname of An,' Jim explained when Joan asked. "Mr Peace" we called him. I wanted to highlight the plight he and his church face. There is another group of Nosu, a far wilder bunch than Pastor An's clan! When the Qing Dynasty suppressed the Nosu 200 years ago, some accepted Han rule but others retreated to an inhospitable region to the south of here, Daliangshan, the Great Cold Mountains. There are maybe three quarters of a million Nosu there, untouched by the gospel and lacking decent medical care.'

As he spoke Joan began to see the intense desire that Jim had to use his skills to bring God's message of salvation to these tribal people.

'I first read about them in a book on China – an intriguing description of brutal tribesmen inhabiting a mountain territory which strangers entered at their peril. And then, shortly afterwards in another book set in the Antarctic,' he laughed, 'believe it or not! I was about twenty-five when I got hold of a book written by Captain Scott. On an expedition he and his companions told stories to pass the time. I was fascinated by the tale of a British lieutenant, one Francis Brooke, who had ventured into the Great Cold Mountains. There he had encountered the Nosu, the "Black Tribe", ruthless men clothed in red-dyed buckskin. The expedition failed. Things turned sour and

Brooke was left fighting a futile battle from the vulnerable shelter of a mud shack. When his ammunition ran out, the Nosu killed him with a rock thrown from the roof.

'These wild Nosu mustn't be forgotten,' went on Jim. 'Headquarters have given permission for us to explore the possibilities of establishing a clinic amongst them. There are two other missions getting involved. Leshan is our base until we find a way in.' As he spoke Joan looked across at Jan and Pauline playing in the courtyard. The question was unasked. 'We will go as a family,' said Jim. 'Janet is definite about this. Our mission is unequivocal. To go where Christ has not been named.'

A few days later, the third member of the Nosu team arrived in town. If the prospect of taking a family into the intimidating harshness of the Great Cold Mountains was to most minds foolish, the choice of a 54-year-old, single woman as co-worker did not particularly seem an astute addition. But then it rapidly became clear that Ruth Dix had chosen herself. Jim and Janet's open letter, aimed, as they thought, at spirited young men, requesting help in their new initiative from CIM colleagues, had brought one response – Ruth's.

Jim and Janet had left Ruth in Chengdu to bring the transport Jim intended to use for his first visit to Daliangshan. His first objective was to get to the town of Xichang, the main administrative centre in the region. From there he hoped to ride into the hills of Nosuland and negotiate with one or more of the Nosu chiefs for land on which to establish a mission station.

'I got tired of waiting for Wang to get the truck sorted out,' Ruth offered by way of explanation as she settled herself in. 'If that vehicle gets to Xichang and back we will know that the age of miracles is not over.'

Ruth was all that Jim described, 'a game bird for all her silver hairs'. Now an experienced midwife, she had joined CIM in 1920, ironically at a time when the mission was appealing for more men to come forward for missionary service. Her first mission stations had been in Sichuan Province, working in a dispensary, an opium refuge and a girls' school. She too was no stranger to evacuation, having been forced to abandon her work in two cities as Nationalist and Communist forces clashed in northeast Sichuan. On the second occasion the city was in uproar as people fled from the Communist advance. Ruth, having secured an inadequate boat for thirty to forty Chinese, the aged, the infirm, and mothers with babies and small children, found herself stranded with them mid-river for twenty-eight hours. There was little to eat. Being effectively in command of the boat, she spent much of her time wrangling with persistent Nationalist soldiers threatening to requisition the vessel for their own flight.

Ruth's silver hair was kept in good order, reflecting the attention to detail she brought both to her appearance and to her work. For a woman she had a deep voice, which unfolded into a likeable chuckle when amused, but there was a striking and appealing femininity in her looks. She had developed great versatility and efficiency and was driven by a desire to persevere no matter what the personal discomforts might be.

Ruth was in many ways a mirror of Jim himself and an able match as their ongoing banter often revealed. Both had an innate passion for their purpose in life and had worked together in Guizhou. Ruth had been with the Broomhall family on their flight to India and had assisted at Pauline's birth. Such was her involvement with them that, having become Pauline's godmother, she had established herself as a valued member of the family. There was little doubt that Ruth would give Janet and Jim remarkable support.

The truck, when it finally arrived with the hapless and irresponsible driver Wang, was the wreck that Ruth had described. Overloaded, unbalanced and in dire need of maintenance, it was coerced back to life for long enough to heave itself out of the yard and head south on the 300 mile makeshift road which would take Jim to Xichang.

Jim wedged himself alongside Wang and two other travellers in the cab and took his last opportunity to wave to Jan and Pauline. Saddened to see him leave, they could not imagine the hazards that he was facing. Apart from the ever-present dangers of travel on inadequate roads, such as the one on which Beryl had died, the route from Leshan to Xichang was by no means secure. The lack of adequate government meant that it was plagued by Chinese brigands and bands of Nosu with little respect for life. Merchants and their goods were easy targets unless they travelled in large groups. Jim must then ride unarmed into the mountains. The team knew that of the seven or eight foreigners who had braved the climb into this territory, three had been killed.

Behind him he left the two children, his pregnant wife, Ruth Dix and Joan, charged with maintaining their missionary outreach to the local community and praying for his success and safe return.

* * *

Jim's trip began in April and he returned in July, having spent forty-five days in Nosuland, traversing the territory from west to east. The journey had not started well...

'Wang's truck met its end just before we got to Fulin, three days from here,' Jim told Janet, Joan and Ruth. 'We had endured more than enough breakdowns, wasting hours with inadequate repairs. Wang was too close to the edge of the road once too often. The truck somersaulted sideways down an embankment to destruction. One of the passengers died. I was a bit shaken up but no serious damage.' He had been away for two and a half months. 'After that I got lifts with bands of merchants and made it to Xichang.'

For some while he described his journey into the mountains and painted pictures for them of the independent Nosu: their unharnessed violence and immorality, their deplorable fickleness and the tragic conditions under which they wrested an existence out of penury. 'In a location called Zhaojue we fell in with a friendly Ba'chie clan chief called Agu. Zhaojue also has a Chinese presence. It's definitely a strategic centre. A three-hour mule ride north of Zhaojue I met the chief of another tribe, the Hma, at a place called Zhuhe. The Ba'chie and Hma clans are literally at each other's throats but I was able to heal some of their sick and was given safe enough passage from one to the other while a gun battle raged. Eventually I negotiated escorts to get across Nosuland to the east and into the Yangtze valley. From there the journey home seemed easy!'

Jim slipped his hand into a pouch and drew out two

letters. 'This is what you were praying for...' The letters were succinct. Jim translated them into English. 'The first is written by Vuda, chief of the Hma in Zhuhe: "This letter is to greet the directors of the China Inland Mission. Dr Hai has come to our Nosuland. We welcome him warmly. If he comes to build a hospital, to dress our wounds and give us medicine we will be very pleased indeed. We Nosu know nothing about medicine and have no drugs. If we are taken sick we are helpless. If we develop leprosy or chronic diseases we are powerless, knowing no effective medicine or treatment. But now that Dr Hai has come, the Nosu are greatly pleased. No Nosu will oppose or molest him. The twenty-fifth day of the fourth moon.[33]"

'The other one is also written to HQ: "This Mr Hai's coming to our Nosuland makes us very pleased and respectful. We Nosu are very glad of medicine for our sick." And here's a note for Janet... "Later when Mr Hai's wife comes there will be nothing to fear, and no trouble will arise. We Nosu Blacks fully guarantee this. Fifth day of the fifth moon.[34]" That's from Vuli, one of the Ba'chie clan in Zhaojue. Took him an hour to compose it in his own script.'

Janet placed a third sheet of paper alongside the two letters. 'This is the telegram you sent us from Zhaojue.'

'Courtesy of the affable Mr Qiang, the telegraphist of Zhaojue!' smiled Jim. 'A telegraph office was one of the last things I expected to find. Mr Qiang hails from Shanghai. He was keen to study the Bible with me.'

Janet read the script: '"Everywhere cheerful respectful welcome. All Nosu factions grateful hospital". A little jolly in the circumstances as you have described them now! But we praised God to get it.'

Jim grinned at the three women sitting opposite him. 'God has prepared the place. We need to go and occupy it. First to Xichang, and then on into Zhaojue and Zhuhe.'

The next major preparations, however, were not for ministry to the Nosu, nor travel to Xichang. Janet's baby was due in the autumn and everything needed to be ready for the new arrival. On the 23 October Janet and Jim delivered Margie, their third daughter, into the family. For Joan this pause in preparations served to confront her with both her past and her future. She found herself increasingly drawn to the Broomhalls. The opportunities to help with the care of Margie brought out her natural affection for children. Jan and Pauline enjoyed her attention and were growing to love her as much as she loved them. But it was in Janet and Jim's relationship that she found role models through which God challenged Joan about marriage. Their obvious, earnest and romantic expressions of the deep-lying love they enjoyed, in circumstances that continually tested their constancy, revealed dimensions to matrimony that she had failed to see fully. It was here that she found a source of healing to the hurts of her childhood and teenage years. Balance was being restored.

God was also speaking to Joan through the very prayers she was offering as she worked alongside Jim, Janet and Ruth. A constant request was for missionaries to supplement their team. She was sure God was telling her that she was an answer to their petitions. Her future did not lie amongst the Chinese in Leshan, nor in one of the many existing mission stations across Sichuan. She needed to focus on the summons to serve the Nosu.

Ruth was the first to leave Leshan, taking the road south, matching Jim's earlier exploits. Her goal was to establish a base in Xichang for Jim and the family. Taking only an old male Chinese cook as her companion, she set out in the bleak of winter just after Christmas 1947. She and the servant carried little and dressed as inconspicuously as they could, not eager to catch the attention of bandits.

Food and shelter proved difficult to find. A diet of coarse buckwheat, corn cakes, turnips and bean curd was often the only fare on offer. Lack of daily progress meant finding abandoned shacks in which to sleep on armfuls of dry bracken. Added to that were the perils of natural hazards as they traversed hill ranges in the wintry weather, once narrowly missing death as an avalanche of rocks fell just yards away from their party. It was some relief to the Broomhalls and Joan in Leshan when the news arrived that Ruth and the cook had finally reached their journey's end.

Jim and Janet's route to Xichang was to be more circuitous, involving a boat ride south to the Yangtze and downstream to Chongqing. There they would wait for a plane to carry them to their destination. As the day of their departure, early in the New Year, grew closer Joan found herself increasingly distressed at the prospect of having to say farewell to the Broomhall family. Their leaving exposed feelings that far exceeded her emotions on her departure from England. They had accepted her in a way that she had not enjoyed for so long. Finally she searched out Janet and in moments of true tenderness unburdened herself.

'Joan?'

Joan looked up through her tears.

'We have been thinking to ask you to be Margie's godmother,' said Janet. 'We aren't sure how you will feel about it.' Joan was elated at the proposal!

Before they left, the Broomhalls gathered for an informal dedication service in which they drew Joan into the embrace of their family. For Joan there was a sense of belonging to the Broomhalls and they, through Margie, would belong to her. For the family, there was also the realisation that, despite giving up the security and support of their extended family in Britain, God had restored these comforts to them through Joan and Ruth. Although nothing had been said of Joan's desire to join them in Xichang, Jim and Janet had instinctively recognised her longing to work with the Nosu and in their prayers began to ask for her release from the work at Leshan.

The Broomhalls' departure left Joan alone in Leshan, working with Pastor Wu and the church. While she remained convinced that her future service lay with the Nosu, for the time being she needed to be content to minister amongst the Chinese. Her commitment, however, was to be tested. She was approached by another member of the mission whom she had met while studying at Mount Emei. He found her attractive, wanted to deepen their friendship...

Marriage? Once again Joan was confronted with conflicting emotions. Her father's hopes still lay in her finding a husband. What should she do? She declined the man's advances. His interest lay in work with Chinese students. She was drawn to tribal work. She must be obedient to God's calling. To demonstrate her commitment she contacted the Broomhalls, telling them of her hope to join their team.

In March, Joan carefully wrote a letter to CIM headquarters, now re-established in Shanghai. The kind response from the directors was not what she had wished for. She should complete her language training. It would be a number of years before she was ready for exposure to such a difficult ministry. Disappointed, she accepted their reply with her customary loyalty to the leadership of the mission. Once again, God would have to work out his plans.

Joan's letter was not the only one to cross the desks of the CIM directors. Jim also wrote, echoing her case: 'Joan Wales feels absolutely certain of a specific divine commission as clear as her call to China – that is to join us in Nosuland... She is already a first-rate missionary and speaking Chinese as well as I could after four or five years in the land. If she is allowed to come without delay it would be all the more possible for Ruth to pack up and mount her black horse for Zhaojue.'

Unaware of Jim's strong support, Joan was surprised to receive a second letter a few months later, in July 1947. The directors had relented. She was to take her final language exam as soon as she was able and then fly to Xichang at the earliest opportunity. By this time, the missionary team at Leshan would be replenished with workers from elsewhere.

Joan's first views of the Great Cold Mountains were in early November from the windows of a Douglas DC-3, the *St Paul*, a transport plane owned by the Lutheran Church.

Beneath her lay the creases and folds of high mountain ranges, cut by crevasses, arrayed around small valleys. Under the scrutiny of the autumn sun the landscape appeared as barren as the lives of the people who inhabited its slopes.

The plane began its descent into the narrow confines of an upland valley. The crescent of a large lake came into view. 'That's Qionghai Lake, just to the south of Xichang,' pointed out her travel companion, an American CIM missionary from Wisconsin, Floyd Larsen.

If Joan was the team's answer for more workers, then Floyd was the answer to the plea for single men. Floyd was in his thirties, dark-haired and of average height. He had already established himself as a valuable member of the Nosu team working alongside Jim in Xichang and up in the mountains. His need for urgent dental treatment due to damage caused by biting down on grit hidden within mouthfuls of boiled rice had taken him to Chengdu and provided the pleasant opportunity of returning with Joan.

Thickset and considerably stockier than Jim, Floyd had joined the Nosu team from his work amongst the Lisu in Yunnan Province. He and Jim had travelled to China for service with CIM on the boat from Canada in 1938 and he had graciously offered his services to Jim for a few months. Having had considerable experience of working in tough situations, he was proving ideal in negotiating and organising the buying and bartering of building materials and then arranging their transport by pack mule up to the building site for a clinic in Zhaojue.

The plane banked steeply down between the hills that protected the town to the east and west, before straightening for the final descent onto the rough field that served as a landing strip. Janet and the children were waiting for Joan and gave her a very loving welcome.

Xichang was a compact town, numbering around 35,000 inhabitants, which had grown in importance with the threat to Chongqing from the Japanese. Preparations to establish the town as a seat of government had transformed it from a place of little consequence, plagued by troubles with Nosu raiders, to a comparatively modern town with electric lighting, telegraph office and an occasional air service. Protected by thick stone walls with a moat on the north side, the town had been built between two rivers. Relative peace in recent years had allowed the residents to venture further afield. Houses and markets had started to appear outside the walls, which were now falling into disrepair through neglect and vandalism. Within the walls there were two decent roads running orthogonal to each other, crossed by more pleasant lanes lined with hedges and trees.

At length they arrived at a set of large double doors that faced onto the street. 'This is home for the time being,' explained Janet. 'We call it "Komfort Korner". With two "K"s, that is. We've cleared out a "prophet's chamber" for you. Ruth has the room opposite yours. We live downstairs.'

The compound was shared with a Muslim family named Ma who had once been wealthy. The sickening sweet odour of opium that embalmed the night air betrayed the cause of their descent into poverty. Far more pleasing was the verandah adjacent to Joan and Ruth's bedrooms. From there, they took great pleasure in an arresting view of the banks of mountains that they truly desired to call home.

Chapter 10

"'There's no sense in going further - it's the edge of cultivation,"

So they said...'

Before Joan's arrival in Xichang Jim had carefully drawn together a team of foreigners, Chinese and Nosu to renew contact with the Nosu chiefs in Zhaojue and Zhuhe, Vuli and Vuda. He had sought out a Nosu interpreter, Zhao, who had accompanied him into Nosuland on his first visit. Zhao was aged around 24 and was a high-ranking 'Black' Nosu, one of the superior caste who had not married outside the Nosu tribes. He carried with him a certain dignity, tall and gracefully energetic, with a frankness that appealed to Jim. Zhao's family had fallen into hard times with the death of his father and had moved out of the mountains into the valley where he had been educated in a Chinese school. Whilst in Nosuland, under Jim's guidance, he had confessed to faith in Christ.

Two other Nosu, from tribes that lived more easily alongside the Chinese, had also joined the team, though one had returned to his home after just four months' service. The other was Ming, a friend whom Jim, Janet and Ruth had worked with in Guizhou Province. Ming was married, but his family had remained in his home town. Having attended Bible school, he had become a recognised worker within the Nosu church. He was tall like Zhao, but did not have the same air of nobility and lacked Zhao's strength. A willing and practical worker, he had an ability to swiftly learn new skills.

The Chinese member of the team was a man by the name of Hong. Hong had been appointed the business manager. Based primarily in Xichang, his contribution to the work was invaluable. An older man, married with a son, he had the natural guile and the abundant enthusiasm of his countrymen for a bargain. Joan's arrival coincided with the recruitment of another Chinese man. A nurse, Tang, had come from Chongqing to strengthen the team. Added to these were a number of servants employed at various times, care being taken to distinguish their role from that of the slaves the Nosu held in bondage. Amongst them was the cook Ruth had travelled with. Of an evening, his duties complete, he would sit by himself and read his Bible, muttering his prayers into the dark.

The team's efforts had advanced on two fronts, establishing a presence in both Zhaojue and Zhuhe. The fort at Zhaojue, with its Chinese administration, provided an excellent location for a medical centre and a base for the team, but none of the existing buildings was suitable for their purpose. Jim and Floyd had negotiated the use of a corner of the fort compound and set about constructing a clinic and accommodation. In Zhuhe the team had purchased a dilapidated tavern for the inflated price of eight bars of silver, about £16. This had been converted to a dispensary, where Ming and Tang were now working.

If Jim had envisaged Joan coming to Xichang to allow Ruth to 'mount her black horse for Zhaojue', he had not anticipated Ruth's determination to get up into the Great Cold Mountains. Joan's arrival in Xichang in November 1948 was not the occasion to release Ruth from her duties in the town. Ruth was already in Zhuhe. She had waited ten months for her opportunity and when it came she was not going to miss it.

The previous month, in October, the team had faced a crisis. Jim and Janet were with Ruth in Xichang, Ming was isolated in Zhuhe, and Floyd was in dire need of a break from Nosuland, requiring treatment for his broken teeth. Tang had not yet arrived. 'I can't leave Xichang until I've organised the builders and pulled them into some sort of order,' Jim had explained to Ruth. 'They are so loath to go into the mountains. It's like being a taskmaster, whip and all.'

Ruth could not see any problem. She and Zhao, the interpreter, would go into the mountains at the end of the rainy season and help maintain the dispensary at Zhuhe. Jim could travel to Zhaojue when a sufficiently large and competent workforce had been assembled. Janet would be left in Xichang with the children, Hong, the manager, and a helper, Mrs Yang. Joan and Tang would provide more help when they turned up in November. 'We'll go once the rainy season abates,' Ruth had declared. The matter was settled; there would be no dissuading her. She and Zhao had departed as soon as they were able.

The dilapidated tavern at Zhuhe resembled little more than a glorified outhouse with stables and pigsty attached. The main room, which had previously functioned as an opium den, was entered through a makeshift doorway reaching no higher than a man's shoulder. Holes, punched in the newly whitewashed mud walls and faced with paper, barely illuminated the ash circle of the wood fire at the centre of the crude earthen floor and the gospel posters the team had pasted up. To complete the ambience of decay, the roof leaked.

Ruth was lodged in a minute, newly built loft above the stables, while Zhao and Ming shared a small room below. The privacy the loft afforded was scant. Conversation filtered up through the shoddily lain floorboards along with smoke from the fire, which irritated and inflamed her eyes and throat. The only latrine available was an open pit behind the tavern.

As the first white woman to enter the area, Ruth had rapidly become a lure for all the Nosu in the districts surrounding Zhuhe. They invaded her home incessantly, coming as soon as daylight permitted and settling themselves around the fire with little desire to depart until their almost voracious appetite for information had been sated. The questions at times seemed interminable and new visitors demanded the same responses day after day. Most were not averse to prying into her possessions, often mounting the stairs to the loft and examining the articles she had hidden there. In the midst of this intimidating inquisitiveness she was required to maintain her composure, pray for good health, patiently explain the gospel and continue to dispense medicines.

Life for Joan and Janet at 'base camp' in Xichang was a different ordeal. They needed not only to feed and clothe themselves and the children, but to meet the requests of Ruth, Jim and Floyd, provide wages for the team of builders in Zhaojue, and to buy construction materials for transporting to the clinic building site. Komfort Korner was stacked with baskets, cones of salt, rolls of cloth, sacks of rice, petrol drums, hammers, nails, mattocks, pickaxes and coils of ropes. In the rafters and piled under beds were heaps of straw and firewood. To make matters worse, rats had free rein in raiding their food stores, as the cat had died due to the bitterly cold weather.

The two women and the manager, Hong, faced major economic and logistical problems. With the momentum increasingly turning to the Communist armies, the Nationalist government was finding it difficult to maintain any semblance of economic order. Inflation had torn a gaping hole in the marketplace and ineffective efforts were periodically being introduced to shore up the battered currency. In just ten months of the previous year, the official bank rate had soared from 3,400 *yuan* to one American dollar, to 12,000 *yuan*. Black market evaluations had doubled, then trebled the official rate. Now the exchange values were escalating again, the trend alternatively confounded or exaggerated by local circumstances.

Previous generations of older banknotes had lost their

value. Huge wads of notes were needed for the smallest transaction. Sometimes there was simply not enough cash available to sustain the local economy. Promissory notes quickly lost their value. Cheques were worthless. Silver was now being bought at three-quarters of its market value and shipped to Nanjing to bolster the issue of another new form of currency.

Joan launched herself in the direction of the market. Towns folk sat in the doorways of shops, sparsely stocked with few goods of any quality. Sometimes it was just impossible to buy meat or vegetables or even firewood. At the roadside peasants were sitting on the dusty earth, hunched over small baskets of unappealing vegetables, calling to Joan in an effort to secure a sale. A pig ambled ahead of her, nosing the piles of debris strewn along the street. Tethered to a post was a goat being milked by a dark-skinned Chinese woman.

A Nosu man and his wife stood motionless against a wall and followed Joan's progress with blank eyes, their expressions revealing little. There were other Nosu, wearing turbans, wrapped in their distinctive blue cloaks, drifting around the town, disengaged from the daily routines of the Chinese. In an effort to bridge the gap, Joan had begun language classes with a Nosu teacher, but progress in half an hour's daily tuition through the medium of Mandarin was protracted.

'*Jiaoshi!* Teacher!' A peasant man waved a cabbage in her direction.

'How much?' asked Joan. Wiser now to the subtleties of bargaining, she affected a disinterested tone.

'One bar of silver.'

Joan looked aghast. A rough conversion was two pounds sterling. 'Too expensive.'

The man laughed. 'I'll give it to you for half a bar. No less.' And despite Joan's protests he refused to change his price. 'Half a bar.' Walking away with her purchase Joan reflected that she could never envisage a day when a plain old cabbage would cost her a pound in Britain.

As Joan returned home she heard strident voices being raised outside one of the shops. A fight had broken out over the price of salt. A few days before, a riot had occurred in the street near their home. Several of the combatants had suffered broken limbs. With the loss of confidence in currency transactions, the bartering of goods, rather than purchasing with cash, had become the predominant practice. It was not, however, the simple process of exchanging one item for another. 'It's like a convoluted treasure hunt. You get something you don't want and trade it for something else you don't want, until you get something you can trade for that you really want...' seemed to be the best advice available.

It was in this respect that Hong, their business manager, was priceless. He was forever scouting around the market, calculating how items could be traded for the products they needed. Substantial quantities of cloth, cotton, needles and salt were hoarded as basic commodities to trade. Joan's accounts, requested by CIM HQ, became lengthy, ever-fluctuating conversions of *jin*[35] of rice into hanks of yarn, to silver, to gold *yuan*, and finally into American dollars. However, as the state of affairs worsened, nothing they owned became indispensable for exchange.

At the end of November Jim and Floyd were together in Zhaojue. Ruth, having been relieved by the arrival of Tang, the Chinese nurse, had returned from Zhuhe to Xichang. Plans, however, were once more thrown into doubt with the receipt of a telegram from the American Consulate in Chongqing, warning of Communist advances in the area. The official message was not encouraging: 'View generally deteriorating... likely means of exit from China may later be unavailable... plan at once to move to places of safety'.

'We will stay,' decided Jim. 'CIM is still working in Communist-held areas. HQ is determined that all missionaries remain in their post for the time being.' The emergency forced him back to Xichang, leaving Floyd to do daily battle with the builders. Jim needed to reassure his own team of his determination to continue working and to canvas the opinions of other Christian agencies in the region. If these missions pulled out, CIM's ministry would be seriously hampered.

The first formal missionary outreach to minority peoples by the indigenous Church of Christ in China, the Border Service Department, had already established a church in Xichang. Among their staff were two couples from the UK, Ernest and Edna Madge and Bill and Win Upchurch. With the end of the Second World War Major Levi Lovegren had resumed his full-time missionary activities with the Conservative Baptist Foreign Mission Society. Under his leadership, their presence had grown to about a dozen American missionaries. They had plans to start a church and to expand their ministry to other major towns north and south along the river valley.

Joan had been disconcerted on meeting Major

Lovegren on her arrival in Xichang. Painful memories of Beryl's death had resurfaced. Dorothy, Edith and Joan had met him briefly at the Chengdu Mission Home for a few awkward minutes in the days after the funeral. None of them had known what to say to him. Joan had set out for language study at Leshan with no thought that they would meet again. His presence in Xichang challenged her. There was no doubt that, as the driver, she held him in some way responsible for the accident. Now they were working alongside each other, worshipping together. She must let her feelings go.

There was considerable relief when both organisations decided to stay. Jim resolved that, with the success of Ruth's stay in Zhuhe and the progress in building in Zhaojue, all the team could prepare to relocate from Xichang to Zhaojue. There were, however, some basics that needed to be tackled first. The ability to ride a horse, for instance, was essential...

Joan measured in her mind's eye the leap that would be required to get her astride the pony standing patiently in front of her.

'Take your time,' called Ruth from the other side of the animal. 'There's no rush.'

Joan braced herself and leapt, pushing hard on her left leg and thrusting her right leg up and over the pony. There was a gasp from Ruth as Joan sailed completely over the creature's back and dropped into her arms. The assembled onlookers exploded into mirth.

'Such enthusiasm is commendable,' remarked Ruth. 'Measured enthusiasm better. Shall we try that again?'

In January 1949 Janet and Jim, riding up to Zhaojue and on to Zhuhe, left Jan, Pauline and Margie in Joan's custody, content that her care for the children would be as complete as their own. The couple would be away for two weeks; this would be Janet's first venture into the mountains.

With Janet's departure imminent, Joan had been moved to share her inner disquiets from the past – this time, her concern for her father. She still did not know whether he was reconciled to her decision to go to China, let alone her desire to move into the uncivilised wastes of Daliangshan.

'Janet, can we talk about my father...?' Joan described the love she had for her father and her longing to see him restored in his faith, the faith he had enjoyed when her mother had been alive. 'I think he blamed God when my mother died. He wasn't able to accept what happened. I want to share with someone in prayer for him...'

On their return to Xichang, Janet and Jim were decided – they would move as a family to Zhaojue as soon as was feasible. Ruth would join Floyd to prepare a home for them in the first of the three buildings under construction, the aptly named 'Barn'. Once this basic structure was complete, the family would set up home there temporarily until they could move to the 'Cottage', a more homely residence being purpose-built for the couple and their three girls. Ruth and Joan would then relocate to Zhaojue as well.

The Broomhalls were acutely aware that there would be great opposition to taking the children into Nosuland. The risks were considerable. The family would be exposed to an environment of licentiousness, drunken orgies and witchcraft, to a culture of tribal violence and drug abuse. No one could guarantee their long-term safety. As parents they were under no illusions about what they were proposing to do. But the Nosu needed Christ; their eternity was at stake. And the family must be together.

Chapter 11

'...*a woman, waiting at a window open to the sky.*'

'Building materials required – tiles, wood, lime. Wages/barter items needed – cloth, cotton, cones of salt, lump silver...' Joan painstakingly matched bales, hanks, ounces, planks, pounds and skeins to dollars and cents. 'All told, around 500 US dollars...'

'And not a beansprout in the HQ kitty,' commented Jim.

Two telegrams had arrived from the CIM offices in Shanghai with the terse news that funds for the Nosu initiative were exhausted. It had been agreed that only gifts specific to Nosu outreach should be used for the work in Zhaojue and Zhuhe. General CIM funds were not to be touched. 'If God doesn't supply, then we need to reconsider our plans,' Jim added.

'Then we must pray,' interjected Janet. 'It's vital to keep

building. If the workers stop now it could be months before we motivate them to start again.'

There was no embarrassment as the three of them got down on their knees on the hard stone paving in earnest prayer. The China Inland Mission had been fashioned on a policy of non-solicitation and all the promises of 'Jehovah Jireh'. Each of the trio had their own stories of God's timely provision of their unspoken needs. This new 'crisis' was no different.

'Hai Yisheng![36] Hai Yisheng!' The hammering on the courtyard gates was urgent. 'Hai Yisheng!'

Jim, responding to his Chinese name, clambered out of bed. Someone needed a good reason to drag him to the door at 11pm.

'Hai Yisheng. *Dian bao... dian bao!* '

'Urgent telegrams are rarely good news,' he told Janet and went out to the gate. He returned in a better frame of mind. 'You'd better go and get Joan. She can't be asleep after all that racket.'

Joan joined them downstairs.

'This is from HQ,' said Jim cheerily. 'The equivalent of 500 US dollars has been received for the Nosu project from our supporters in Britain.' There was a moment's silence as the news sank in and then a joyous roar of laughter. 'God will supply all our needs. This is all the assurance we need. We can go ahead and move to Zhaojue.' In one very undistinguished corner of Xichang the jubilant sound of three foreigners praising God was to be heard well into the early hours of the morning.

On 6 April 1949 Jim and Janet roused the girls and put

the finishing touches to their packing. In the courtyard was a mound of baskets, boxes and drums stocked with clothes, medicines and equipment. Ming, their Nosu co-worker, was quietly checking that everything was in place. A train of sixteen mules was lined up and the muleteers loaded their backs with the baggage. As the mules shifted under the weight, they lashed out in irritation at the chafing of their saddle sores, giving lie to the gentle tinkling of the bells around their reins.

Two wicker armchairs, facing each other and padded out with blankets, had been bound onto bamboo poles beneath a small awning of oilcloth. This homemade contraption was a *huagan* made especially for Jan, Pauline and Margie. It had been suspended in the courtyard for two days to allow the three girls to get used to sitting in it. With the children secured in place, hired carriers lifted the bamboo poles ready to settle in step to a steady jogging pace.

'Where is Mrs Yang?' asked Jan.

'I'm sure she will come,' Janet reassured her. Mrs Yang, their Chinese house-help, had agreed to join them in Zhaojue, though not without some trepidation. But by the time she arrived, running breathless into the courtyard, the mules had already left. She was a charming woman but had previously been addicted to opium. Under Ruth's stringent supervision she had been cured of her habit. 'I am sorry, Hai Yisheng. My mother is unwell. I must care for her.'

Jim frowned, suspecting a ploy to avoid accompanying them. 'Let me come,' he said.

A short while later Jim returned, nodding at the unasked question that both Joan and Janet had. 'The lady won't last long,' he sighed. There was a moment of indecision. Should they postpone the journey? Wait for their helper to accompany them? 'The mules have gone...' said Jim. 'We can't get them to come back. We will have to go.'

Joan followed them out of the courtyard onto the earthen road and watched as Jim and Janet, both wearing wide-brimmed bamboo hats, mounted their horses. Jim had saddled Floyd's lively horse, Smuts. Janet would ride the reliable Bclinda, Jim's mule. Ming and one of the servants were to accompany them. The old cook, who had travelled with Ruth from Leshan, had decided that he would spare himself the deprivations of Nosuland and stay in Xichang enjoying the teashop gossip.

When they had gone Joan knew she would miss the family, and particularly the children. She would be alone until Ruth returned in May. There was, however, plenty to keep her occupied. Manager Hong would need managing and the provision of materials for building and food supplies to Zhaojue must be maintained. Mrs Yang would need comforting and there were others whom Joan had befriended and could visit.

'Mrs Lu!' called Joan at the door to the bank manager's home. She had been to the post office and smothered a letter to Leshan in several layers of glue to paste on 200 stamps. The highest denominations were far too low to meet the cost of postage. It was an absurd situation when the additional mass of stamps made the letter far heavier than its original weight, requiring yet more stamps. 'How are you, Mrs Lu?'

Mrs Lu met her by the door. 'Come in, come in. See, I can walk again!'

When Joan, with two Chinese companions, had first visited she had found the lady propped up inelegantly on her wooden slatted bed beneath a thick eiderdown. She had been bedridden for six months. The three visitors had squatted on wooden seats beside her. Looking around the room it was clear that this was one of the finer residences in the town. The room was decorated with pictures of folk gods and other figures from Chinese mythology. On one wall hung a shrine to some wooden deity, laden with small oranges and spiced plums.

The bank manager had roused himself from the book he was reading and gone to make them tea. He returned with a tray of minute cups and a miniature teapot. Carefully he washed the cups in the hot tea he had prepared before refilling the teapot and pouring them their drinks. '*He ba!*' he told them. 'Drink!' Politely they thanked him and, as etiquette demanded, left the tea to go cold.

'I want to tell you about Jesus and how you can get his help,' Joan had explained to Mrs Lu. She had shared how Jesus healed the sick, and read stories from her Chinese New Testament.

'I want to believe in your Jesus,' Mrs Lu had said when she had finished.

Joan had waved her hand around the room. 'Then you must stop worshipping wooden statues and these other paper gods. If you want Jesus to help you, then you need to trust him alone.'

To some astonishment it was the bank manager who,

having returned to his reading and apparently oblivious to their conversation, had jumped to his feet. '*Hao le!* Then that is what we will do!' Without further ado he had stripped the pictures from the walls and had ripped the idol shelf down. 'It is done!' he had announced to his wife.

Joan had thanked him for his very enthusiastic help and taken Mrs Lu's hand in hers. 'Now we can pray together...'

Since that first visit Joan had called on Mr and Mrs Lu many times. Now they sat together and Mrs Lu showed Joan the letter she had written to her relatives. 'I am asking them to follow Jesus. I have told them how the Living God has helped me.'

On other occasions Joan visited the women's prison with another Chinese Christian. There was always a warm welcome.

Joan handed out gospels. 'Who can read?' Two of the women put up their hands. 'Then you must read to the others when we are not here.' They had taken posters to brighten up the dank, squalid cells in which the women existed. They would be a good reminder of their weekly messages.

'You will come again?' asked the women as they left and Joan promised that they would visit each Wednesday.

By the summer there remained only two obstacles to Ruth and Joan joining the Broomhall family in Zhaojue. It was essential to have a Westerner to work with Hong on keeping the trains of equipment and stores moving; Hong's enthusiasm needed curbing from time to time and the meticulous demands of the CIM accounting system could not go unsupervised. The second necessity was finance. Their HQ oasis had not failed, but a 200 pound sterling reserve was required to ensure that provisions did not dry up. Jim returned to Komfort Korner prepared to escort the two women into the Great Cold Mountains early in September. In preparation for the four-day trek Joan took up riding over rough ground amongst the graves on the hillside above the town.

The provision of help in Xichang came from the American Baptists through Major Levi Lovegren. It was strange to reflect that it should be he, after all her reservations, who provided the means by which Joan could fulfil the ministry God had called her to. God did indeed have his own plans! Now they had only to pray for God's supply of the appropriate finances before they could leave.

A few nights later, Joan awoke and lay still in the darkness. There were sounds of movement. The crack of a shifting roofing tile. A board creaking on the verandah. The door to the passageway outside her room slowly opening. Bare feet shuffling carefully forward, step by step, on the wooden planks. Then the disturbing rhythmic breathing of a man just a metre from where she lay, separated from her by no more than a thin paper partition.

He had been before, two nights ago. Soap and blankets left on the verandah had gone missing. Now, emboldened by his success, he had returned and was exploring the house. Joan switched on the light. There was a clatter as the man retreated swiftly to the verandah before leaping onto an adjacent roof. And then a return of the midnight quiet.

'He'll be back,' opined Ruth as she retrieved a discarded pair of sandals from the roof the next morning. 'He won't be easily deterred.'

'What do we do?' asked Joan. 'Bed down on the verandah?' Jim, who was sleeping downstairs, had an alternative idea.

It was three nights before the burglar reappeared. Joan's senses were fully engaged as he slipped carefully down onto the verandah. He stepped inside the house. Joan could feel him alongside her, turning his head, listening, checking no one had detected his presence. He moved towards the stairs. Joan forced herself to remain in control. Slowly she stretched out her hand and found the rope Jim had left by her bed. A swift pull would ring a bell in the bedroom below.

The building erupted into commotion. Stealth gone, Jim pounded up the stairs and sprinted down the corridor past her room in pursuit of the man. A roof tile smacked against the boundary wall as he flung it at the intruder balancing precariously on the coping. There was a yell as a second tile found its target. Then, a cry as the man half fell, half leapt onto the dirt track below. Noises in the street. And finally quiet.

Jim knocked on the frame of the flimsy paper bedroom door. 'You all right, Joan?'

Joan gathered herself and went out into the corridor. 'Did you see him?'

'Just his outline. Too dark to see his face. I need some practice at tile throwing.'Whatever the merits of Jim's abilities with roof tiles, the burglar did not dare return.

On the first Sunday of September the team's prayers for

finance were answered. Another telegram, confirming the receipt of another substantial gift for the Nosu work, arrived from Shanghai headquarters. It was the final confirmation they needed. As soon as a mule train could be assembled Joan, together with Jim and Ruth, would set out for Zhaojue.

Chapter 12

*'Sweet meditations and discoveries are the peculiar
treasure of mountaineers. And they always find, I
think, that far more than the toils of the climb, they
remember the places where they gathered the
edelweiss of God.'*

AMY CARMICHAEL

Heavy rainfall, the consequential intrinsic dangers of the
route, and the capricious whim of the muleteers kept Jim,
Ruth and Joan in need of patience for a further five days.
On 9 September a crowd of Chinese gathered once more at
the doors of the compound to see what the foreigners were
doing. Their desire to leave the, albeit transient, comforts
and security of Chinese territory for the deprivations of
Nosuland was a 'madness' that few locals could
understand.

Joan hoisted herself onto Ruth's mule, Blackie, and Jim

158 POINT ME TO THE SKIES

settled himself astride Belinda. Ruth, having loaned her smaller mount to Joan, had a hired mule they had named Laddie. With them would ride Manager Hong and his son, along with the muleteers. Seventeen pack animals carried their personal belongings and loads of flour, rice, salt and sugar: provisions to feed the team and the twenty builders still on the site.

Jim gave orders to the muleteers and the convoy headed down the street to the town gates and out towards the surging river that lay across their route. The tributary had its source in Nosuland and flowed down to Qionghai Lake. On this Friday its banks were overburdened with torrents of runoff from steep hillsides. Upstream, racing currents marked out the thalweg until they broke on an insubstantial bridge. The flood threatened to engulf those who stood on its approaches, weighing the risks of crossing. In a shallower stretch downstream travellers had formed chains, grasping outstretched hands and linking arms to brave the waters. Some of the sturdier men carried women and children on their backs, making several journeys until all their party were safely across.

'Put your legs up behind you!' shouted Ruth. 'Blackie'll get you across.' Joan adopted this rather ungainly posture and allowed Blackie to take her own course. With a surety that was immensely reassuring the mule followed the lead horses, picking her way forward without hesitation. With each step the water rose, climbing high on her flanks but then receding as they climbed the opposite bank. '*Hao le!*' Jim was wringing water from his trouser legs. 'I knew that you having short legs had to have its advantages.'

For an hour the muleteers led the way to the rim of the

valley and then called the company to a halt, insisting that the mules graze before starting the ascent into the mountains. As they had travelled, the better cultivated pastures of the Xichang valley had given way to barren, poorly farmed tracts that bordered Nosuland. Joan dismounted and joined Ruth, who was surrounded by a group of Chinese children.

'Can we teach them *Jesus loves me*[37]?' asked Joan.

Ruth nodded. 'Why not?'

'*Yesu ai wo, wo zhi dao...*' The children stumbled over the words, giggling at their own awkwardness, yet growing more confident with each repetition.

'Jesus loves you. You can pray to him. He can help you.' Joan shared her straightforward message with them.

A group of Nosu men and women stood to one side. Not all the men had turbans with the distinctive horn above the forehead; some went bare-headed. Their fashion of blue tunics of rough cloth and loose cotton trousers varied little. One or two carried rifles with ammunition belts, strung with cartridges, draped over their shoulders. Others had knives scarcely concealed in sheaths. There was a general griminess about their appearance, accentuated by legs caked with mud and unwashed faces. For the most part, the women were as poorly dressed as the men, but the older wives were wearing silver earrings. Joan went across and attempted her few phrases of Nosu. 'The God of Heaven, *Mo'm Apu*, loves you.' The language didn't matter. The message was the same.

It was six in the evening before they forded the last of the swollen streams and trekked wearily into their stop for the night. The hamlet was no more than a collection of meagre fortified farms arrayed along the road. They were to spend their night in a 'horse-inn'; stables and fodder would be provided for the animals, but their riders must do with makeshift accommodation in the loft above or sleep outside. A Chinese woman emerged from the farm carrying a kettle of flavourless tea and offered them bowls from which to drink. Thirst prevailed over any judgement of the palate and they drank indulgently.

The fare that followed, however, a meal of undercooked rice, poor quality potatoes and bitter cabbage soup, left a lot to be desired. Appetising it could never be. Seated on a hard bench at a low table Joan, fatigued and pallid, stared at the food on offer. Jim and Ruth watched her, wondering if she could bring herself to eat. For a long moment her hand, clutching the crudely carved wooden spoon she had been given, remained at her side. Jim and Ruth reached to the pot at the centre of the table and scooped out a spoonful of the broth. Joan would have to eat. She followed their example... the red peppers scorched the back of her throat and tears sprang to her eyes.

Jim nodded and smiled sympathetically. 'I don't suppose it helps to say you get used to it?'

Joan didn't answer. She heaved a determined sigh, plunged her spoon in for the second time and ate. However nauseous the menu, the meal would stay down.

The inn offered little in the way of rest. The natural noises of the night were augmented by the vitriolic wrangling of the muleteers. In the loft Joan and Ruth contended with mosquitoes. At dawn there was the peculiar sensation of horses reaching up and snatching straw from between the boards beneath them. Bleary-

Map of Daliangshan and surrounding area

Chengdu

Ya'an

Mt Emei   Leshan

Min River

Fulin

Dadu River

Anning River

Daliangshan

Zhuhe

Zhaojue

Xichang

Qionghai Lake

Yangtze River

- - - boundary of Nosu territory

Joan with Eric (LHS) and Vivian (RHS), Children's Special Service Mission Camp, Paignton, Devon, 1925

Photo: Bertha Wales

Beryl Weston, 1945

Photo: OMF International

Language students at Leshan, 1946
Back row: Joan Ipgrave, May Polhill, Mary Welander, Dorothy Jones, Ellen Lister
Centre row: John Lockhart, Jean Lockhart, Marvin Dunn, Miriam Dunn, Edith Cork,
Gordon Harman. Front row: Isabella Davidson, Joan, unknown, Margery Sykes

Photo: Mary Welander collection

Jim Broomhall
Photo: Broomhall collection

Janet Broomhall
Photo: Joan Wales Collection

Floyd Larsen
Photo: Broomhall collection

Ruth Dix
Photo: Broomhall collection

Joan
Photo: Broomhall collection

Nosu team, Xichang, 1948
Pauline Broomhall, Ruth Dix, Ming, Zhao, Janet Broomhall with Margie, Hong,
Nosu colleague, Cook, Bottlewasher, Jim Broomhall, Jan Broomhall, Floyd Larsen
Photo: Broomhall collection

Agu – Black Nosu chief of Ba'chie clan
Photo: Broomhall collection

Zitu, leprosy patient,
Zhaojue fort
Photo: Broomhall collection

Black Nosu, Zhuhe
Photo: Broomhall collection

Janet Broomhall with Joy, Jan, Margie and Pauline, 1950
Photo: Broomhall collection

The Cottage at Zhaojue, with covered passageway and clinic to LHS, Great Hen in distance
Photo: Broomhall collection

Joan with picture of Jim Broomhall, Daliangshan, 1996
Photo: Joan Wales Collection

eyed, the two women climbed down at 5am. Breakfast was the same as the previous evening's meal – reheated, served and eaten with little relish.

The next two days would see the party covering fifty of the seventy miles to their destination. Now they would climb high into the mountains, deep into Nosu territory. It was, Jim pointed out, as though the Chinese government controlled a corridor of access to Zhaojue, the county seat, no more than ten miles in breadth. And what they controlled of the region around Zhaojue was limited to no further than the eye could see from the walls of the 'fortress'. Beyond these boundaries the land was in the hands of the Nosu clans.

Joan delighted in the flowers they encountered along the way. Anemones, bugloss, columbine, dwarf azaleas, gentian, monk's hood and periwinkle. And amongst them one of her favourites, edelweiss – sturdy green stems supporting silvery white leaves crowned with golden floral gems. No two flowers alike, paradoxically symbols of the fight against evil and tokens of love. The flora were more usually found growing on the face of hazardous crags, on the remotest ledges, inviting danger to the casual collector and jeopardy for an ardent lover. The missionaries were entering a kingdom remote and hazardous, a tribal fiefdom known for its malevolence. There was a wickedness they dared to defy. And like hesitant suitors they came with messages of love. Their own imperfect, faltering feelings and the deep flawless passion of God.

The company climbed to a pass at 10,000 feet. Below, in a narrow gorge impeding the path, were grouped Nosu men, squatting with their knees tucked beneath their chins, swathed in their blue cloaks. Even at this distance the muzzles of their rifles were intentionally on view. Joan had been warned of the unpredictable Nosu gangs who set up roadblocks and demanded payment before travellers might proceed. These were rarely peaceful encounters as the Nosu sought to extract as much gain as they could while the travellers tried to minimise their losses. A show of weakness was not advocated; the Nosu had minimal regard for meekness.

There was relief when the posse proved to be a sanctioned checkpoint. They would be asked to pay for safe passage through the region. Each mule would cost them half a *jin* of salt. A lack of iodine in the Nosu diet was responsible for a prevalence of goitres amongst the population and the commodity was in great demand.

The party were met with smiles and a request for their dues. Here on the mountain the Nosu were stronger, more sure of themselves than their clansmen down in the valleys. There was something noble about them that, but for the grime of their bodies and shabbiness of their attire, would have been appealing. As cones of salt were produced and the official scales set up to weigh the correct amounts, the men conversed cheerfully with the muleteers. They had heard of Janet and the children living in Zhaojue and quizzed Jim after their health. They asked questions about Joan and Ruth.

On the periphery of the group stood a few Nosu children, some naked, watching the proceedings intently, captivated by any movement of the peculiar white foreigners. The braver ones dashed forward as fragments of salt fell to the ground and carefully retrieved them, moving swiftly back to the others and displaying their plunder with animated shrieks of laughter.

Accommodation for the night was found in one of the larger collections of makeshift dwellings, where around fifty impoverished families of the Hma clan had congregated. The inns were huddled together along the route and provided a substantial proportion of their occupants' paltry income. The company were invited into a mud-walled home, a modest-sized abode with stables adjacent to the living area. Small as she was, Joan had to lower her head to gain access to the single-room living area. The fading daylight barely lit the room through the rifle-slit windows and it took some moments before her eyes adjusted to the dim light.

'Do you see the stairs to the loft?' asked Jim, bending double to enter behind her.

Joan stared into the gloom. 'No...' Beyond the opposite wall she could make out moving forms. These, she realised, were the mules in their stable. The stairs were simply crude steps formed to create a partition wall. Warily, not keen to fall into the stable area, she felt her way up into the bare hayloft. The loft floor was no more than a web of woven bamboo, slung insecurely above the stables. It moved disconcertingly as Joan dragged her bedding across to the far wall where Ruth would join her. No straw was available here. Jim, Hong and his son would occupy space alongside another wall and the muleteers along the third. There could be little privacy for the night. Joan would have to sleep in her clothes, stained and soiled from two days' riding. She was conscious of a peculiar mix of wood smoke and the distinct, vile aroma of opium. Above her the ceiling planks of wood provided no more than scarce shelter. She prayed that the rain would hold off. There seemed little prospect of sleep for a second night, but remaining dry would be a bonus.

Cautiously Joan made her way down the 'stairs' to where the others had gathered for supper. The evening meal was eaten by the light of a little oil lamp around a rickety table. Eggs had been purchased at the price of one ounce of salt each and provided a welcome side dish to the apparently ubiquitous serving of vegetable soup and rice. Joan, Jim and Ruth were handed slabs of buckwheat, a staple for the Nosu. The heavy dark-brown cakes were filling but virtually indigestible. Joan really did not like them. But... she took another chunk, scooped up a sizeable spoonful of soup from the shared pot and persevered. If the meal proved to be another ordeal Joan had one reason to be grateful – at least it didn't rain in the night.

The sudden appearance of more than fifty Nosu, blocking the path ahead at a point where the route narrowed, did not look good. The company had heard whistled signals from unseen scouts on the rocks above them and the band now standing in front of them had clearly responded to this obvious communication of their approach.

'Do you see a flag or scales?' Jim called cagily to Ruth who was several places ahead in the line. These were the telltale signs that the checkpoint was official.

'No. And I don't think we are going to either.'

'Let me get ahead,' said Jim, urging Belinda forward. 'You and Joan keep back for the time being. Hopefully it will be no more than a delegation curious to see *Yari*. I think they are Asu clan, not Hma. On a poaching trip perhaps!'

There were six brigands standing on a bench they had placed across the path. The rest of their mob lined both sides of the path, funnelling the mule train into their 'trap'. The first exchanges were cordial enough, preliminary pleasantries as each party sized up the other. In number the team and their company were at a definite disadvantage. Jim, anxious to maintain the positive atmosphere, produced the sweets and biscuits they had brought for their own consumption and distributed them. The Nosu accepted them greedily.

'Time to go!' shouted Jim to the head of the muleteers once he felt the gifts had achieved the desired effect. 'Move the mules on.' Immediately there was a yell from the Nosu and a dozen of them sprang forward and blocked the path again. 'Push on!' ordered Jim. Reinforcements crowded onto the path and there was some ungainly shoving of men and beasts as the two groups tried to gain the upper hand. 'Back off,' Jim shouted to the muleteers, throwing his hands up. 'These fellows aren't going to give up easily. Find me the headman.'

Jim approached the Nosu. There was a strangled cry as he was stopped by a short, scrawny man brandishing a rifle just inches from his face. Jim eyed him warily. 'Are you the chief of this clan?'

The man thrust the rifle forward. 'Yes.'

'We'll give you salt, but we want free passage through these lands.'

'How much?' The rifle was not lowered.

Jim offered the going rate per mule. The chief was not

easily swayed and bargained the price up by several *jin*. Only when the salt had been weighed did he step aside. His comrades, however, were less easily satisfied and pressed in on them again. Jim grabbed Belinda's reins and pushed forward into the crowd, calling for the muleteers to follow. Joan and Ruth hurriedly remounted and tried to move forward, but there was no way through. Reluctantly, more salt was handed over before they were allowed to continue.

'That was relatively peaceful!' were Jim's few words of 'comfort' once they had put some distance behind them. 'Shame about the biscuits.' With no food left for the day, they picked blueberries from bushes that they happened upon as they descended towards the river in the Sanwan valley. As evening fell they finally found themselves on the banks of the river and Jim rode ahead to find shallower water for their crossing.

'We're less than ten miles from Zhaojue and home,' said Ruth, 'but we won't make it over Great Hen tonight. There are places to stay less than quarter of an hour away.'

The Nosu home they found was smaller than the previous night but was blessed with two modest loft spaces, one offered to Joan and the other for Jim and Hong. Ruth would occupy a bed on the earthen floor. Hong's son and the muleteers would have to find whatever shelter they could. With only one ladder to serve both lofts, Joan was marooned till morning in her sleeping quarters once she had climbed up to bed. Her solitude was, however, no precursor to undisturbed sleep. The squabble and fluttering of hens and mules munching on a diet of corn and straw kept her awake for long periods into the night. The dawn was as readily disturbed by the screech and squeal of a litter of piglets grubbing inside the hut for food.

Jim, Joan and Ruth emerged from the house the next morning anxious to be away before the mule train, knowing that only one remaining peak stood between them and Zhaojue. Great Hen afforded them awesome views of the mountain ranges stretching away in every direction of Daliangshan. The summit brought them high above the Zhaojue plain, a poor tract of infertile, treeless land against the stunning beauty of the mountains, about four miles long and a quarter of that wide. The Zhaojue River, a substantial watercourse meandering south to meet the Sanwan, lay in the shadow of the mountains on the north and east sides of the basin. The valley periphery of dry brown foothills was fringed with thickets of poplars and a small number of tumbledown villages, home to the local clan, the Ba'chie.

'There's home,' said Ruth, pointing to the very centre of the plain. Joan could make out the Zhaojue fort, isolated both by location and status as a Chinese stronghold. A small Nosu village lay within a few hundred metres, but a distance of kilometres would have better represented the antagonism between the two cultures. Cradled in the southwest corner of the high walls of the fort she could distinguish the whitewashed buildings of the newly constructed Zhaojue clinic.

The soreness of travel-weary limbs, the struggles over an unpalatable diet, the apprehensions of violence and the burden of insufficient rest fell away as quickly as the path ahead. Joan experienced a revitalising awareness of the purposes of God. This was what God had been preparing her for. To see the Nosu of the Great Cold Mountains turning to Christ. Joan reached her hand up to her lapel and touched the silvery leaves of the small edelweiss bouquet she had pinned there during one of their stops. God's edelweiss. An encouragement for weary travellers. A treasure to be gathered in hard places.

The party descended from the peak, forded the Sanwan River once more and started across the plain. Another hour and a half brought them to the arch of the south gate of the fort and beyond this onto a rubble-strewn dirt track that passed the hovels and offices of the local Chinese officials. The administrative premises had signs announcing their purpose – Tax Bureau, Law Department and Telegraph Office – though there was little else to distinguish them from the shanties in which their workforce lived.

Their arrival brought people out onto the lane, a mix of dark-faced Chinese peasants and farmers, the tough traders Joan had frequently met in Xichang and the better-educated staff of the magistrates' entourage; the last were a curious fusion of reprobates, who had escaped to the margins of the law, and honest denizens ordered into the mountains to fulfil a tour of duty. Amongst the onlookers were a few Nosu who frequented the fort in the daytime before they were ejected each evening.

At the crossroads adjacent to the magistrates' hall they turned left and came to the door of the clinic compound. Janet, with Margie in her arms and Jan and Pauline holding onto her skirt, appeared at the gateway.

'Daddy!'

Jim jumped down from Belinda and scooped up Jan

and Pauline.

'Auntie Ruth!'

'Auntie Joan!'

Joan eased herself out of the saddle and into Janet's embrace.

'Tea?'

'Please...'

Chapter 13

*'I have been sceptical of some of the stormy pictures
painted of these parts, but ... more flashes of
lightning and bent trees could be added to them.
Independent Nosuland is wilder and more lawless
than the Kiarung or Tibetan territory I have been in.'*

FLOYD LARSEN, WRITING FROM ZHAOJUE, 1948

The Barn, in which the Broomhall family were
temporarily accommodated, was a spartan mud-walled
stable, standing in the lee of the south wall of the fort and
facing onto rough land where the team could keep
livestock. In the weeks before their arrival Ruth and Floyd
had organised the laying of flagstones and the
construction of steps to the loft that was divided into
bedrooms. Items of furniture in the form of Chinese board
beds, a table, desk, stools and a washstand had been made
from scratch. The carpenters had bartered with the Nosu

for trees, before felling them and then cutting, drying and shaping the planks. This had been a time-consuming process that needed to be supervised continually to ensure the maintenance of reasonable standards. Leniency in one area of workmanship invited shoddy efforts in another. At first there had been only a roof of wooden planks, held down Nosu-style with stones. The girls slept more soundly beneath sheets of oilcloth, but for Jim and Janet judicious rearrangement of the planks on rainy nights was essential to keep the drips of water from disturbing their sleep. Eventually the primitive roofing was replaced with traditional Chinese tiling.

'You and Ruth are to live in the Cottage until the clinic is completed,' Janet explained to Joan. 'I'm afraid you will have to sleep on the living room floor, but that should be for no more than two weeks. Then you can move into your own rooms in the clinic and we'll occupy the Cottage. Come on, I'll show you around while Jim sorts out the mules.' Janet led Joan past the goat and the large guard dogs chained in the yard and down a narrow path between low earthen walls.

Janet was five months pregnant, with a baby conceived within days of her arrival in Zhaojue – a fact that was now clearly evident. 'No problems to report,' answered Janet when Joan asked her. 'That's the beauty of having a doctor for a husband. Jim would like a son, of course. And the girls want a baby brother. Actually, the whole Chinese nation seems to think a boy is better than a girl.'

On the fort parapet above them Joan could hear both Chinese and Nosu discussing her, speculating about her age, marital status and nationality; the speculation crystallised into 'fact' with each retelling of the scant information available. Amongst the gossips Joan noticed three or four petite Chinese girls in their late teens, similar in height to herself, dressed in plain tunics. She waved to them. They shyly waved back and giggled in embarrassed laughter, covering their mouths with their hands.

'Jan, Pauline and Margie have loved living here,' continued Janet. 'We keep a tight rein on their activities. Within the compound we feel they are safe enough. But we do not allow them outside the walls without adult supervision. For a while we had Mrs Yang with us, but as you know that arrangement came to a sad end.' Towards the end of April Mrs Yang had come up to Zhaojue with Zhao, the interpreter. Tempted by opium addicts who made profit out of trapping others into their own obsession, she had taken to smoking the drug in secret at night. Confronted by Jim she had brazenly denied any wrongdoing. But the discovery of the eggshell pipe and a quantity of the drug carelessly concealed between the roof planks had revealed her complicity.

'Jim was all for sending her back to Xichang,' said Janet. 'I felt she should stay. I would rather have had her here, stealing our goods to feed her addiction, while we still had a hope of her salvation. But to no avail.' For a few weeks Mrs Yang had promised to reform but had rapidly lapsed again. Finally, Janet had taken to sleeping in the rat-infested kitchen across the bottom of the stairs in an attempt to prevent Mrs Yang indulging herself. A second exposure of her inability to break her habit had been too much. Mrs Yang had left of her own accord.

In front of them stood the Cottage, a building of

adequate size for a family, with 'proper' windows and a verandah, surrounded by the beginnings of a garden. 'The Nosu couldn't get over the fact that Jim and Floyd insisted on not having rifle-slit windows. Took them a while to believe we were to be unarmed. Caused a lot of head shaking and very earnest lectures on how to live here.' Janet led Joan into the house. 'Downstairs is the living room and kitchen, with our bedroom, an area for storage and a place for guests. The attic has a large room for the girls to use. We've divided off a section to act as a classroom for Jan. Eventually, she and Pauline will be leaving, of course. They will board at the Mission's school.'

Joan pushed open another door. Wedged neatly within the four walls was a canvas bath. 'Ah... a luxury apartment after all.'

'Did I tell you what Margie got up to in there? Found her fully clothed in the bath after Jim had finished bathing and was getting dressed in the bedroom. The following week I found her fully clothed in the pig trough...'

A short, covered connecting passageway, adjacent to the Cottage, took Janet and Joan down to the rear entrance of the clinic. They passed storerooms, the servants' quarters and a laundry. There was a well in the centre of the courtyard and a grindstone by the door into the alley which led to the compound gate. The clinic was a similar size to the Cottage with rooms on the ground floor for the medical work. 'This is the waiting area,' Janet explained. 'We have our Sunday services here. And Jim does his surgery in this room.'

'There's not a lot of light for operations,' observed Joan.

'He uses oil lamps. Not ideal, but he copes... There are

other rooms designated for opium addicts who are trying to rid themselves of their craving. And there's a kitchen and dining area.' They climbed the stairs to a small flat, a larger space than Joan had occupied in Xichang, as yet sparsely furnished and without decoration. 'A room each for you and Ruth. With a sitting room... and that's the pharmacy. You can sort out your own breakfasts and then come over to us for other meals.'

Joan carried her few belongings to the Cottage. Everything of any value had been left with the Lovegrens in Xichang. It had been decided that even her better clothing, her few silk dresses and cloaks, which would not have seemed particularly pretentious in the valley, should be dispensed with. Larceny was rife and there was no point in attracting it. Clothes must be as plain and practical as possible.

With time on her hands to explore, Joan climbed up onto the fort wall and wandered along the parapet. Zhaojue was little different than she had imagined from the descriptions of the others. The magistrates' compound and the soldiers' barracks dominated the north side of the enclosure. By the crossroads was the circle of an inconsequential parade ground, overlooked by a knoll bearing a flagpole from which hung a worn flag of the Nationalist government. The dwellings and offices lining the main path were dead-beat structures, a few burdened by traditional roofs, comprised of rows of broken or absent tiles. Not a shop amongst them. Over the north wall she could see graves, arrayed in ranks like miniature Nissen huts for the bones of the dead. Only the north and south gates allowed entrance and exit. To maintain a semblance of security the west and east gates had been blocked off and rendered redundant.

Joan's circuit of the fort brought her back to a point on the rampart above the barnyard, where Jan, Pauline and Margie were engrossed in a game. Still unsteady on her feet, Margie was excited by the cackle of the hens. 'Eggs! Run!' she ordered her elder siblings and stumbled off over the rough ground towards the stable shed that leant against the angle of the parapet walls. As the sun finally lost its daily struggle, the sudden chill of the dusk drove Joan indoors, to find warmth in the smouldering baskets of charcoal that they kept close to their feet during the autumn and winter evenings. Outside, only feathered clouds, harbingers of snow, remained clinging to distant summits. But as the sun dipped from sight, shadows stained them first grey, then black, until they were lost in the dark wells of the night sky. In the distance Joan heard the crack of a rifle and a volley in reply.

* * *

The immediate consequence of Joan and Ruth's arrival was the loss of Floyd to the team. The American had come to help Jim supervise the building of the clinic compound and that task was near completion. His involvement had always been temporary and now he had his own neglected ministry amongst the Lisu tribes to return to. He left for Xichang with the mules Joan and Ruth had arrived with.

His going, though always anticipated, was not easy. Jim missed the companionship and counsel of another male Western missionary. Of the indigenous team members, Hong, the manager, was planning to take a holiday. Even if he remained on the team, he needed to be based in Xichang, not in the mountains. As a new Christian, Zhao, the interpreter, was finding old partialities to gambling and drink an attraction his young faith could not resist. Ming and Tang continued their vital, but distant, labours at the old tavern in Zhuhe. Jim wrote home – 'Needed: men. Husbands!' But his requests for members of the mission to join him seemed, ironically, to resonate only with single female missionaries.

For Joan and the other two women, there was the loss of reassurance in a male presence when Jim was away, dispensing medicine in the villages. More particularly, there was the loss of a good friend. What Joan was not prepared for was the oppression that, without warning, assailed her. Evil, seizing his chance, drove her into his depths, stifled her sense of God's presence and challenged her commitment. Had she promised to follow Christ wherever he led her? Had she promised to follow Christ whatever the cost? Yet from somewhere she heard the reassurance, 'This is my place for you.'

The next two days after Floyd's departure were little better. Joan struggled with a tangible atmosphere of hell that shrouded her, confined her within her own thoughts. In her prayers she pleaded for relief... Determined not to wallow in feelings of self-pity, Joan escaped from the confines of the compound and started out along the street, gladly accepting an invitation to sit outside the home of an old Chinese lady. Within a few minutes a small group of passers-by had gathered, fascinated by the fort's newest arrival. She stayed for a while, telling them stories of Jesus, asking them to come to the weekly services. When she left them to continue her walk, she took some encouragement that a few of the listeners had seemed interested in her message.

Her relief was short-lived. With Floyd barely back in Xichang and beyond reach, Ming announced he must go back to his home town in Guizhou Province, some ten days' journey away. A Nosu Christian family he was close to had lost everything in a barbaric raid by self-styled insurgents; the women had been stripped of their clothing and whatever possessions could not be carried away had been burned. Now his father and family were threatened. He must leave to protect them. He would not return.

The nurse, Tang, would not stay in Zhuhe by himself. Throughout his ten-month occupancy of the exposed tavern he had endured aggravation and personal peril. His attempts at ministry had frequently been frustrated by frenzied spirit worship and witchdoctor activity in the town. In recent months the makeshift dispensary had been burgled several times by thieves burrowing through the walls. Being Han Chinese, he had been threatened with a loaded gun by a Nosu shaman, disgruntled that the medicine he had received failed to cure him immediately. He had suffered the additional ignominy of hiding behind a woman whilst bystanders struggled to wrest the rifle from his assailant. With Ming's leave-taking, Tang left too.

Joan felt aggrieved for them. Their departure seemed like defeat, a capitulation to the unrelenting physical pressures and spiritual onslaught that disquieted them all daily. Once more, the viability of their outreach was being called into question. Without reinforcement of the team, the tavern dispensary could be no more than an outstation manned only as frequently as Jim could make the journey to Zhuhe. Unable to resolve her dilemma Joan again looked for refuge in reaching out to others. In the comparative safety of daytime she and Ruth visited one of the hamlets nearby, taking opportunities to ask people to the Sunday services.

Their invitations bore fruit. Two dozen Chinese and Nosu filled the hall where Jim welcomed them. Speaking in Mandarin, with Zhao translating into Nosu, Jim told the story of Elijah's battle with the prophets of Baal on the heights of Mount Carmel. He described the miraculous way in which the holy men who served an idol were defeated by Elijah's God and how God had formed clouds in the sky to bring rain to a drought-stricken land.

In their worship Joan was aware of God close to her once more. Although neither she, nor any of the team, would ever lose the awareness of an ongoing, intense spiritual battle whilst they lived in Zhaojue, Joan was restored into a special sense of God's presence. The deep wells of dark oppression were sealed – for the time being.

Chapter 14

'*A girl is reared without joy or love ... no one sheds a tear when she is married off.*'

FU XUAN, C. THIRD CENTURY AD

Joan looked up from *Miss Nowack's Chinese Primer*, a teaching aid prepared by a CIM colleague, at the group of Chinese girls sitting on bamboo stools arranged around her new bedroom above the clinic. It was strange to be teaching them to read their own language, but they could recognise no more than a few basic characters. All of them were dressed in coarse cotton smocks of blue, brown or grey, over trousers. With their almost identical black hair, smoothed down, uniformly parted on the left and tied in short pigtails, Joan had taken a while to distinguish one from another.

Closest to her was Meihua. She had a congenial oval face and amiable smile and was very eager to learn. In her late teens, a similar age to the others, she was already engaged to be married. Beside her were two sisters, Baoli and Baodan, daughters of a village headman. Baoli, also engaged, was the prettier of the two and a definite leader within the group. Baodan was a far more dignified and serious individual.

'This is the character for "sin" - *zui*.'

In rote fashion the girls repeated the word after her.

'And this one is "hate"... Now we can make a sentence. "God hates sin". *Shangdi hen zui*.' It was difficult to keep the girls' attention. None of them had had any schooling and, consequently, sitting for a prolonged period in one place seemed an impossible proposition. Songmei, a tall, slim girl, fidgeted, eager to be out and see Janet and the children. Her family ran a wine-distilling business from their home, a larger property by the north gate. The profits they made, however, were consumed largely by the opium habit of Songmei's elder brother.

'Do you remember this word?' Joan turned back to a previous lesson. For a moment the girls looked puzzled.

'*Ai?* ' said Baoli.

'Well done. "*Ai*" – love.' She flicked the pages forward again. 'What about these two characters? This one again?'

'*Zui*.'

'And this one?'

'... *Ren?* '

'*Zui ren* - "sinner". Now we have two sentences. "*Shangdi ai zui ren. Shangdi hen zui.*"'

Joan reflected that even this simplistic telling of the gospel was going to take a while to sink in. Brought up in an environment of animism, confused with a mythology of miscellaneous Buddhist and Daoist deities, the teenagers had no comprehension of one God, *Shangdi*. How would they ever grasp the truth of Jesus and his death and resurrection?

'*Xia ke*.' Joan announced the end of the lesson. 'Can you tell Feng we missed her today?' Feng was amongst the slowest in the class. She seemed to be frequently at odds with her peers and her demeanour was generally dark and moody. The team had discovered that she was the daughter of opium addicts. Her parents had made their obsession first priority, frequently causing the family to go without food. It was little wonder that Feng was so surly and lacked social graces.

The group dispersed, leaving Songmei behind. 'Can I come with you to the villages?' she asked Joan.

'That would be good. I am going out to the blind man's village tomorrow. Is that convenient?' Joan knew the answer already; Songmei was always keen to spend time with her, even if there were household chores or labour in the fields to be finished.

Jim had encountered the blind man, suffering with double pneumonia, on one of his regular forays to the neighbouring villages to provide healthcare. The family had blown hot, then cold, over Jim's proposed treatments, at first welcoming Jim with the gift of a live cockerel as payment and later refusing an injection. When Jim returned he found relatives and friends already crowded into the home, preparing for the feast that the blind man's anticipated demise would occasion. The man, not inclined to appease the appetite of his relatives, had called Jim back and his swift recovery had brought the gift of an ox tongue and kidneys to the clinic. Deep-seated traditions, however, were well entrenched. Jim's success must be shared with the local witchdoctor whom the family had also summoned.

The payments that folk brought to the clinic varied greatly. Some were unable to pay and the more influential Nosu, insisting that their position and protection made them exempt from the obligations of others, were not always inclined to pay, particularly when their ailment had not yet been cured. However, whenever possible, the team insisted on some gift in kind. Most patients could manage a few eggs, counted carefully into clutches of ten, or a collection of vegetables, or even an odd assembly of animal parts – some more edible than others! Occasionally someone would appear with unusual gifts such as an otter or fox cub. Whatever the contributions, they were meticulously entered into the clinic's accounts.

Joan had been amused by an old Nosu lady who had arrived at one Sunday service clasping a large melon. Having sat patiently through part of the proceedings, she had taken Jim's sermon as the signal to approach him and ask for eye medicine. Jim, halted in full flow, had politely explained he would dispense medicine after the service. Satisfied that she would get the attention she needed, the woman had shuffled back to her seat and cradled the melon on her lap until he was finished.

It was while visiting the blind man with Songmei that Joan met one of the first Nosu girls to befriend her. 'What is your name?' the girl had asked. Surprisingly she spoke good Mandarin. Joan judged she was about 18 years old. Markedly darker than her Chinese peers, she was quite striking, having the precise features of her race and long black hair, which she had plaited down her back.

'I am Teacher Wei, Wei Zhu'an - Bamboo Peace. And you?'

'Jinfeng – Golden Breeze.'

Jinfeng, a lower caste White Nosu, lived with her brother and his family. She was clearly an intelligent young woman, but had been married off by her brother to a coarse Nosu man from a village along the valley. It was obvious she hated the thought of moving to his home. For the time being she remained with her brother, visiting her husband only occasionally until she became pregnant or his family decided she was needed to help them permanently.

'Come and learn to read.' Joan offered Jinfeng an invitation to join her reading classes for the Chinese teenagers.

'Songmei, you need to help me understand these marriage arrangements,' requested Joan as they made their way across the fields back to the fort before nightfall. 'It seems very complicated.'

'You must come tomorrow. Jielo is to be married.'

'And who is Jielo?'

'She is Nosu, like Jinfeng. She lives in another village. I will come for you as soon as the sun rises.'

Songmei and her elder sister, Songan, appeared at the clinic as promised early the next morning. Songan was much older than Songmei, about 30, and married with two children. The recent rains had turned the footpaths into slippery, ill-defined tracks. Clods of earth clung to Joan's shoes. It would be impossible to arrive looking neat enough for a wedding. This, however, was seemingly of little consequence. Grouped around the hut when they arrived were a small collection of Nosu, most apparently oblivious to the gritty mire in which they were sitting. Songmei and Joan climbed onto a low wall to watch. A steady trail of Nosu were arriving with brass basins, earthenware jars and small tubs. These they took into the home, emerging moments later with them filled with wine. One of them offered Joan a drink, '*He ba!*'

'*Bu hui*,' Joan refused him robustly. He laughed at her and drank noisily from his pail.

Finally, the bride came out from the house. Disappointingly, she was dressed in the attire that she normally wore: a soiled ragged outfit that clearly had seen too many days.

'How old is she? Fifteen?' guessed Joan.

'Yes. But she will stay here for another four or five years. Nothing is happening yet; let's come back later,' Songmei suggested.

'The rules are quite simple,' Songan explained to Joan as they negotiated the way back to the fort. 'Black Nosu, the pure Nosu families, can only marry Black Nosu. Their serfs can never marry Black Nosu.'

'And what happens if they do?'

Songan made a slow deliberate motion of her hand across her throat. 'The clans usually try to marry within a clan because they don't want to lose money to another tribe.'

'Isn't that a problem?'

'Not if they are from different sections of the clan,' said

Songmei. 'And there are rules about cousins marrying. The related parents have to be brother and sister, not two brothers or two sisters. There are three inferior castes, the "Whites", who are ranked second to the Black Nosu, then the "house slaves", and, at the lowest level, the "cooking stove slaves". Obviously, the higher-ranking castes don't want to marry beneath their status. But the lower ranks are just in bondage, some treated no better than animals. Their Black Nosu masters force them into marriages for their own ends and dictate the fate of their children.'

'Course,' sniggered Songan, 'there's plenty of other relationships going on. Girls are there for the taking once the wine starts to pass their lips. You have to watch the men; they think they own you until you're married.'

When they returned after breakfast the bride was dressing. Standing barefoot at the centre of a straw mat she had donned a dramatic blue, deep-pleated skirt, bordered with a band of intense blue, which reached to the floor. The skirt was complemented by a matching blue felt tunic with a yellow collar. She slipped her arms into a loose outer jacket of beige, elaborately embroidered with threads of red, blue and yellow.

One of the young women produced a tin mug. The lid was lifted to reveal an exquisite pair of silver earrings, strung with finely worked chains from which hung minute silver ornaments. 'The dowry was 200 ounces of silver,' whispered Songmei. 'It is paid to the bride. If she wants a divorce she must return it with interest. If her husband divorces her he forfeits it all.' There was a struggle to remove the bride's earrings. Finally a Nosu teenager, encouraged on by her friends, obliged, using her teeth to bend the metal away from the girl's earlobes. The stunning jewellery was fixed in place and the tin mug sewn to her skirt. She shook out her plaits of copious black hair and her companions combed it carefully for several minutes before winding it back into a tight bun, held in place with a scarlet cord. A cotton scarf was then wound into a turban and covered with a piece of towelling, the edges of which were sewn together down the back of her neck. Finally she donned a pleated, black felt outer coat. The transformation was astounding – the grubby diminutive mountain girl had become a tribal princess for a day.

There was a commotion outside the hut... the unmistakable sound of a chicken clearly in distress. Amidst much shouting, a small boy rushed into the living area clutching the unfortunate fowl in his thin fingers. He swung the hen over the bride's head while her friends laughed and clapped. Joan instinctively moved back against the wall, keen not to be caught by the flailing arms of the boy. As the boy ran out again a Nosu man, his face blacked with soot, stepped into the dim light. With clumsy and unnecessary aid from her friends the bride was hoisted onto his back, before he expertly negotiated the low door lintel and carried her outside.

Songmei darted out of the door. 'Come on!' They emerged from the house into the abating of a heavy shower. Joan saw the man already some distance away, racing across the fields followed by a chasing crowd of Nosu men, women and children. Joan joined the helter-skelter muddy pursuit, arriving at the gates of Zhaojue just as the man swung his black woven cloak from his shoulders, spread it on the ground and lowered the girl, still barefoot, onto it. A horse sent by her husband was brought forward and she was lifted onto its back. As she was led away the towelling veil was pulled forward to cover her face.

'What will happen when she arrives at her husband's home?' asked Joan.

'Oh, she won't see him. She sits in hiding for two days and then comes back to live with her family, just like Jinfeng is doing. She won't get to see her husband until she goes to visit.'

'She hasn't seen him before?'

'No...'

'Never?'

'Never.'

Chapter 15

'*This truly is the devil's throne.*'

JIM BROOMHALL

At Joan's reading classes that afternoon the Nosu teenager, Jinfeng, joined her Chinese counterparts, Meihua, Songmei, and the sisters Baoli and Baodan. They were eager to listen to Joan's opinions of the events of the morning and discover more about Joan herself.

'Why aren't you married?'

'I haven't found a husband.'

'Haven't your father and mother arranged a marriage?'

'It's very different in my country.' This caused some energetic discussion that Joan found hard to follow. The girls were genuinely incredulous that her family had failed to find her a husband – they had clearly failed in their responsibilities. Joan smiled at the girls. Any partner of her father's choice would definitely not suit her current situation! 'But *Shangdi* is also my Father,' she told them. 'He can arrange a husband for me when he wants.'

A comment from Jinfeng brought the conversation to a sudden halt. Embarrassment rippled around the group until Baoli received a hurried nudge from her sister. 'The Nosu say Dr Hai has three wives: Qi Furen[38], Di Lude[39] and you...'

'The Nosu are wrong!'

'But... you live together. And you and Teacher Di have no other husband.'

Joan frowned deeply. 'Hai Yisheng and Qi Furen are married. Di Lude and I are not married,' she stated firmly. 'Besides, Teacher Di is far too old to be the wife of Hai Yisheng.'

There was a chorus of protests. 'Teacher Di is 36 or 37!'

'She is 56.'

Again there were cries of disbelief. 'No way! She is too active to be so old.'

'Teacher Di is a very energetic lady, but she is 56 and nearly old enough to be Hai Yisheng's mother.'

'If she were Nosu, she could marry her grandson,' said Jinfeng. Joan hurriedly got out the Chinese primer and turned to a new lesson. The maze-like mores of the polygamous Nosu were beginning to get beyond her.

Strangely, just four days later, after the morning service on the last Sunday in October, Joan found herself once more on the way to observe a wedding, this time at the invitation of the groom's family. The request had come from Vuda, chief of the Hma clan local to Zhuhe, who had given the team consent to open the old tavern dispensary in his village. His son was to marry a bride from the Alu tribe a few hours to the north. 1100 ounces of silver had exchanged hands for the match to be completed. It was, apparently, going to be quite a party. It also provided a timely opportunity for Ruth and Joan to show themselves independent of Jim and Janet.

Ruth rode Belinda and Joan took Blackie. With them came Zitu, one of the Nosu servants; Zhao, as interpreter, would follow on the next day. As they passed over the mountain in the chill of the late afternoon the crimped rice-bowl valley of Zhuhe, chequered with cultivated fields, opened up more than a thousand feet below them. Zitu reined in his mule and sat looking wistfully at one of five small villages scattered along the valley. 'I can never go back,' he muttered mournfully. 'There are my wife and my children. And I will never be able to live with them again.'

Zitu's 'real' name defied pronunciation, transliterating into something akin to 'Zz-t-pp'. The man had been employed to look after the animals, collect firewood and draw water from the well some while before Joan had arrived in Zhaojue. Consternation amongst the builders had taken Jim away from his work to find a badly deformed young Nosu man sitting amongst a heap of bricks, detached from the gaggle of patients around the clinic. He was hunched beneath his cloak, staring down at his hands, rubbing away at the fingers of one hand with the other, searching for feeling, chafing away the vestiges of optimism. His dark skin carried tell-tale discoloured patches of leprosy. Through a translator, Jim discovered he had been driven from his village by the headman, leaving a family of three children behind him. Shunned by Nosu and Chinese he had made his way to the clinic.

Zitu was fortunate. Fear of the disease had often driven the Nosu to violent remedies to protect themselves. Some victims were given food, wrapped in a shroud and flung down the mountainside. Others were reduced to the condition of helpless drunks before being burnt alive.

'I can help you,' Jim had reassured him. 'Your leprosy is at an early stage. It is treatable.' Jim had offered Zitu work at the clinic during his treatment, fetching water and tending the animals. Besides his innate desire to see the wretched man healed, he had ambitions that the local chiefs might be persuaded to allow the building of a leprosarium on the hills between Zhaojue and Zhuhe if Zitu's stay were successful.

The dispensary at Zhuhe lay on the far side of a pretty copse of firs and poplars, adjacent to the more impressive home of Chief Vuda. As the three of them approached, several inebriated Nosu greeted them. 'Looks like the celebrations have begun,' said Ruth disparagingly.

Chief Vuda's wife was sitting by the roadside having a thorn extracted from her soiled foot by a servant. 'She's the one the Chinese nurse, Tang, hid behind when he was being chased by the shaman with a gun!' Ruth pointed out. 'Not a bad choice as it turned out. There would have been the equivalent of a Nosu world war if she had got in the way of a bullet.'

Saddle-sore, Ruth and Joan dismounted and made conversation before retreating to the dispensary. They unpacked their few belongings and then sat on the mud bench which ran around the walls of the living area, enjoying the welcome warmth of the fire Zitu had lit indoors. The old tavern was in the state of decay Ruth had vividly described. Apart from the protection provided by a gatekeeper the team had employed, the building had been unoccupied since Ming, the Nosu worker, and Tang, the nurse, had departed, seven weeks previously. A patchwork of inept repairs where the burglars had burrowed through had disfigured the lower rooms. Furniture had been kept to a bare minimum – a low table and three stools in the dining room. The posters adorning the mud-grey walls were in poor condition, having been handled by the many Nosu who had crowded into the waiting area, but were still useful enough to explain the gospel to visitors.

Trying to sleep in the undersized loft above the dining area proved a vain hope. The cacophony of drunken babble from Vuda's home and the road below kept the two women awake well into the night.

Little of ceremonial significance happened on the second day. Ruth and Joan watched as a party of Nosu on horseback, with their servants driving a gift of a black cow and two goats, set out on the 30-mile round journey to collect the bride. Then the two missionaries wandered out to another village and found a group of Nosu women squatting idly by stacks of straw. One or two were young mothers, shielding their restless children from view within the sanctuary of their blue cloaks, the heavy folds of material bulging and subsiding with movement. Using their limited Nosu Ruth and Joan chatted for a while.

'Talk longer with us,' the women pleaded when they made respectful excuses to leave. One of the women thrust a handful of walnuts into Joan's hands. Joan courteously declined the offer but the woman insisted she accept them.

Ruth and Joan continued their walk, scrambling along

narrow pathways across scenic hillsides, taking time to
exchange greetings with the Nosu they encountered along
the route, and, finally, returning to Zhuhe just before Zhao
arrived. With his help, they spent the evening entertaining
Nosu, guests at the wedding, who were anxious to meet the
foreigners who had also been invited.

The bride arrived the following afternoon. A throng of
300 Nosu crowded into the village to welcome her. The
bride's horse, riderless, led the procession. Some distance
from Zhuhe the girl's floral costume had been swathed in
a black cloak and her head completely covered by a heavy
veil. Two men had lifted her and her maidservant, similarly
clad in black, onto their backs and taken a position at the
heart of the procession. Any hope Ruth and Joan had of
seeing the bride herself was quickly lost. She was taken to
a newly erected bamboo shed surrounded by a bamboo
fence in a nearby field and deposited there in the company
of her servant and two or three male relatives. She would
stay enclosed in this temporary shelter until evening and
then be taken to the home of a White Nosu some distance
away for the night. Twenty-four hours after her arrival she
would return home unseen by the groom, his family and
the guests.

The arrival marked another opportunity for raucous
feasting which was to last two full days. The Hma chief
had prepared three huge tubs of alcohol. Three cows,
fourteen pigs and over a dozen sheep and goats had been
slaughtered for the festivities. Local White Nosu had been
press-ganged into bringing quantities of half-cooked rice
and oversized wedges of buckwheat. Young men scuttled
between the visitors with baskets laden to extravagance

while the guests grabbed at the food with soiled hands, using bowls of straw or wood and even their cloaks as plates. Their uninhibited gluttony was washed down with wines of fermented rice and sorghum made freely accessible to all.

Joan and Ruth found a more secluded position on a bank at the edge of the proceedings to observe the event. They were centres of attraction themselves and it was difficult to escape the attentions of groups of women who crowded around. A Nosu man approached them, swaying unsteadily. Joan's Nosu was not fluent but it was clear that the man was propositioning her quite graphically. She stepped aside as he tumbled over another man and landed across the lap of a young woman as inebriated as himself. Wild laughter and a volley of abuse rose from those around him. The man clutched salaciously at the girl, repeating his intentions, before finally rolling into a heap at her feet to more jeers.

'I think we should go, Joan,' said Ruth maternally. 'This is not going to get any better.' As they made to leave, some of the women tried to stop them, asking them to stay. Ruth was firm. 'We'll be safer in the loft.' Without further discussion she set off for the dispensary with Joan in her shadow.

As night fell, revellers encamped beneath the loft window. Glancing out, Joan was intrigued to see them pressing sticks upright into the earth in a crude circle. There was an atmosphere of acute anticipation, the group chattering like impatient children.

'Ruth? What's happening?' She called Ruth across to the narrow gap between the shutters.

Ruth shrugged, 'I'm not sure.'

The Nosu dropped to their haunches and began to summon the spirits. Their incantations rapidly drew a throng until there were a hundred or more men and women chanting a primeval mantra. 'They're calling out the spirits,' said Ruth, turning away. 'I've seen this kind of thing before. Then they had a puppet: a basket dressed in a woman's skirt with a tunic and a wooden dipper for the head wrapped in a scarf.'

Below them the excitement level was rising. And rising. Joan's previous encounter with the presence of evil just a few days before was only a preparation for the feelings that now overwhelmed her. She gasped. One of the sticks seemed to be dancing in the air, jerking up and down. The Nosu began to shriek as more sticks started to move. Erratic, uncontrolled jumping. Up. Down. Up. Excitement gave way to frenzy.

Joan pulled back from the window, shocked at the sensations that had suddenly assaulted her emotions. Evil seemed to pour in through the shutters, through the cracks in the walls and ceilings. Frighteningly real. Dreadfully close. Suffocating. 'We must pray...'

Ruth and Joan got to their knees and in the darkness deliberately declared that Jesus is Lord. They prayed, claiming the protection of the blood of Jesus. They prayed for God's victory over all of Satan's power. They prayed for the Nosu and the shattering of demon supremacy in their lives. They prayed for Zhuhe and that God alone would be worshipped. They prayed on until the oppression they had encountered lifted. Below the window the sticks had ceased to dance and the clearing was deserted. The crowd had dispersed, looking for thrill and gratification elsewhere in the merrymaking.

The morning brought little respite from the revelry. An invitation for lunch with Chief Vuda's family was summarily cancelled with a message brought over to the dispensary – 'Please stay away. Vuda and his family are still drunk.' They wandered to the outlying villages, as they had done on previous days, where folk were still sober enough to receive them and to listen to the gospel message. It was a relief to get away from the carousing for a while.

'The sticks... was that real? A trick?' asked Joan.

Ruth shook her head. 'It seems real enough. Others have reported seeing something similar. That time with the puppet. Our co-worker, Ming, was still here in Zhuhe. He got very close and told me he couldn't see anyone manipulating the vile thing. He, at least, was convinced it was the work of demons.'

Zitu returned for Joan and Ruth the following afternoon. As they prepared to leave, the local people turned out in great numbers, begging them to return. There was a peculiar charm in their manner for all their dirtiness, sores, drunkenness and superstitions, that Joan could not ignore. A veiled loveliness that pleaded for liberation.

Finally, the three riders said their goodbyes, promising to return, and climbed away from Zhuhe, up towards the pass which led back into Ba'chie clan territory. In the barren soil Joan discovered wild herbs that she had not observed before: marjoram and St John's wort. And for a while she delighted in the colours of the autumn leaves.

Chapter 16

*'One wishes that among these brave but superstitious
hillmen some modern medical men would set to
work to relieve the suffering that abounds, and to
lead these people out from the distressing fear of the
all-powerful demon.'*

SAM POLLARD, C. 1902

Jim bent over the body lying on the table beneath his
surgeon's knife. The pith and vegetable oil lamps lacked
sufficient strength and the flickering of the flames cast
distorted shadows. 'Shame about the kerosene,' he said, as
Ruth rearranged the lamps to better advantage. He had
ordered fuel for new lamps they had secured, but petrol
had been delivered instead.

Jim, Ruth and Joan were standing in the clinic's twelve-
foot square 'theatre', starting a thyroid operation. They,
along with Janet, made a unique and unusual team. Jim

put his surgical expertise to good use, performing surgery in the clinic, and occasionally out in the villages, with local or general anaesthetic. Ruth, in line with her general housekeeping responsibilities, performed the unscrubbed-up theatre duties, ensuring that Jim received the requisite implement at the required time. Joan relied entirely on her two months of operating theatre practice, acquired ten years previously at the Bermondsey Medical Mission Hospital, to help Jim in the operation. Following Jim's instructions she held arteries in place with forceps, applied swabs and gave any assistance Jim requested, a role that Janet also performed when appropriate. There was one occasion, a bowel operation, when first Janet, and then Joan, overcome by the spectacle, required resuscitation. Ruth carried on regardless, resolutely helping Jim complete the task in hand.

The environment itself was a challenge to safety and cleanliness. The Nosu, curious to see what would happen, gathered in throngs of up to thirty, settling themselves in the theatre alcove and maintaining a running commentary on the likelihood of the patient surviving. Jim had brought in surgical gowns and had a supply of gloves for each of the team members. Effective cleansing agents, however, were hard to find. The soap brought in from Xichang was of poor quality. Locally there were no supplies. The Nosu did not wash...

The clinic had quickly gained a good reputation for its success rate. Demand for treatment came in the form of rugby scrums or a bedlam of pleas each morning: crowds of up to a hundred patients and visitors eager to secure attention. Attempts to maintain any semblance of order were in vain. The concept of queuing was alien to both Chinese and Nosu cultures. Jim was required to deal skilfully with amputations, eye conditions and inversion of eyelashes, fevers and pneumonia, melanomas and malnutrition, typhoid and typhus, and the aftermath of attempted suicides. Wounds from local warfare, damage done by wild animals, or injuries sustained in animistic rites appeared regularly on the waiting list. The news of Zitu's improving condition brought patients with leprosy to the clinic two or three times each week, but without the provision of a leprosarium there was little progress to be made. Tragically, the Nosu women, reluctant to let Jim examine them and asking Ruth to act as doctor, often remained untreated through their own decorum.

Jim, unexpectedly, found his work greatly helped from time to time by his father back in Britain. Dr Broomhall, wanting to encourage his son, wrote detailed notes of his own experiences of surgery in China. Letters, written weeks before, would slowly travel a third of the world's circumference and arrive in Zhaojue when muleteers or some official delegation brought the post from Xichang, usually no more frequently than once a month. Providentially, these notes provided instruction just as Jim was contemplating undertaking a similar operation or a procedure he had not attempted before.

The thyroid operation Jim, Joan and Ruth were presiding over was not a success; the patient died. While it was the only occasion where Jim failed to operate successfully, he was greatly troubled. For a few days doubts were raised publicly about the efficacy of the clinic. Jim knew that the ability of the team to remain in Zhaojue and, more importantly, the physical safety of his family and co-workers depended on the tolerance of the local communities. If the clinic failed to provide good medical help, the mood of acceptance would swiftly change. Mercifully, this sad event was soon accepted as unfortunate and the air of antagonism faded away.

The clinic, as a means of bringing healing and opening opportunities for the gospel, was also undermined by the culture of shamanism within the community. Patients and their families set great store by the contribution of witchdoctors in the healing process. It was difficult to persuade patients that the slaughter of fowl, pigs and goats or the wild incantations of witchdoctors had no part in their healing. Fear of demons and the need to appease them ran deep. The Nosu were haunted by spectres of malevolent spirits who affected their daily lives. The clinic was recognised as 'God's ground', free from devilry. Many patients begged for permission to stay on the premises so that demons would not affect them during convalescence. Only those recovering either from operations or opium addiction were, however, accorded the privilege.

While medical duties and planning for their weekly services consumed much of Jim's time, the three women combined their duties in the clinic with the daily necessities of survival and care of the three children. Aided at various times by two or three servants, there was the continual cycle of food purchase and preparation to sustain. With no shops in the fort, they were chiefly reliant on gifts brought in payment for treatment, and on provisions exchanged in barter at the clinic doors. Periodic deliveries of supplies from Xichang served to keep them in salt and cloth for trading. The frequent distraction of vendors of unwanted goods and the need to haggle over bartered items employed time that was often in short supply. Sometimes the team lived hand to mouth, the needs of the children being a constant concern. Praying for 'daily bread' was a practical necessity, not a duty-bound devotion.

There was an incessant struggle against stealing. No matter how unsophisticated a lifestyle the team had adopted, their possessions remained superior to anything the Nosu could hope to own legitimately. In their dire poverty, patients would carefully preserve the cotton wool used on their wounds. Pestered by pilferers throughout the day who surreptitiously palmed items beneath their cloaks, the compound was invaded at night by intruders dropping from the parapet walls while the guard dogs howled at the end of their chains. Anything not secured was liable to be purloined, while their carefully cultivated crops were often ripped from the ground.

Milk teased from the goat and eggs lifted from the hens helped to improve their diet. Jim had thoughtfully brought in quantities of seed to establish a vegetable garden of peas, beans, sweetcorn and cabbages, supplemented by potatoes and turnips. There was an orchard of sorts, in the form of apples, pears and loganberries, while honest beauty had been introduced with the planting of rose bushes.

Food preparation was hard work. Water must be drawn from the well. Adequate stores of firewood needed to be maintained. Their meals were cooked using a wood-burning mud stove, positioned beneath a makeshift oven constructed from petrol cans. Steamed bread had to be prepared from scratch. Grain was roasted, ground and mixed with chicory to create instant coffee postum. Jams and marmalade were boiled and set as mountain strawberries, wild plums and oranges came into season. As a 'treat' the team would sit down to a dinner of peas, potatoes and mint sauce and imagine they were enjoying roast lamb.

Around the storerooms and kitchen, Ruth was in her element. Efficient and versatile, she was always ready to give her helpers direction, whether it was considered beneficial or not. 'Joan,' she instructed her junior missionary, 'never take the kettle to the teapot. Always take the teapot to the kettle.'

Janet was predominantly concerned with the children's welfare and, as her pregnancy entered its final weeks, there was the need for rest and preparation for the baby's arrival. With Joan's help she had embarked on the primary stages of Jan's education in the loft above the Cottage, whilst Pauline, playing in a corner of the small room surrounded by pictures of historical characters, absorbed everything Jan was being taught. With books and toys in extremely short supply, entertainment had to be provided by Jim, Janet and the children's 'aunties' once the girls tired of amusing themselves. When weather and circumstances allowed they were able to escape to the river for picnics.

Joan and Ruth had the better opportunities for ministry, with more freedom to sit alongside convalescing patients and share Bible stories, to lead and preach in the services or take time visiting local homes and villages.

Both had established Chinese reading classes, Ruth teaching the older women and Joan the younger ones. Joan's group often numbered up to seven Chinese: Meihua, Meihua's fourteen-year-old niece, Baoli, Baodan, Songmei, Feng and Shan. Though of a similar age to the others Shan was married to a man from the only Han Chinese family in Zhuhe and already had a son. Dissatisfied with the marriage, she had left her husband and had returned to live in one of the local villages with her parents, both opium smokers, and an ageing grandmother. Joan found her interested in the gospel but often distracted by her situation. 'I don't want to go back to that family,' was her usual and final refrain whenever they talked.

Joan also had three Nosu teenagers regularly attending her lessons, Jinfeng and two friends, Aji and Lanlan. These girls had tried to teach Joan Nosu songs – an endeavour which came to an abrupt halt when the lurid nature of the lyrics was revealed.

'Where is Jinfeng?' Joan asked at a lesson in late November, noting the Nosu girl had not come.

'She's going to her husband's home.'

Afterwards Joan hurried out to Jinfeng's village and was relieved to find her still there. Jinfeng was sitting outside the hut sewing clothes for herself. She appeared quite desolate. 'I don't want to see him. His family just want him to get me pregnant. Then I'll have to go and live with him forever.' She turned her head and pushed aside her tunic top to reveal bruising, visible on her dark shoulders. 'My brother hits me if I don't go when the family sends for me.'

Joan shared how God could help her. 'God can go with you wherever you go.' Jinfeng seemed genuinely touched by the care Joan showed her.

It was close to Christmas before Joan was able to visit Jinfeng again. This time she found her weeping.

'I hate him! My husband's a useless yokel. An idiot!' Jinfeng swore and burst out into a series of profanities which were well beyond Joan's Nosu vocabulary. 'What can I do? How can I escape?' she asked between her sobbing. 'I hate him...'

'Jesus can help you...' encouraged Joan. 'He can heal the broken-hearted.'

Jinfeng's distress was acute. 'Come again. Come every day. I must find a way out.'

Joan's opportunity to help was short-lived. Lanlan found Joan at the clinic just three days later. 'Jinfeng has gone to her husband. Her brother forced her to go.'

'How was she?' asked Joan.

'Desperate. I don't know what she will do.'

It crossed Joan's mind that suicide might be behind Lanlan's words. For Nosu women self-inflicted death was the ultimate solution to their crises. Girls, unhappy in their marriages, were capable of consuming poisonous herbs found on the mountain slopes or overdosing on opium to draw attention to their plight.

'Auntie Joan, can I come with you today?' Jan was now six-years-old and had not lost her passion to be involved in converting anyone and everyone. A lack of language ability apparently did not concern her.

'Yes, Jan, you may. But you must stay with me and

never leave my side.' Joan gripped Jan's hand as they passed through the fort gate. 'We are going to visit Lanlan's village.'

Lanlan was not at home but others were eager to invite them in. Despite the cloudless, sunny skies the team had layered themselves with warm clothes against the raw winds of winter. The Nosu, however, were as scantily clad as when Joan first arrived in September. They crouched indoors around a smouldering fire. A blackened pot of vegetable soup simmered away in the failing embers.

'Will the little foreigner sing for us?' asked the wife.

'Jan, will you sing?' Joan translated for her.

'Auntie! I can't sing in here. It's so smoky!'

'Don't you think you could, Jan?'

Jan's face suddenly lit up. She stood up, disturbing the hens that were scratching at the earthen floor of the hut. 'Yes. I will. I'll do it for the Lord Jesus.' Jan broke into 'Jesus loves me', first in English, then in Mandarin. Joan ventured to repeat it in Nosu and explain the meaning. Jan was elated as she sat down. She had helped Joan. She had helped these Nosu. And she had helped Jesus.

As they left to return to the fort, Jan twisted around to get a last look at the village, reluctant to leave.

'Well done, Jan.' Joan thanked her with a squeeze of the hand. 'You must come again.'

A children's Christmas party was scheduled for 23 December. There was a strict moratorium on mentioning it until noon the same day. A prior announcement was likely to draw children from a radius of several miles. The slaughter of a pig by a local family gave Ruth her chance to barter for portions of the meat. Quantities of turnips were procured and peeled, chopped and boiled in pans of soup.

The team watched in amazement as fifty young Chinese and Nosu, under instruction to bring their own bowls and soup spoons or chopsticks, appeared in the late afternoon, skidding along the snow-laden fort walls to the compound, carrying an array of receptacles – brass bowls, wooden tubs and earthenware pots in small, medium and huge. Some were even dragging buckets behind them!

'Did we make enough soup?' asked Ruth wryly. Janet and Joan did not bother to answer. Ruth would be more than well prepared for any eventuality.

The team ushered the minor invasion into the clinic where they had made a considerable fire on a stone hearth, using the wood chips left by the builders. With much shuffling and shoving, the youngsters settled themselves on the cement floor, squatting back on their heels with a practised ease that Joan could never achieve. Jim produced his mouth organ and broke into a tune. Those who had attended the Sunday School recognised it and in their own chaotic manner sang along. As the hubbub subsided, Joan, with Zhao's interpretation, began to tell the Christmas story, placing figures on large flannelette pictures as the narration unfolded. Afterwards, Jim taught the children a carol he had composed that afternoon whilst waiting for them to arrive.

Ruth had provided three sizeable chunks of pork for each child, served with ladles full of soup until no more could be consumed. Pictures of the nativity were handed out and then the children were lined up to have their bowls, tubs and buckets filled with the last of the soup to take to their families. How much would finally make it home was debatable...

The Christmas services and celebrations were over as promptly as they had started and the team quickly went back to the demands of their daily routines. With the arrival of the New Year, the birth of the Broomhalls' fourth baby was imminent. Once Janet's contractions started it was Joan's task to supervise the three girls.

Later in the day Ruth looked in at the living room of the Cottage. 'Shouldn't be long now. I'm ready to help Jim.'

Jan, Pauline and Margie had become embroiled in their childhood fantasy world, the 'Doorway People'. Joan glanced round at them. 'Do you think I could slip away? I'd love to be there for the birth.'

'Why not? They're happy enough.'

The first Western child to be born in Daliangshan, Jennifer Joy Broomhall, was delivered shortly afterwards without undue difficulty, on 6 January 1950. Joan returned to the living room to fetch the children. 'Mummy has had the baby,' she told them. 'You have another sister.' Jan and Pauline ran to the bedroom, Pauline colliding into her elder sister as Jan suddenly stopped by the door. She looked back at Joan uncertain for a moment. 'It's OK. Go on in,' Joan reassured her.

Tentatively, Jan pushed open the door. She and Pauline peeped in. Janet summoned a weary smile and beckoned them over, putting her fingers to her lips. They tiptoed to the bedside and peered into the bundle of cloths that Janet held. 'This is your new sister. She's called Jennifer Joy. And she's very happy to see you.'

Jim opened a drawer in the cabinet by the bedside. 'This is such a special occasion that you have a special present.' He handed home-made boiled sweets to each of the girls. An immense treat. Sugar had to be brought from Xichang to make such luxuries. 'And for you, my dear...' He slipped out of the room and re-entered a few moments later with a bunch of Japanese anemones for his wife. 'A unique occasion.'

Later in the evening Joan prepared the children for bed and read them a Bible story. 'Prayer time...'

Pauline spoke up. 'Thank you, Lord Jesus, for giving us another baby sister, but do please send us a baby brother SOON.'

Chapter 17

*'When science in general and medicine in particular
were liberated from... ecclesiastical chains, the
original happy relationships between bodily and
spiritual health were virtually forgotten. Then, the
wheel of history coming full-circle again... Medical
missions today form an integral part of the Christian
missionary enterprise.'*

DR STANLEY BROWNE, 1946

Jim inspected the Nosu child standing on the doorstep of
the clinic. After breakfast he had walked over to the
building in preparation for the day's surgery. As Jim had
opened the main doors the boy had leapt to his feet and
declared emphatically, 'My name is Jiha. I am here to look
after your horses.'

'We already have someone to care for the horses.'

The boy was scrawny – a wiry, ragged urchin with an

optimistic grin. He was wearing no more than a pair of soil-flecked, baggy cotton trousers, a short Nosu cloak and insubstantial straw sandals. In his hand he carried a piece of sacking, which held the crumbs of buckwheat he had begged for that morning.

'We don't have work for you,' Jim repeated sympathetically.

The smile faltered. 'I have nowhere to go.' The boy pulled back the hem of his cloak, revealing discoloured patches and ulcers on his skin.

'How long?'

'Two years...'

Jim bent down to get a better look. 'You'd better come in. I will find you something to eat.'

Jiha's story, like Zitu's, was one of rejection. Fearful of falling victim to his leprosy, his M'po family had escorted him south to Zhuhe and abandoned him to Hma Nosu. They, in turn, had ushered him to the Ba'chie border and now he had been left at the clinic door, alone and afraid.

'We need a leprosarium,' said Jim. 'I have tried getting the clans to give up a piece of land. But can I get the chiefs to see further than feathering their own nests?' The question needed no answer. Every overture to the Nosu had met with either utter refusal or manipulation of the unfortunate victims of the disease for their own gain.

'But what are we going to do with Jiha?' asked Janet. The boy was sitting in the courtyard, slurping soup noisily from a bowl, occasionally glancing in their direction to listen to their unintelligible conversation. 'How old did he say he was?'

'Fourteen, but he looks younger to me. Ten, maybe. '

'He could help Zitu with the animals,' suggested Ruth. 'It might do Zitu some good too. He hasn't got over losing his family.'

Jim weighed the risks. His stay would cost them something. Clothing, food and treatment. But, more importantly, his condition was further advanced than Zitu's. He would be a risk to the health of the team... and to the children. There was, however, something so pathetic about Jiha that no one had the heart to follow the clinic rules and send him away. 'OK. Let's get Zitu up here. I'll tell Jiha our decision.'

Jiha's stay lasted three days. Homesick and not welcomed by the servants, he slipped away one evening. He would have to return voluntarily; there was considerable danger in chasing him in the dark. In the end it was the bitter reality of his situation that forced him back to the compound. His second appearance was more pitiable than his first. A well-aimed stone had caught him on the head, leaving a scar still encrusted with dry blood. The team took him in once more, bathed and fed him and restored him to his role working with Zitu. Their attempts at rehabilitation, however, soon floundered. Within a few months the boy began to resist treatment and engage in petty pilfering. The team had to find a Chinese family in the valley willing enough to accept him and, with regret, let him go.

The first of February was marked by frenetic activity. The winter snows were still falling and the clinic had attracted a large number of Chinese and Nosu looking for shelter. The waiting hall was crammed to capacity with the sick and their relatives. Order and decorum were rarely in evidence but any sense of protocol had been completely lost amidst the skirmishes that had broken out.

Jim, Joan and Ruth had a number of operations scheduled. Impatient pounding on the door, raucous insistence on immediate and individual attention and incessant interruption made progress next to impossible. Jim was repeatedly forced to abandon the surgery to answer appeals for medication and advice. Nevertheless, no sooner were those with needs satisfied, than they were replaced by new patients, equally demanding.

'Let's see if we can establish some order in here,' called Jim. 'Anyone who hasn't got a problem can go.'

'There's a man in a bad way here.' Joan waved him over.

'He's dying,' said Jim after examining him. 'Prepare plasma.' The crowd were unmoved. Ambivalent to the plight of the man, they continued to obstruct the team as they hurried back and forth, creating yet further frustration.

'Hai Yisheng! We have come.'

Jim looked up to find two young Nosu vigorously pushing their way through the obstinate throng. The first, quite small in stature, he immediately recognised as Yu, one of the students who had visited Zhaojue from a Nosu Bible school in north Yunnan Province the previous year. With him was a companion, Chang.

'You are more than welcome. We had heard you had arrived in Xichang.'

Yu greeted him warmly. 'My wife is outside with the mule train...'

Jim called to Ruth. 'Ruth will sort her out, don't worry. As you can see we are very busy today.'

'Hai Yisheng, we are here to help,' said Yu earnestly. 'Tell us what to do.' It was not long before the two men, faces still streaked with dust and grime from their journey, were caught up in the chaos that characterised the day.

The arrival of Yu and Chang as reinforcements to the team brought a sense of relief. The dilemma over the sudden departure four and a half months before of their Nosu worker, Ming, and the nurse, Tang, had been resolved. Zhao, lacking any Christian Nosu companionship, had been sucked into the drinking and gambling habits of the locals, making him a hindrance rather than an asset. His input had become erratic and, when interpreting the gospel message to patients or in the villages, his own life displayed little of appeal to draw people to Christ. With the additional help of stronger indigenous Christians the team could once again consider advancing the work, political uncertainties permitting.

Yu and Chang brought news of the unfolding situation in the conflict between the Communists and Nationalists. The Communists were making significant gains into the remaining Nationalist strongholds in the southwest. Having entered Beijing on the final day of January 1949, Nanjing had fallen to the People's Liberation Army in April and Shanghai in late May. On 1 October, from the distant, elevated balcony of Tiananmen, the triumphant Communist leader, Mao Zedong, had responded to the adulation of the masses with a spontaneous but historically significant riposte of '*Renmin Wansui* – Long Live the People' and declared his party to be the sole legitimate rulers of the People's Republic of China. The Nationalist capital city of Chongqing had surrendered to the Communist advance in November, followed within four weeks by the capitulation of Chengdu.

Xichang had now assumed strategic significance and had been declared the Nationalist military headquarters. Tension in the town was high. If Xichang fell to the Communist forces advancing north from Yunnan Province, then Zhaojue would be cut off and the team's supply route would cease to exist. The fort's telegraph office would be their only contact with the outside world.

The welcome calmness that finally descended on the compound as the last patients were dismissed and night fell was not to last. The pandemonium of a bewildering and violent argument outside the clinic suddenly spilled over onto the premises. The clinic door burst open. There was the hammer of hurried footsteps in the courtyard and the frenzied howling of the guard dogs.

'What on earth!' asked Ruth, appearing at Joan's bedroom door.

'Who knows? I'm not sure I want to know...'

Jim raced across the courtyard and sprinted into the building. Joan could hear Jim shouting to make himself heard above the affray. Minutes later there was more upheaval as the magistrate came beating up the path and stormed in through the clinic door. When quiet descended and the building was vacated Jim came to find Joan and Ruth. 'Nearly had cold-blooded murder on our hands! Yu had offered help to a Nosu chief on the journey up and invited him here.'

'That's not allowed after dark...' interrupted Ruth.

'...which would have sparked a riot,' agreed Jim. 'But it gets worse. This particular chief had been ambushed by two soldiers last year. In retribution the chief had killed one and wounded the other. As these things go, the survivor saw him entering the fort this evening and decided to exact revenge with a bunch of his comrades. Eye for an eye and all that. If they had flushed the chief out of here, that would have been it,' Jim added. 'We have to thank God the magistrate sorted them out - took the chief and his gun into custody for the night. It needed a terrible tongue-lashing to make the soldiers stand down.'

The next day Joan returned from a visit to Jinfeng's home deeply dismayed. The teenager had complied with her brother's wishes, albeit unwillingly, but her situation had not improved.

'Her brother has thrashed her again,' she told Janet. 'Appalling bruising. The abuse is awful.' She shook her head sadly. 'I can't communicate with her any more. She has just become cynical. That initial interest in the gospel seems to have been beaten out of her completely.'

'She might be better off living with her husband,' suggested Janet. 'He might be simple but perhaps he will protect her.'

'Maybe. But she won't go. And now Aji tells me that Jinfeng has a shiftless Chinese trader hanging around the house.'

It was Aji who turned up breathless at Joan's room. '*Wei Jiaoshi!* Teacher Wei!'

'Good morning, Aji. Why the rush?'

'It's Jinfeng. She's run away. Eloped!' Aji rattled on with her news. 'Her brother and the soldiers have gone after them. Everyone is talking about it.'

Joan groaned. 'That was a very foolish thing to do. She must know what will happen if she is caught.' The prospect of seeing Jinfeng dragged back to the fort in chains and to imprisonment was not something Joan wanted to witness.

'It will be worse if her husband's family find her. They will burn her alive.' Nosu justice could be crude and cruel.

'Then we must pray they won't find her...'

Around the fort rumour rapidly began to flourish. The soldiers had captured Jinfeng and her lover, some reported... They had returned in the night, said others... The magistrate would hand Jinfeng over to her husband's family for punishment... The couple had escaped after all. What was true was that Jinfeng was pregnant.

The chase after the two errant lovers across the mountainside lasted three days. The dejected couple were unceremoniously prodded and pushed through the fort gate by soldiers and deposited at the magistrates' offices. Jinfeng, in a futile attempt to disguise herself, had donned the clothing of a Chinese peasant and chopped erratically at her hair. She looked bedraggled and scared. The young man shuffled along beside her, contrite and submissive, not daring to raise his head. Jinfeng was fortunate that the magistrate tried the case according to Chinese law. Both received sentences of six months' imprisonment. The trader was thrown into the fort prison, a dark, unventilated pit with no redeeming features. Jinfeng was incarcerated just a few feet away in the guardroom, locked in the foulness of a cramped metal cage.

When Joan visited Jinfeng she found her squatting in filth, contained like a zoo animal, surrounded by churlish soldiers. Sick in the early stages of her pregnancy, there was little immediate comfort to be offered. Jinfeng's family wanted nothing to do with her. The family of her husband had requested that she be turned over to them. The magistrate, however, was determined to protect her. 'Tell her not to try and escape,' he instructed Joan. 'She is safer here.'

At times Jinfeng seemed to respond to Joan's offers of advice and prayer. Other days she adopted an altogether arrogant attitude, feeding off the scraps of praise for becoming 'Chinese' tossed condescendingly to her by the Han soldiers. Jinfeng's troubles had a notable effect on her friends. Aji and Lanlan, like other Nosu, rejected her completely. The Chinese girls through their discussions with Joan began to understand the deeper consequences of sin. There was profound astonishment expressed that Joan should continue to visit Jinfeng.

'Do you remember our reading lesson?' Joan asked the group. '*Shangdi ai zui ren, Shangdi hen zui*. That is why I go. To tell her that God still loves her no matter what she has done.'

* * *

Joan was starting her daily prayers when she heard a small but recognisable thump on her door. 'Good morning, Margie, have you had your breakfast?' Margie nodded with all the candid vigour of a two-year-old and squeezed her way past Joan's legs into the room. 'Yes, you can come in,' said Joan, 'but Auntie is reading her Bible, so you must be quiet.'

Joan found Margie a book and settled her on the bed

before returning to her own reading for the day. Margie turned the pages of the book, muttering to herself a story to fit the pictures. Then she stopped and said, 'Auntie, talk to Jesus.'

'A very good idea, Margie. We can always talk to Jesus, can't we?' When their prayers were over Joan got up to lift Margie off the bed. Reaching out she glanced at the ugly, dark-red swelling on her own right forearm. She ran her fingers over the hard protuberance. This was something that concerned her. 'Come on, Margie. I'll take you back to Daddy.'

Jim examined the button-sized blister. 'I'll keep an eye on it. Hopefully it will turn out to be nothing to worry about.' His immediate lack of reassurance was disturbing. Doubt and difficulty quickly began to beset Joan. What did that mean? Was it malignant? Where would she go to deal with the problem? The current partition of China made travel to Chengdu, Chongqing or Shanghai uncertain. Hadn't local officials said that there would be fighting in Xichang before long? Rumours of a Nosu rebellion had been in the air since before January. And who would go with her? The team were stretched to the limit even with Yu and Chang at work. Could she travel unharmed alone to Xichang? For a while the secure shelter of her inner peace was splintered. She must let the matter rest until diagnosis was made.

A week later Jim examined the swelling again. His forehead furrowed in concern. 'I think I should operate. Get yourself ready and I'll find Ruth to assist.'

'It seems Satan has been allowed a little more leeway,' Jim

said as he cut into the flesh below Joan's elbow. 'God's workers aren't immune from his interference. Let's see what we can find.'

'There's a cold abscess,' reported Jim as he sewed the wound together again. 'And sinus which leads up above the elbow. It possibly could be TB.' He scooped Joan up in his arms and carried her upstairs to her room. 'I don't do this for all my patients... but this once,' he laughed as she protested. 'I'll telegram Shanghai for streptomycin. Till then you're to keep it immobilised. There may be infection in the bone. A secure sling will be fine.'

'How long for?'

'Till we get it sorted. Don't want to aggravate anything.'

'But...'

'Doctor's orders!'

Joan contemplated the limitations. The loss of the use of her right hand would present all kinds of difficulties. Her ministry options would be severely restricted. How could she aid Jim in the clinic? Getting out to the villages regularly might be too demanding. The additional burden of chores would put greater strain on Janet and Ruth. Typing her occasional letters home with her left hand and completing the accounts would be time-consuming and tiring. How would she cope? 'What about bathing Joy?' asked Joan tentatively.

Jim mulled over the question for a moment, well aware of Joan's care for his children and the depth of her feelings. 'OK. It will probably do you more good than harm. Ruth! Write this down. "Doctor's orders to Miss Joan Margaret Wales, Missionary Extraordinaire to the

Great Cold Mountains of Inland China, Esteemed Member of the Nosu Team, Godmother of Margie. One bathing of Jennifer Joy Broomhall permitted per day. To be enjoyed to the full."'

Next morning there was a small, but recognisable, thump on Joan's door. When Joan opened it Margie was standing looking very pleased with herself with her arm neatly held in a sling made from an old cotton rag.

'She wanted to be like Auntie Joan,' Janet said later. 'You are very loved.'

Chapter 18

'...the root of Liangshan's inaccessibility lay in the threat to human life.'

ZHONG XIU

The crack of a rifle shot in the night, the clatter of a minor battle taking place down the valley or even the fort guards discharging off several rounds from the walls above the compound at unseen enemies had become so commonplace that it was unusual for the team members to be woken by anything but the worst aggression. Their situation was rarely peaceful. The intensity of tribal warfare ebbed and flowed between flimsy treaties of fragile harmony: agreements made and broken on the whim of impetuous chiefs. An accidental intrusion into land held by another clan, an insult fuelled by alcohol, an old score to settle and downright belligerence could all trigger fresh fighting. Cold-blooded murder was not uncommon.

221

Every skirmish would bring new casualties to the clinic. Or Jim would find people lying injured in their homes as he travelled around on Belinda offering aid. At times he would start out for one side of the valley, binding up wounds, then trek across to the other to stitch up the opposition. The local chiefs, grateful for his ministrations and ignorant of the irony, were ever sympathetic for the exertion they had created for him. It was some time before they recognised that ceasing their hostilities altogether would spare him the trouble of repairing their wounds. Tribal pride would not allow them to seek a lasting solution to their enmity.

These erratic, yet frequent, episodes of mayhem were played out against the larger backdrop of the Communist and Nationalist conflict now anticipated in the Xichang valley – a scenario, which, in turn, stirred renewed uncertainty and unrest locally between Chinese and Nosu.

As March advanced, the team were not immune from internal upset and strife. Illness took its toll, consuming energy, threatening hope, as each team member in turn fell sick. Yu and Chang, as newcomers, had misunderstood the strength of the mission's finances and had initially expected better provision for their livelihood than the team could afford. Indigenous churches needed to support their own workers, not leave them dependent on Western resources. They should not be viewed as hired employees of the mission, no different than servants, ministering out of duty rather than personal commitment to Christ. Yu's wife could not settle and both she and her husband were quickly homesick. Discord then flared as Yu and his wife engaged in an unseemly public argument. She was adamant that they had made a mistake in coming and wanted to return home to Yunnan Province. Only timely intervention was instrumental in encouraging them to stay and helping them as Nosu to meet the unanticipated challenges of cross-cultural adjustment amongst their 'untamed cousins'.

The team were temporarily boosted by the arrival of Lo, a young Chinese ex-officer and graduate of the Bible college in Chongqing. He had arrived in Xichang with his new wife and his mother shortly after Yu and Chang. Initial impressions of a strong, capable co-worker proved premature. He had little appetite for the aggressive nature of the Nosu. Although in looks he resembled the local tribesmen, once they discovered that he was Han Chinese he found they quickly despised his efforts to help them. The repetitious winter diet of dried shredded vegetables soaked overnight for cooking was not to his liking. He also found the district's Mandarin dialect as foreign as English. As his list of complaints grew ever longer he quickly became discouraged and keen to leave.

'We are going to find it hard to sustain any meaningful outreach without a stable team,' lamented Jim as he spent his time bolstering the confidence of the young men, Yu, Chang and Lo. Once again, prospects of doing any more than maintaining a clinic at Zhaojue and a sporadic presence at the dispensary in Zhuhe seemed beyond their grasp. There was, however, some blessing in it all. Their interpreter, Zhao, had returned from a trip away from the area determined to put behind him his indulgence in vice and recommit himself to Christ. His attitude and the growth in his faith now became a major contribution to the team's outreach as he shared in the services and meetings.

'What's the situation with servant Yang?' Joan asked Janet when visiting the Cottage.

Janet shook her head. 'He is becoming impossible. He's drunk before lunch. Then he sits in the house smelling of alcohol and swears and threatens us all. The children are frightened. We will have to dismiss him.'

'It means more work for you about the house,' Jim said. 'Joan can't do more with her arm in a sling.'

'Ruth has offered to milk the cow morning and evening.'

Joan laughed. 'Perhaps that will be a good thing. She reckons if she sings to her we'll get more milk!'

'But...'

'Jim,' Janet interrupted him, 'we can cope.'

Jim never ceased to be amazed at his wife's resilience. In Ruth, Joan and Janet he had missionaries who asked for no comforts and whose dedication to the work far surpassed his natural expectation. To work amongst the Nosu was his vision, the compulsion that drove him day in, day out, to minister despite the dangers. Yet these women had embraced the same vision and refused to withdraw in the face of opposition.

There was a cry from the walls above the compound. 'There are soldiers approaching the fort!'

Jim strode up onto the rampart. In the distance he could make out formations of soldiers descending from the hills. Several units of infantry were heading in their direction, some peeling off to occupy villages on the periphery of the valley. 'Who are they?' Jim asked the local

Chinese, but got no reply. Heavy-hearted, he returned to the house and lay face down on the bed. He felt sick. The responsibility he carried for his wife, children and the team bore down too keenly. What could... what would happen to them?

He did not hear Janet enter the room after him. Gently she placed her hand upon his shoulder. 'Jim... it will be all right,' she comforted him.

Within an hour the fort was swamped with the vanguard of Nationalist troops – a battalion of soldiers retreating in the face of the Communist advance. Brash and overbearing, arrogant and imperious, despite the seeming futility of their resistance, they vowed that Zhaojue was to be their guerrilla headquarters. Men and officers immediately invaded the clinic, demanding doors be removed as makeshift beds, requisitioning anything they had failed to bring with them. Officers took up residence in rooms used for patients and walked at will into the compound. It was only the arrival of their commanding officer, a General Liu, that brought order to the mayhem. He instructed the soldiers to vacate the building and assured the team that he was sympathetic to Christianity. The soldiers, shamed by losing face before foreigners, took petty revenge by removing the best of the guard dogs with them.

In the days that followed there was a frenzy of activity. The breaches in the fort walls were hurriedly repaired and a machine-gun post erected, aerials to establish communication with Xichang were assembled and on the drill ground there were regular exercises for the troops. Jim was requested to attend parades of the sick and add his advice to that of the army doctor. Unexpectedly, the influx of armed forces brought opportunities for ministry that the team had not envisaged. The men were encouraged to attend meetings; a special service was arranged on Sundays for the soldiers. Evening Bible studies for smaller groups were also asked for. At one of these an adjutant stood up during a time of prayer and announced his desire to follow Christ. As the uncertainty in their situation grew, others also showed interest in the gospel.

Lo and Yu, as ex-military men, seemed for a short while to be in their element, mixing well with the soldiers. After the first Sunday service Lo, however, latched on to a group returning to Xichang and promptly left to join the work of the Conservative Baptists in the valley. He had survived just ten days amongst the Nosu. His abrupt departure served to unsettle Yu and his wife and within a few days they were again arguing about staying.

The apprehension in Zhaojue had become palpable. 'Will the Nosu rebel?' was a question that was increasingly heard. The arrival of the Nationalist troops had done nothing to quell speculation that the clans would seize the opportunity of civil war to strengthen their claims upon the land. The amounts demanded as Nosu protection levy on supplies brought up from Xichang increased rapidly. The sequestration of a whole packload of valuable salt by a young chief brought swift and terrible reprisal. Two Nosu villages were attacked in the night with grenades and set alight. Those who escaped the flames were shot at indiscriminately. The wrath of the Nosu seethed beneath the surface.

Jim and Janet were in bed when they were disturbed by the wife of the fort telegraphist. She stole quietly into the compound and made her way discreetly to their door.

'Who is it?'

'Mrs Qiang.'

The door was opened. The lady refused the offer to enter. 'I have news from Xichang,' she whispered. 'The Communists are half a day's march away. There are three columns of soldiers. The Nationalist generals are going to escape by plane...'

On the evening of 25 March 1950, five planes sped across the airfield just outside Xichang and rose into dark skies, carrying high-ranking Nationalist officers to safety above the massive heights of the Great Cold Mountains. Behind were left the tattered rank-and-file troops of a defeated army. The much-trumpeted last stand had come to nothing and the Communist forces continued their progress unchallenged up the river valley. The fall of Xichang occurred without aggression, under the cover of night. Quantities of American weaponry and resources accumulated over a period of weeks for the resistance passed unchallenged into the hands of the victors. Zhaojue was now isolated as a Nationalist stronghold.

The news of the 'liberation' of Xichang preceded the arrival of Nationalist fugitives. Amongst the first were a group of four. Pursued into the mountains, they had fallen foul of Nosu eager to take advantage of their plight. Gifts and bribes were ineffectual. The Nosu, exacting revenge without fear of retaliation, had stripped them naked and bound them. The men had, however, escaped once more and arrived dressed in meagre cloaks and with pieces of felt tied about their feet. 'We were fortunate,' one told Jim as he bent over him to bind up his wounds. 'So many were murdered by Nosu. Others were handed back to the Communists. Who knows what fate awaits them?'

Their coming, and the arrival of scores of men, women and children, with similar tales of loss and harassment, shook the military stationed at the fort. It was clear they were cut off from reinforcements and essential supplies. The loss of senior leaders and high-grade armaments meant resistance could only be limited. The Nationalist general mustered his officers together and in tears told them that their cause was lost. Within a few days he had left, heading northeast in the hope of getting to the Yangtze River. An influential Nosu prince, Ling, who as a child had been adopted and educated by a local Chinese warlord, was left in nominal charge of the despairing remnants of Nationalist troops.

As each day passed the tension increased, with confusion over which of the combatants to fear the most – Communists, Nationalists or Nosu. There were rumours that the forces holed up in Zhaojue would riot and loot the little spoils that remained in the fort. Local women were hurriedly employed to sew jackets and trousers for the soldiers to flee as civilians. Food was stockpiled and hoarded away ready for flight. Local Chinese whispered of their plans to dress as Nosu in the hope that they would escape unharmed.

The team were also prepared, sleeping at night in their clothes, bags packed with provisions, medicines and extra clothing. Jim put aside drugs to make the children sleep should they be forced to flee and seek shelter in Nosu homes. Prince Ling came with a warning for Jim. 'You must arrange for your children to hide in the home of a local chief.'

'Whom would you recommend?' asked Jim, but Ling would not commit himself. Jim made his way back to the Cottage and gathered the others. 'I have no idea what news Ling has, but he looked very drawn and worried.'

'What choices do we have?' asked Ruth.

'We could do as he says and move out of Zhaojue to a Nosu village. Risky, of course. All the villages around here will be vulnerable to attack. We could move to Zhuhe... not particularly attractive if the Nosu turn hostile. Or we can stay here.'

There was no dissension. They would stay in Zhaojue and trust for God's help in whatever events transpired.

The renewed fears for their physical safety drove both the Nationalist troops and locals to seek spiritual help. The Bible studies with the soldiers were well attended and there were indications of greater understanding of the need for salvation and definite commitments to Christ. Yu and Chang found themselves fully employed in preaching. Mother Hu, the mother of one of Joan's pupils, Songmei, came looking for Joan, asking for opportunity to study the Bible with her.

Joan's afternoons were spent with Prince Ling. Aware of the team's love for his people, Ling offered his services to them despite the precarious position he found himself in. While others moved listlessly from distraction to distraction to alleviate their fears, the two of them worked together for unbroken periods of up to three hours, translating key verses of scripture into Nosu. Joan found the prince remarkably friendly and open to the Bible message.

Joan also continued her regular visits to Jinfeng, still held in prison.

'Give me silver to pay off my in-laws,' begged Jinfeng.

Joan shook her head. 'Silver and gold have I none; but such as I have give I thee,'[40] she quoted and told Jinfeng the story from Acts 3. 'Jinfeng, you need to respond to God's love for you. You cannot buy your way to Heaven.'

The next day Joan was called to the prison. The place was in a state of confusion. 'Take Jinfeng with you,' she was urged. 'The Communists are coming. If you hide her in your compound maybe she will be all right.'

Joan refused. 'We cannot do that. Besides, our compound is no safer than any other building. If you want to help her, then release her.' Joan spent a few minutes by Jinfeng's cage, but the teenager seemed lost in her own troubles.

As at Xichang, the 'liberation' of Zhaojue was not the final battle that everyone expected. After lunch on 6 April an insignificant delegation consisting of three men appeared on the horizon, unarmed and clearly not expecting trouble. Their leader, an official with the surname Mao, was arrayed in a silk cloak lined with leopard skin and was most polite in accepting the surrender of the Nationalist troops from Prince Ling. He, then, courteously asked Jim to join him at the front of the 'victory parade' as he took control of the fort and occupied the magistrate's quarters.

'We have no wish to hinder your work,' Comrade Mao later reassured the team. 'I know missionaries who live in

Leshan. Perhaps they are friends of yours. I would be honoured to attend one of your services.'

'Then you must join us tomorrow,' said Jim. 'It is our Good Friday service.'

'Tomorrow I must go to Zhuhe and then return to Xichang. We have much work to do in this region.' Mao made his apologies and took his leave of them.

The Communist delegation left Zhaojue with the remnants of the Nationalist army and, amongst them, the soldiers who had expressed interest in Christianity. A small platoon remained as a token presence under the command of a young man designated as the acting magistrate. Nervous of the intentions of the Nosu he immediately implemented a high level of surveillance. The Chinese who had lived in the villages around Zhaojue sought the protection of the fort. Gunfire continued to punctuate the night. The violent deaths of two soldiers confirmed the fears of the beleaguered watchmen on the walls that little had changed.

The sorry plight of Jinfeng was finally settled with the onset of the new administration. She was released from her cage but not to freedom. Protesting vehemently, she was dragged into the road and handed over to her in-laws, who sold her into slavery for 150 ounces of silver. Her new owners, with an eye for profit, then sold her again. Four months pregnant, she was consigned to work as a menial slave in a village a considerable distance from Zhaojue. Joan was distressed to see her treated so shamefully but nothing could be done to save her from the injustices of the system. It was difficult to know what effect, if any, Joan's teaching and expressions of concern had made on

Jinfeng. The girl was intelligent enough to understand something of the gospel message. But when the opportunity had been offered she had not responded and, as the web of her own misfortune had closed in around her, it seemed that Satan had won that battle. If there was anything good that had been achieved it was the influence of Joan's example on the teenagers in the reading class and their embryonic comprehension of Christian love.

As life gradually returned to what was depressingly considered normal, the eye of the storm provided an opportunity for the team to recommence their work in the villages. Services attracted some of the local Chinese who had shown little inclination to come before. Renewed interest was a great encouragement but there seemed to be no sign of personal response. The progress, however, was tempered by the departure of Yu and his wife for Xichang in early June, never to return. Once more the ranks of indigenous Christians in the team were depleted, leaving only Zhao and Chang to continue the work.

There was now a growing frustration in the team that, despite all their efforts over two years, there had still not been a single lasting response to the gospel from the local population, Chinese or Nosu. While there was little thought that they could not continue in Zhaojue with their humanitarian work, the opportunity to preach and teach might well in time be restricted. Their resolution was to instigate a week of prayer and fasting when every available hour would be devoted to seeking God for an end to the resistance.

Chapter 19

'Hell has had many disappointments.'

BISHOP FRANK HOUGHTON, 1949

As the Nosu and Chinese congregation filtered out of the clinic at the end of the Sunday morning service that followed their week of prayer, the father of Shan, one of Joan's reading class, shuffled forward and asked to speak with Jim. 'My wife and I want to become Christians,' he said. Jim was taken aback. While they had prayed for and believed a breakthrough was possible this was certainly not what they had anticipated. The man was racked with an obsession for opium and it was difficult to believe that either he or his wife had any inkling of the implications of devotion to Christ.

'He must be drawn by the notion that Christians are rich and thinks he can gain from associating with the mission,' Jim told Chang as they set out to make a visit.

'The attraction of wealth has caused too many miscarriages of "rice Christians"! We must emphasise the cost of commitment to them.'

The family's hut was primitive and poorly furnished, shorn of all but the basics. Whatever possessions the couple had owned had been bartered to finance their addiction. Shan was also there, sitting with her friends, Baoli and Baodan, in one dark corner on a pile of rough boards that the family had procured to make a coffin for Shan's grandmother. Chang carefully explained the essential elements of the gospel, laying out plainly to the family the need for the rejection of their immoral lifestyle and a complete change of heart. Shan's father and his wife listened in silence, but it soon became apparent that this was not the message they had wanted to hear.

Baoli and Shan were far more receptive. 'I want to believe,' declared Baoli when Chang had finished.

'Me too,' added Shan.

'Then you need to talk to Joan. She can help you. And you?' Jim asked Baodan, who had not expressed any views of her own.

'I am not sure. I have not decided yet.'

When Joan searched out Shan it soon became obvious that, despite her declaration the previous day, Shan's marriage into the only Chinese family in Zhuhe remained a major obstacle to believing. She was not prepared to return to her husband and was trying to secure a divorce. 'I cannot return. If Jesus helps me and makes sure I don't have to go, then I can believe.'

Joan was at pains to explain that commitment could not be conditional. 'You need to give your future over to

God too. You must trust him whatever your situation.'

Shan, however, simply refused to be convinced. 'I don't want to be married to that man...' There seemed to be no way forward.

Hugely disappointed, Joan returned to the fort. She was deeply concerned for the girls who attended her reading classes. Their lessons in the Chinese primer had slowly built up for them unfamiliar concepts of a God who loved them and who had cared enough to live on earth and die for them. They had learned about sin and the need for forgiveness. The team had prayed for personal responses from each of the teenagers. Shan and Baoli's comments to Chang and Jim had seemed at last to open the door of understanding. Meihua had remained interested. What of the others? Feng? Songmei?

Further disappointment awaited Joan as she walked up towards the north gate to the home of Songmei and Songan. To her dismay the house was crammed with Nosu. At the centre of the room sat a witchdoctor, a small drum clasped between his legs from which he was pounding out a tedious rhythm. The Nosu swayed uneasily back and forth.

'What is happening?' Joan asked Songmei, beckoning her to the doorway.

'Mother's eyes are bad. The shaman is exorcising the demons.'

'She would be better off seeing Hai Yisheng,' Joan insisted. 'This isn't going to help her at all... Mother Hu!' Joan stepped audaciously into the gathering. 'If your eyes are hurting then you need to see a doctor. Come back with me. Hai Yisheng will give you ointment.'

Not averse to trying any remedy, Songmei's mother, whom Ruth had also befriended and spoken to about the gospel, was firmly steered in the direction of the clinic. 'This medicine has nothing to do with your shaman's chants or your spirits,' Jim made plain as he handed over the ointment. 'Come and see me when your eyes are better. Songmei, take your mother home and turn that witchdoctor out!'

Songmei was soon back at the clinic, bringing Meihua in support. 'Can we talk with you, Wei Jiaoshi?' she called from the bottom of the stairs.

'Of course, come on up.' Joan rearranged her room and fetched stools for the girls to sit on.

'We want to talk about believing in Jesus.'

'And I would be very happy to do that...'

'I don't want to wait,' interrupted Meihua. 'I mean, I want to do it now... but I don't know what to do...'

'Well, I'll pray and you can repeat what I say,' Joan encouraged her. 'I'll go slowly so you can think about the words.' Joan felt a strong sense of jubilation as Meihua followed her prayer. Here was the first unambiguous answer to their prayer and fasting. Meihua was crossing a threshold in eternity. The twenty-six months of danger, privation and struggle that the team had endured suddenly assumed meaning. Joan looked across at Songmei. 'What about you, Songmei?'

Songmei shook her head. 'I am still not certain. I need more time to make a decision.'

Surprisingly, it was Songmei's elder sister, Songan, who was next to find Joan. 'I want to finish with the wine-making trade,' she declared after her reading lesson.

'Whatever it costs I want Jesus' way. Will you pray with me as you did with Meihua?' Joan had no hesitation in guiding her to Christ – the second significant answer to their prayers.

In turn, Songan's decision finally precipitated Songmei's commitment later the same day. Joan was walking along the fort wall. Above her, rain-laden clouds were tumbling from the mountain summits and cascading over each other across the valley skies.

'Wei Jiaoshi!'

Joan looked back to see Songmei clambering up the steps onto the rampart, dragging her young nephew behind her.

'Songan has told me she has become a Christian. Can you pray with me?'

'Of course.'

'Now? Here?'

'Of course.' As Joan began her prayer the clouds burst open and the rain poured down, soaking the three of them instantly. 'We can't pray here!' laughed Joan. 'You must get your nephew home and dry him off.' Songmei hurriedly scooped him up and, doing her best to shield him, started back to the steps. 'You can pray to Jesus by yourself!' Joan shouted after her. 'Don't wait until tomorrow!'

'Three commitments in two days.' Joan was ecstatic as she brought the news to the others at prayers that evening. 'Meihua is revelling in it. She even prays out aloud in front of the others. Then Songan. And now Songmei.'

Two weeks later there was another standoff with the shaman. Opposite Mother Hu's home was a hovel with an evil reputation which was occupied by a woman, her late husband's brother and her daughter, Yingying, a girl of 19. Yingying had participated in Ruth's reading classes from time to time, but had shown little curiosity in the gospel, often scorning the other teenagers for their interest. Foolishly, the girl had deliberately grazed a pony in a crop of oats belonging to a Nosu chief. He had discovered her and, riven with insanity, had beaten her viciously before putting his brutal hands around her throat and throttling her. Finally he had thrown her to the ground and left her for dead. Her mother, on finding her, had called for a witchdoctor to divine what damage Yingying had suffered.

The shaman had brought a chicken into the house, battering it against the walls and floor to replicate the beating Yingying had received. Then, slitting open the fowl, he had revealed the bruised entrails and torn organs. 'See,' he had declared triumphantly. 'The bird's bowels are black. Yingying's bowels are black. The spirits must be placated.' Yingying, however, had not recovered. She lay on her bed in the small loft, oblivious to the clamour of invocations that were offered on her behalf. Slowly she slipped into torpidity, and the frightening pall of death closed in around her. 'Get Hai Yisheng. Get Hai Yisheng!'

Jim examined her. There was no doubt that Yingying was dying, yet there was nothing in her injuries to suggest that they were life-threatening. 'The witchdoctor is wrong,' he told the crowd that had gathered. 'There is nothing wrong with Yingying's organs. She is in fear of your demons and no longer wants to live.' His words provoked vehement protests from the shaman and his supporters. Jim went on: 'If you fear the demons that live here, then bring her to "God's ground" where there are no demons. She will soon recover.'

After lunch Jim and Janet returned to the hovel with a dessert Janet had cooked. The mother had gone off on another spurious errand to consult the witchdoctor once more. Free from the attentions of the shaman, Yingying responded more readily to their care and later in the afternoon was brought to the clinic, carried on the back of her uncle. Taking her in, Jim dismissed the family and called for Joan. 'Joan, get Songmei and Meihua up here to care for her. She'll respond to them better. Now she is out of that hell she calls home, she may have a chance to learn about Heaven.'

It was several weeks before Yingying returned to her mother. The witness of the new believers had begun to bring light into the darkness of her life. With Ruth's determined teaching and guidance she gradually groped her way to knowledge of God's power to overcome the demonic forces that she feared. Some months later she committed herself to Christ.

Shan's battle over the issue of her marriage raged for three weeks before she approached Joan again, bringing with her Songan, who seemed to have assumed the role of 'big sister' to the young Christians.

'I know that Jesus will go with me if I have to go to my in-laws,' said Shan. 'I have decided to trust him with every part of my life. Please pray with me.'

Within a few more days first Mother Hu, helped by the medicine for her eyes, made a commitment following the Sunday morning service, then Feng, Baoli and finally Baodan also found Joan and asked to become Christians.

Within one month of their call to prayer and fasting, six of Joan's reading class – Meihua, Baoli, Baodan, Songmei, Shan, Feng – together with Songmei's mother and elder sister, had come to know Jesus as their Lord and Saviour, all making their commitment with Joan's help. Only Meihua's young niece had not yet responded. It was a remarkable answer to the team's prayers.

In the midst of these thrilling events, Jim called Joan to the Cottage. 'Post has arrived.' He handed her a letter from Shanghai. 'I thought you might like to see this.'

Joan opened the envelope and scanned the neatly typed script on thin opaque paper. It gave details of a gift received for the work amongst the Nosu. 'Fifty pounds! That's generous...' She read on: '"...the gift of Mr G. H. Wales, Bournemouth, UK". Oh, Jim, it's my father. I can hardly believe it... that's a lot of money.'

She read the letter again. Slowly. Savouring its significance. 'He is interested... he does care about what I am doing.' It was as though her heavenly Father, now he was liberating the captives for whom she cared deeply, had chosen this moment to unfetter her own bonds.

* * *

It came as little surprise when, after some respite, problems and crises began to reassert themselves. The Hu household was reduced to a state of turmoil. Following the conversion of Songan and Songmei's mother, Mother Hu had ceased to make wine. The elder brother was outraged. The loss of such a lucrative trade would cut their income drastically. Without regular earnings his opium habit could not be financed. Enraged by their refusal to acquiesce to his strident demands, he threatened to turf the three women out of the house. The tensions further intensified when Songmei's sister-in-law ran off with a soldier but was caught and brought back. Songmei's elder brother moved his errant wife to a nearby village in a vain attempt to keep her at a distance from her lover, before landing himself in prison over an alleged plan to sell his wife as a slave. The woman, keen to be rid of him, was suing for divorce.

Meihua was the next casualty, brought in some distress to the clinic with a leg infection. 'It's osteomyelitis,' Jim told Joan. 'And it doesn't look good.' Meihua had to undergo an operation and a period of acute illness before she recovered and was well enough to return home.

Ruth was deflated by the progress Yingying was making. The teenager had begun a relationship with one of the soldiers and there was no doubt that their entanglement had stepped beyond the bounds of propriety. 'She'll have to marry him. Why can't these girls see beyond cheap bracelets and look at the scoundrels that offer them?'

Then Feng stopped coming to prayer times and reading lessons. It transpired that the family were destitute and lacking even basic food. Feng, aware that the team frowned on anything that smacked of association with the mission for personal gain, had stayed away. She did not want to be considered a 'rice Christian'. To save her from impoverishment the team employed her around the compound to aid Janet and Ruth.

A letter from Yu, the team's former co-worker now resident in Xichang, caused the greatest grief. He was insisting on wages for his 'employment' while in Zhaojue. The missive carried a threat that he would appeal to the Communist officials if the money were not forthcoming. Chang and Zhao, wiser to the situation than their Western colleagues, argued strongly that the ultimatum should be met. There was little advantage in stirring up official animosity. The incident created considerable disquiet for the new believers, shocked that such a strong Christian as Yu could so easily lose his way.

The spiritual battle continued into September when the team proposed a 'Short-Term Bible School' – five days when the girls would live in the compound for concentrated teaching from all the members of the team, combined with a programme of crafts and games. Their families, particularly those addicted to opium, were not happy with the arrangements; without their daughters to work, they insisted, they would not cope. Prayer was, however, answered again. The teenagers were allowed to come to the Bible school, with an agreement that they would return to their homes for a couple of hours each morning.

'It is incredible to see the changes in these girls,' remarked Janet to Jim. 'Just a few months ago they were no different from any of the others. Caught up in innuendo, flirting with anyone who showed no more than a passing interest in them. Lewd, rude. Barely able to read. And now look at them. Studying their Bibles daily. Praying aloud. Concerned for their families. Genuinely aggrieved if they fall out with each other. Repenting openly for even the smallest sins. Last night they were up way after we went to bed singing, *All for Jesus*[41]!'

'Would that the men showed such promise,' said Jim, thinking of Yu's sad example. 'But Chang is doing a remarkable job. His influence on Zhao has been profound.'

The teenagers were sent home with Jim's final talk to them on Joshua chapter 1. 'Be strong and of a good courage; be not afraid, neither be thou dismayed: for the Lord thy God is with thee whithersoever thou goest.[42]' The choice was apt. Before October 1950 was out Communist troops had fully asserted their control in Zhaojue. Their uniforms were little different from those of their predecessors, save for the small badge above the stiff peaks of their mushroom-like cloth caps, which bore the gold characters '*bayi*'[43] on a five-pointed red star. Another insignia on the left breast-pocket of their grey tunics identified them as '*Jiefangjun*' – the People's Liberation Army. The few months of relative freedom for worship and Bible-training the Christians had enjoyed were at an end. There would be fresh ordeals that both the team and the new believers would have to meet.

Chapter 20

*'As for prospects? Who knows? All that matters is
that the Lord knows, and he has said, "Stay put and
await further orders!"'*

JIM BROOMHALL, LETTER TO LEVI LOVEGREN, 1950

Baoli, with her sister, Baodan, met with Shan by the fort
gate. Above them on the wall lounged two soldiers.
'Comrades!' the men called out. 'Where are you going?'

'To the clinic.'

'Why? Are you sick?' His companion sniggered: 'Sick in
the head.'

'We are going to see Wei Jiaoshi. She teaches us to
read.'

'So we have heard. Fills your heads with fairytales. A
god who dies and flies into the sky.'

Baoli scowled. 'Let's get on. These two are
troublemakers.'

The girls passed through the gate. As they emerged into the fort a stone fizzed past Shan and struck Baodan. She screamed. Another stone was aimed in their direction. Baodan yelled again. 'Run!' The girls dashed up the lane as a couple more missiles missed their targets. Baoli glanced back. The twisted expressions on the guards' faces told her this was no horseplay, the absurd male notion of a joke. This was pure intimidation.

Baodan inspected her arms and legs once they made the safety of the clinic doors. Her brown skin had been stung into shades of bruised puce. Songmei, who was waiting for them, was sympathetic but excited. 'You'd think we were some sort of threat. But listen, Meihua's niece is going to become a Christian! Teacher Wei is going to pray with her. Come on, I don't want to miss it.'

'What do we do about the stone throwing?' asked Baodan when she showed Joan her bruises after their lesson.

'We are going to have to think how we can continue our studies,' replied Joan, shocked that the situation had deteriorated so quickly. 'Go carefully. And remember we need to pray for those who persecute us.'

The simplest solution was to meet during the daytime when there were plenty of people around and it was less easy for the soldiers to mistreat the teenagers. Whenever possible, Joan would go to the girls' homes rather than have them come to the compound. Sometimes they would meet in the fields or on the verge of the tracks within the fort.

'Comrade...' Joan spoke to the officer who stood observing them as she and the young believers sat on the roadside.

'This is a copy of what we are reading.' With only the use of her left hand she had painstakingly typed out several sheets of their study to distribute if soldiers insisted on standing around their meeting. 'You are most welcome to read it,' she said politely and then returned to her instruction of the group as though they were completely alone.

The initial campaign first to constrict, then stifle, the expanding ministry of the team became a contest of ever-shifting tactics. For a while the administration tried to persuade the new believers to desert the mission with the organising of dances – a vain presumption that the glamour of social events would quickly entice them away from their meetings. The girls' established friendship with Joan, however, would not be so easily broken with inducements borrowed from a way of life they had so recently rejected.

Then it was decreed that Sunday services could no longer be held in the clinic waiting room. They must be conducted in the courtyard: a trial as the increasingly cold weather set in. When this also failed to deter the believers from congregating, propaganda meetings were organised, calculated to coincide with the services and forcing the new Christians to miss their opportunity for worship. Pressure from public questioning persuaded two of the girls to deny their faith, causing great grief to the beleaguered young believers. Ostracised by their peers, the two rapidly repented and were eventually restored to the fellowship. But the incident revealed how vulnerable they all were.

The team themselves were by and large immune from direct interference for the early months of the autumn. Officially they were made welcome but privately the team were denounced as imperialists, spies with only harm of the community on their agenda. Both Nosu and Chinese were asked to protect their own position by disclosing the malevolent nature of the team's 'covert' deeds. The ploy failed. The people would not be easily deprived of the only local medical facility available to them, nor was the goodwill earned by the team's treatments to be so readily repudiated. In response to the threats to their welfare the residents wrote to the Xichang authorities and the Beijing government requesting that the mission be allowed to stay. For the time being their work could continue. Sometimes opportunities arose when least expected.

'Auntie Joan?'

Joan was in the compound patiently pegging out her washing with one hand.

'Auntie! Up here.' Above her on the wall sat Jan.

'What is it, Jan?'

'Can you please come up here and talk to Lili? I have told her all I can about Jesus.'

Lili was the nine-year-old daughter of Mr and Mrs Qiang at the telegraph office. The two girls were squatting back on their heels with the practised air of Chinese adults when Joan joined them. 'I have run out of Mandarin,' explained Jan. 'Please tell her all you can.' Joan squatted down beside them and began to tell them stories of Jesus.

'You did very well,' said Joan to Jan when the two girls decided they needed to go and play somewhere else. 'Lili understands a lot about Jesus. We need to pray for her mummy and daddy to love Jesus too.'

'We will!' shouted Jan as they dashed off along the wall and down to the Cottage. Joan got up very slowly and stretched. Her right leg had gone to sleep. Would she ever be able to squat for hours like the Chinese, and like Jan? 'They don't teach you this in orientation...' she moaned as she hobbled back to her washing.

'Auntie...'

This time it was Lili standing at Joan's bedroom door. Since their talk on the wall the little Chinese girl had been coming daily to listen to a Bible story.

'Come on in, Lili, I was just waiting for you.'

Lili pushed her little brother into the room with the invested authority of a big sister. 'Mummy asked if he can come too. He's been very naughty. She says, can we pray for him?'

'Of course we can.' Joan lifted the boy onto her knee.

'I've been telling him about Jesus. Can you tell him a story?'

'We can do that as well. What would be the best story to tell him?'

'Auntie... Can I bring a friend?' Lili peered around the door of Joan's room. 'She's called Wan.'

Joan became aware of a girl of eight or nine peering shyly over Lili's shoulder. 'Come in, Wan. And you too, Lili.'

'I've told her about Jesus,' explained Lili, leaning over confidentially. 'And she wants to know Jesus just like I do.'

'Well, we shall pray that she does. Now, which story shall I tell you today?'

Other unexpected encouragements came as the team's contacts, unconcerned about the opinions of the authorities, continued to associate with the mission. Without warning, Mrs Yang, who had left their employ more than twelve months previously because of her opium addiction, returned as a reformed character determined to overcome her addiction. Songmei's elder brother, chastened by the loss of his wife and now freed from prison, appeared in the middle of November also wanting the team's help. The love shown him by his converted family had convinced him that he should break his dependency on drugs. He moved into the clinic for a few weeks' treatment. Returning home cured of his opium habit, he declared that he would only worship *Shangdi* and tore down the idol shelves that he had previously refused to allow his mother and sisters to touch. In their place he pasted up posters proclaiming the Ten Commandments and the gospel.

Amongst the new arrivals in Zhaojue was a man educated at a Baptist college in Shanghai, his wife and the youngest of their six children. The other five children had been sold to raise funds for the parents' addiction to opium. Coming, as they did, from respected wealthy families their descent into poverty was all the more tragic. Reduced to starvation, they tried without success to sell the remaining child, who was weak with malnutrition, to the innkeeper. Finally, totally impoverished, they sought refuge in the clinic, both responding well to the treatment and teaching they received.

Aji and Lanlan, the Nosu teenagers, were encouraged towards faith by their Chinese friends. Aji had come to the point of belief, declaring, 'I believe all you have told me about Jesus.' Yingying, who had been close to death through her fear of demons, finally emerged from the darkness that had enveloped her and with Ruth's help made a commitment. Even her disreputable mother seemed to have grasped the basics of the gospel enough to know that she was a sinner and needed help. The telegraphist and his wife were also influenced by Lili Qiang's determination to tell her parents what she had learned about Jesus from Joan. And, fearing exposure like Nicodemus, there were others – a few local people, Communist soldiers and officials – who, in the shelter of night, whispered their desire to believe.

In December, Chang approached Jim. The young Nosu preacher wanted to leave Zhaojue and return with a wife as equally dedicated to the establishment of a local Nosu church as himself. He had written to his church asking their blessing upon his plans. His departure, with no possibility of a Nosu, Chinese or Western replacement, brought the team in Zhaojue to just five workers: the four British missionaries and Zhao, the interpreter. Living with them in the clinic compound were Mrs Yang, Zitu, a young cook and an elderly servant, together with the children, Jan, Pauline, Margie and Joy.

New restrictions on religious activities began to hem the team themselves in, forcing them to concede ground. They were confined to the compound as the local administration slowly squeezed the missionaries into a situation in which they would cease to be effective. The clinic became increasingly hard to manage as Jim had no way to visit patients in their homes. Propaganda classes were instigated in the compound itself and team members and patients were compelled to attend. Their experience was not unique. Across the country a door was swinging slowly, but inexorably, shut on eighty-five years of service for the China Inland Mission in China.

Tuesday, 19 December 1950, brought both good and bad news for Joan. At Jim's request she eased her arm out of its cotton support and Jim inspected her forearm. 'I think we can dispense with the sling. There's nothing to suggest it's still needed. Bathing Joy must have done the trick after all!'

'Definitely good medicine,' agreed Joan, delighted at Jim's diagnosis. 'It's going to be as difficult to get used to doing things with two hands, not one.' Joan pushed the sling with relief into the depths of her pocket. It had been nine months since her operation.

'I'm sure we can find work over Christmas for an extra hand,' laughed Jim. 'Ruth most certainly will; don't worry about that!'

Joan and Jim left the surgery and made their way to where a group of women were waiting for the evening meeting. Jim found a gospel poster and put it up on the wall. The women, all recuperating opium addicts, were quickly engrossed in the message and sat in enthralled attention as Jim preached. Joan sensed their readiness to respond but Mrs Qiang's sudden breathless arrival as the meeting drew to a close broke into the atmosphere, and the attentiveness of the women was lost.

'*Dianbao. Hen zhongyao.*' The lady made her apologies

as she handed a telegram over to Jim. He quickly scanned the note and for a brief moment was lost in thought before folding the paper into his Bible.

'Come over to the house as soon as everyone is settled,' he told Ruth and Joan. 'This we need to discuss. I'll get Janet.'

The telegram was lying on the table when Joan and Ruth entered the Cottage living room. 'You can read it,' said Janet. 'It's from CIM HQ in Shanghai.'

Ruth picked it up and read it aloud. 'Widespread withdrawal missionaries and your circumstances indicate advisability of Nosu team withdrawal after two months final effort. Challenging home churches to pray for establishment infant church.'

The order, unwelcome as it was, had come. The team were to leave. Their work in Nosuland was to end.

Chapter 21

'The waves in the wind lose their fixed place
And are rolled away each to a corner of Heaven
From now onwards long must be our parting
So let us stop... for a little while.'

LI LING, C. 81BC

On her final evening in Zhaojue Joan sat on the edge of her bed and surveyed the scattered remnants of her packing, stacked in ordered piles around the room. She had brought so little. She would take so little away with her. Even the handful of parting gifts she had received had been returned under orders laid down by the local officials. She had her memories, of course. Both precious and painful. All carefully wrapped within the words that made up the meticulous details of her diary. Entries that enclosed her private perceptions of the feral world she had inhabited for sixteen months. Within its pages were her jubilant accounts of the coming to faith of her teenage friends and others who had sought her out to express their desire to serve Christ. She had adeptly folded away incidental minutiae of the humdrum chores that had ensured their survival. And slipped innocently among them were her amusing observations of Jan, Pauline, Margie and Joy.

Entwined around these unsullied reminiscences, like weeds around wheat, were the unembellished accounts of fierce encounters with evil and her occasional submissions to doubt and depression. These she had overlaid with opaque references to the spiritual fatigue engendered by daily contacts with coarse purveyors of atrocity and immorality.

Binding everything together, threaded like the fine links of cherished silver the Nosu women treasured, she had chronicled her quiet moments of inner tenderness, restoration and healing shared with God.

The team's 'final effort', ordained by the CIM leadership in Shanghai, had lasted just one month. Deteriorating circumstances nationwide had forced the mission to revise its instructions. On 7 January a second telegram had arrived from headquarters: Make application for exit visas immediately and head for Hong Kong. The team must join the roll of missionaries from every foreign mission in China who were embarked on the haphazard exodus from their promised land.

Joan's second Christmas in Zhaojue had come and gone so quickly. But there had been good moments to etch into her reminiscences. The carol singing till dusk. The crowd that gathered to hear the Christmas story. A feast they had invited friends to. Even the expressions of sadness at their impending departure.

'We don't want you to leave,' Baoli had sobbed on Christmas Eve. 'There is so much we don't understand. I don't want to be lukewarm. I want to be ablaze for Jesus.'

In the morning, the team would close the clinic doors and walk out beyond the fort gates. They would begin their traverse of the painfully slow miles down to Xichang, putting ever-increasing distance between themselves and the fragile formation of a church that they had established in Zhaojue. Who could return? And when? Zhao? Chang and a wife? God alone knew.

Joan picked up the few remaining items of clothing and carefully put them away. The place looked bare, stripped of the small indulgences that had defined it as hers. Precious letters from home had been emptied from drawers, and the few books that had adorned the rough shelves were stacked into boxes. Posters with Bible verses in Chinese characters that had imbued the barren walls with colour had been passed on to her many visitors during the day. The room occupied an enduring emptiness that signified an end to everything they had endeavoured to achieve.

There was a gentle knock at the door and Joan opened it to Mrs Qiang. They talked idly for a while, her guest plying Joan with questions about the journey, whispering her fears for the children. Finally, when it seemed time for Mrs Qiang to leave she leant forward and took Joan's hand. 'I want to receive Jesus as my Saviour. Will you pray with me?' In recent weeks the lady had become bolder in attending services and at Christmas had made it clear that she was not afraid to sit with the believers.

Joan opened her Bible at Romans chapter 10. 'This is what the Bible says: '...if thou shalt confess with thy mouth the Lord Jesus, and shalt believe in thine heart that God hath raised him from the dead, thou shalt be saved'[44]. Is that what you believe, Mrs Qiang?' Lili's mother nodded her agreement. 'Do you understand what it means to make Jesus Lord of your life?'

'Yes...'

Together the two women bowed in prayer, Joan allowing Mrs Qiang to repeat the words of commitment after her. 'Now, are you a child of God?' Joan asked when they had finished.

'Not yet,' Mrs Qiang smiled. 'I haven't done all that the Bible said. I must go home and tell others.' She got up to leave. 'My husband also believes,' she said softly. 'But he doesn't want people to know. He's afraid... you understand?'

Joan accompanied Mrs Qiang down to the clinic doors and watched her walk the short distance to the corner of the track adjacent to her house. She closed the doors and went back to her room, no longer the barren cavity it had seemed. Even on their final evening God had not stopped his work...

23 January 1951

Chapter 22

'*And what know they of succour who have never ventured in difficult places? We shall press through the mist and the smothering snow; we shall climb and not give way; for there is One Invisible with us.*'

AMY CARMICHAEL

It was Margie's crying that roused me from my introspection. I had been lost in my memories of the past, not keen to acknowledge the constrictions of the path, nor the sharp inclines that from time to time pressed in on us on one side and plummeted away abruptly on the other. We were well into our first day on our mule journey from Zhaojue to Xichang. Margie was perched on Zhao's saddle, dwarfed by the stately Nosu interpreter. Tenderly he smoothed her hair, hushing her tired wails and chatting in Nosu amiably about nothing in particular.

'Poor child must be frozen to the bone,' commented

259

Ruth riding up alongside. 'After a while these hot-water bottles are as useful as a half-inch candle on an iceberg.'

Our company, with Zhao, Mrs Yang, Zitu, Agu, the Nosu chief, and a small number of Nosu and muleteers, were straddling the ridge of Great Hen, our final sight of Zhaojue. A two- to three-hour descent to the Sanwan valley. Ahead of me snaked our mule train, now strung out in single file over a mile from first to last, the leading animals lost in the mist, others temporarily out of sight as they moved by uncertain degrees around the turns of our ice-obscured route. I urged my mule forward along the path, and rode on down the slope away from the mountain summit.

There is something sickening about watching an animal lose its footing, teeter desperately on an edge and then keel over into nothing. In the distance I saw the stiff legs flailing frenziedly for purchase. I felt the instinctive twist of the neck upwards, the spasmodic flexing of the body. The mule fell a few feet and hit the slope. Almost involuntarily I prayed for an obstacle of a shrub or a rock to impede its plunge downwards. But the sparseness of vegetation and the cumbersome imbalance of its burden combined to condemn the beast to an appalling death.

There was the brutal impact of the heavy body on an unyielding spur. I could sense the breaking of bones, snap of the spine, a graceless extinction of life. And then the carcass fell again, beyond the opaque curtain of haze, into its abyss.

The incident lasted a matter of moments. Horror assailed me as I sat back rigid in my makeshift saddle. I knew one of the adults had not been astride this particular mule. But what of Jan and Pauline pinioned like baggage to one of the animals? Had I seen clearly enough? Could I be sure they had not plunged into the valley with the unfortunate creature? We had to ride on until the path widened and we were able to move more freely along the line, praying for sight of the children. I wanted to weep for Jim, behind me, and Janet, some way in front, in their private nightmares. But the tears froze on my lids and would not fall.

As we approached the location of the calamity I could see where the edge had crumbled away, a slight but deadly indentation in the path. I forced myself to look over the precipice, searching for clues, colours of clothing strewn on the slope. But there was nothing and the valley floor was concealed from sight. Gradually the party crept down the track until it broadened out towards the valley floor and we were relieved of our unspoken fears. Jan and Pauline were being lifted from their panniers in front of a collection of Nosu homes where we would stay for the night.

Thankful that the worst of the day was behind us, we dismounted. Gingerly I rolled my body over and felt for the ground. I had ceased to have any feeling in my feet some hours ago. Swinging my legs had done little to ease the problem. There was no sensation in my legs, nothing to tell me that my feet were on terra firma.

'Joan!' gasped Janet as my legs folded beneath me and I crumpled into a heap in the dirt. I forced my upper body to find some sort of equilibrium and lifted my legs with my hands to place them in more dignified positions. 'I'll be all right... once my limbs begin to thaw out... a bad case of frozen feet.'

By the time I made it into our lodgings, the others were already huddled around the small fire in the centre of the room. Ruth was busying herself making porridge for the girls and Janet was regretting that Joy had been given her smallpox injection that morning. 'And we haven't been able to change her nappy all day,' she added.

That evening we slept in the hay loft, our *pugai* wrapped around our clothes, arranged in two rows, male and female. It was not comfortable, but for a while we were warm. At breakfast we consumed large quantities of vegetable soup, unsure when we would be able to eat again. It was here that Agu was to take leave of the party, instructing his retainers to take good care of us. The young chief was genuinely grieved to see us go. He had been a friend to Jim and his goodwill and fearsome reputation had helped us initially to find acceptance amongst the Nosu clans.

'We will not forget you,' he told Jim. 'We will tell our children your story. And you must tell your descendants about us. *Mo'm Apu* will preserve you. Do not forget us...'

'Agu, don't forget the Lord Jesus,' Jim tried to encourage him. 'Nothing matters more. Let him give you a new heart. Let him save your people. Do this and our coming to live with you will have fulfilled its purpose.'

Once again we left behind another we had come to love. Left him by the roadside with a few hopeful words: messages spoken into the chill unyielding air, into circumstances we now could only hope to influence in prayer. Who would encourage Agu now we were going? What would he remember of all Jim had painstakingly told him of Jesus and the need for salvation? Would he and his people ever believe in *Shangdi*?

Our trail brought us down for a while from the narrow paths of the mountain slopes to the respite of a cultivated valley. My mule turned aside and, uninvited, helped himself to the meagre rice stalks. Anxious to avoid the attentions of an angry farmer and afraid to be left behind, lacking a bridle I dug my heels as hard as I could into the mule's flanks. My intention of a sedate return to the path was confounded as the animal broke into a run. With no proper means of control I clung on desperately as the mule careered ahead of the rest of the company. As I passed Jim, he shouted after me. 'Don't worry, Joan! He'll get tired in a while. Then he'll slow down.' The advice was of little comfort. I envisaged finding myself lost on a myriad of tracks while the others lumbered on through the hills without me. It was a considerable relief when the mule finally slowed to a trot and I coaxed him to a halt. To Jim's credit he did ensure that I was provided with a bridle the next day.

The sanctuary of the valley was quickly left behind as we once more climbed up through crags and crevices to 10,000 feet. In the bleak mists that again closed in on us the paths were treacherous.

'We'll have to walk.' Carefully we slid from our saddles and stepped onto blankets of sheet ice. 'Hold hands!' There were desperate moments as we steadied ourselves, leaning heavily on each other, then straightening and shifting our weight to take a step. Progress became painful as we struggled to hold each other up, grasping from time to time at rocks and shrubs to maintain balance. We moved like uncertain ships across a sea made of ice until it was safe to mount our mules again.

Our worries were far from over. In the distance we heard the distraught cries of a child. Hurrying forward as best we could, we found the mule carrying Jan and Pauline slewed on its side across the path and struggling to get up, unable to find secure footing for its hooves on the stone slabs that now made up our road. Pauline was trapped in her wooden box beneath the beast. Jan had slipped head-first out of her pannier over the flanks of the animal as it fell and was sitting several feet away.

'Thank goodness it wasn't the little ones,' was her 'grown-up' response when Janet picked her up and inspected her for bruises.

'I don't want to go back on,' declared Pauline.

Janet cuddled her close. 'Do you know what aeroplane pilots do when they have an accident? They are told to go back up in an aeroplane just as soon as they can. Then they know it's OK again.' She dried Pauline's eyes with her sleeve. 'Shall we do that?'

The incident brought our fears back into focus. We rode on, praying for safety, wanting the day to end. Our stop for the night came at another of the small villages along the route. Our hosts were kind enough to us, but when they saw that Zitu had suffered with leprosy they were adamant – he would not be allowed in the house. We found him a blanket and ensured that he had a fire in the corner of the courtyard where he deposited himself for the night. The house was not large. After supper Ruth and I lodged ourselves on a tiny shelf built into the wall which acted as our bed for the night.

Thankfully the third day of riding left behind the terrors of the previous two. The going was substantially easier with the sun breaking through the clouds to warm us. While we had not passed beyond the borders of Nosuland, the change in the weather matched our growing sense of relief that we would reach Xichang the next day. We received a generous welcome at an inn before sunset, affording us the luxury of washing ourselves and changing our clothes.

The evening was more relaxed. I took time to chat with the innkeeper's wife and her relatives as we sat around the grate in the middle of the living area. They were not enamoured with the new regime. They murmured of their worries over the 'terror' they perceived, a dark menace haunting their future. I encouraged them to believe that Jesus could calm their fears.

It was here that Zitu was to remain behind. In the village we found a Chinese family willing to provide food and a shelter outside of their home. Jim had given him enough silver for six months' keep and we had provided him with a bundle of clothes and bedding. He looked a pathetic figure, riddled with apprehension, as we waved our goodbyes. As we rode towards the gates of Xichang the mid-afternoon sun reigned unrivalled in a cloudless sky. In a closing incongruity to our descent from the bitter cold of the mountains we had shed numerous layers of clothing and now sweltered like holiday-makers under sunhats.

We wound our way through the streets to the doors of the government offices, where we waited until an official eventually emerged, checked our papers and examined our baggage. 'Unpack. Everything. A full inspection is required before you go to your accommodation.'

I looked at the ground. There was no choice but to lay my clothes in the dirt and dust.

'Teacher Wei, put your things here.' Zhao slid his cloak with a graceful movement from his shoulders and laid it at my feet. One by one we unfastened the boxes and bags from the mules and exposed the contents item by item to the protracted scrutiny of the official and the curiosity of a crowd.

There was a movement in one of the doorways. A guard stepped out into the street with Levi Lovegren behind him. I stifled a friendly greeting. He was bound in chains and being led away.

'What on earth...' questioned Ruth and then, catching Jim's eye, hastily turned away and busied herself with repacking. Lovegren passed us without a glance in our direction.

'The 16th of January was a bad day here,' reported Ernest Madge when we settled down later to a meal at the Border Service Department Mission premises. 'That was the day Lovegren was arrested. Accused of being a US spy.'

'That is ridiculous,' said Ruth. 'He is a missionary.'

'The two are not mutually exclusive to this government's way of thinking. He was an easy target. As you know, he did a stint with the American army. They found his uniform in a trunk.'

'That wasn't helpful.'

'There was other old army stuff with it. Maps and the like. And his weather records. A bit of a hobby apparently. Regularly submitted details to the Geological Society of America. That was the same day they also raided the mission's quarters up and down the valley. Most of the missionaries were still in bed when it started! Food, bicycles, photographic equipment, typewriters – all confiscated. Financial assets frozen. Folk were left with a few dollars to survive on.'

'We left a lot of our belongings in Lovegren's care,' commented Janet. 'I guess there will be no way to get that back now. So much for getting hold of more substantial clothing to get us through to Hong Kong...'

'Working here has got increasingly difficult,' continued Ernest. 'The Baptist church is going to close. They'll join with our Border Service Department Mission church. Christians are being pressurised not to associate with us. Everyone is ready to leave, like it or not. When we heard you were coming out of Zhaojue we knew that was it. Game over.'

'Not yet,' said Jim. 'We are playing for eternity.'

The rules of engagement were soon made clear. There would be no rush to see us depart. We must first jump whatever bureaucratic hurdles officials could find for us. Eight guarantors were needed for the next stage of our journey: two for each adult. Their security would lie in our discretion on reporting events once we had left China. A permit to travel would allow us passage to the Xikang provincial capital, Ya'an. There we could make application for exit visas.

We stayed in Xichang for three weeks, occupying three first-floor rooms of a traditional Chinese residence built around a private courtyard. Given the events and uncertainties we were to experience before arriving in Hong Kong, the relative freedom we enjoyed was something of a luxury.

Chapter 23

'While we do not court danger, we are committed to a life which may involve it.'

CIM POLICY DOCUMENT, 1948

Zitu's arrival in Xichang created great consternation. He had heard rumours of plans to murder him for the silver we had given him. Fleeing from his new home, he had come to find us, believing that we were still able to help him. But we were no longer able to influence anyone and had to turn him away to fend for himself. We said our goodbyes to Mrs Yang. And to our business manager, Hong. Finally, to Zhao. Hong was soon in prison for his 'treachery' in helping us spy on the people of China. Zhao was pressed into the uniform of the People's Liberation Army.

We would complete the thirteen-day trip to Ya'an ourselves, making our way as best we could, stopping each night at roadside inns or in friendly villages. For Ruth and Jim it was, in part, a return journey along the route that they had undertaken in their first expedition to Xichang. On the one day of rest we allowed ourselves, the children, free from the constraints of their carriages, pleaded for rides on the horses as amusement.

It was mid-March before we arrived in Ya'an, a small provincial centre surrounded by mountains, west of Chengdu, now a hub of inactivity for departing missionaries awaiting exit permits. Petty officialdom was paramount, speed and convenience of little consequence.

'I must inspect your luggage.' Comrade Yang was among the more gracious officials who were charged with overseeing our arrival and departure. He had been a member of a Bible class run by John Lockhart, my mission home host at Leshan, and treated us with courtesy. 'This could be a problem,' he said, delving for a paperback notebook in the midst of my pile of belongings. He opened it and turned a few pages.

'It is my diary, Yang Comrade,' I said politely. 'I write down what I have done and how God has spoken to me each day.'

'It could delay you if questions are asked.'

I looked crestfallen. 'It is important to me. I don't think others would find it interesting.'

He looked around him and drew a little closer. 'Give me an address in Hong Kong,' he said quietly. 'I will ensure you receive it there.' He slipped the diary into his pocket and after a few cursory questions concluded his inspection.

Comrade Yang's influence was also instrumental in

obtaining permission for us to leave after only a weekend in Ya'an. Others had waited as long as three months for their visas. On Monday morning we vacated our temporary accommodation in a school classroom and found rickshaws for the children and the luggage. Ruth, Jim, Janet and I walked with them to the bus station. Here we underwent yet another inspection of our baggage. Then a female official took Janet, Ruth and me to one side and carried out a more thorough personal check.

Glad to have the inspection behind us, Ruth, with Jan and Pauline, clambered aboard the lorry we had hired to get us to Chengdu, whilst Janet and I sat in the waiting room with Margie and Joy. 'Jim's taking a while,' Janet looked out over the crowds across the room. Jim was coming, Comrade Yang at his side. There was clearly something wrong. Jim's face was drained of colour. Yang's was animated and angry.

'Give me your exit visa,' he ordered.

Jim was reluctant, casting a despairing glance at Janet.

'Give me the visa!' Yang's tone was harsh. We dared not ask what had happened.

'My bedding is with my wife's.'

'Then she must stay too,' retorted Yang. 'Only the two unmarried women can go. You and your family will stay in Ya'an. Take them back to the school. Then you come to my office and report to me!'

I handed Joy to Janet and went over to the lorry. Ruth helped Jan and Pauline down into my arms. The girls burst into tears, confused by the sudden change in circumstances and our separation. The Broomhalls' luggage and the children were hastily bundled into rickshaws and the family trudged away out of the bus station.

Ruth and I sat in the lorry, shocked into silence. While we knew that the journey would be difficult we had not envisaged our team being split up. What had Jim done? Would he be imprisoned? How would Janet cope alone with four children? The truck engine growled in protest as the driver pulled forward and headed for the station exit, his hand never far from the horn. For most of the journey we hardly spoke. There were no stops for food or relief from the discomforts of the journey. I felt as though tears were running down inside me, but I dared not show it.

It was 11pm when the truck reached our destination. Once more we completed our baggage inspection as requested and were ready to leave when a second official arrived. 'It is my responsibility to check baggage. Undo your bags.'

'We have already...' protested Ruth.

The official stared hard at us. 'It is my responsibility. Undo the bags.'

We removed everything from our bags and boxes again, laid out everything for inspection in the dirt of the floor and, only when the official was satisfied, repacked everything as best we could once more.

In Ya'an we had sought permission to stay at the CIM Mission Home in Chengdu rather than be housed in accommodation designated by Chengdu officials. Comrade Yang had readily agreed to this.

'It's nearly midnight,' noted Ruth. 'We can't disturb folk at the mission home at this late hour. We should stay at an inn.' I added my agreement.

'No,' insisted the official, eager to maintain his authority. 'Your papers say you are to stay at this address. That is where you will go.' I gave Ruth a faint smile. There were no further protests from us as we tumbled out into the darkened streets to raise a rickshaw driver from his slumbers.

'When did you last eat?' asked Signe Jeffrey, the mission home hostess. She and her husband, Sam, were determined to make us feel welcome despite the inconvenience of our arrival.

'Yesterday afternoon, about four. We didn't get breakfast at the bus station.' We explained the events that had precipitated Jim's arrest.

'And wash?'

'Some while ago....'

'We'll arrange a bath for you.'

Our luggage had still not arrived when I emerged from the extravagance of the bathroom. Signe was waiting with a pair of Sam's pyjamas. 'These haven't been dragged through the dust of a dozen inspections.' I took them from her and retreated to my room. I held the jacket up against myself. The material dropped to my knees. The pyjama bottoms were no less of a problem. The waistband would be up around my chin! Sam Jeffrey's pyjamas and myself were definitely not made for each other. Decorum dictated that I wear both: a novel spectacle as I flopped around the corridors of the house, rolls of redundant material flapping about my ankles, waist and wrists.

Our concern for the Broomhall family was at the top of the morning prayer list. The meeting, however, was disturbed by the arrival of a telegram from Jim. 'Coming

Chengdu Wednesday'. Our relief that we could continue our travel together was, however, short-lived.

'You will leave for Chongqing on Wednesday,' ordered the official.

'There are no buses to Chongqing on Wednesday,' we protested.

'Then you will hire one. You leave Wednesday. With luggage you will need half a bus,' we were instructed. 'We will find you a bus and driver.' Objections that half a bus was substantially more than the two of us required were similarly dismissed. 'Half a bus with luggage'. The driver inevitably had little compunction in finding passengers to fill the empty seats we had hired before threading his way out of Chengdu and into the countryside.

On the outskirts of a poor hamlet we groaned inwardly as the bus halted, the protesting engine cutting out with an exaggerated shudder. The road was blocked by soldiers. Behind them sun-weathered, rough-clothed peasants were being herded like sheep out of their houses and down into the fields. The excited chatter of the bus passengers dropped suddenly to the nervous murmur of those unsure of their safety as the purpose of our delay became apparent. In the distance a group of ten men, naked to the waist, hands bound behind them, had been separated out from the agitated mass of villagers. Opposite them stood a rank of soldiers with rifles.

Sickened I looked down at my lap. In the uneasy silence we heard the sharp orders of the commanding officer. Crack. An uneasy murmur around us. I counted the volleys. One. Two. Three... ...Eight. Nine. Ten.

The bus started up and we pulled away. Eventually I

lifted my head and looked out of the window. There were the same picturesque scenes we had seen before we had stopped. A scrawny peasant digging in a ditch. A woman carrying a bundle of sticks. Another with a basket tucked under her arm. A boy goading a bullock along a path. So normal. Yet in another field a mile away, frightened villagers would be digging holes to fill with the bodies of men.

The Broomhalls caught up with us in Chongqing. 'My fault entirely,' Jim explained as we pressed them for information about their delay in Ya'an. 'The guards at the bus station were looking through my stuff. The usual questions. Then one of the guards picked up a DDT bomb.' He lifted his hands in a gesture of resignation. 'I said, 'I can guarantee it isn't an atom bomb.' And suddenly the whole of Ya'an was up in arms! Yang Comrade instructed me to write an apology and get it published in the paper. Once the city had read of the proper penitence of the impudent imperialist we could go.'

'More an *imprudent* imperialist,' Janet corrected him. 'Pauline put Jim firmly in his place when we were due to leave. 'Daddy,' she said, 'if you must crack jokes this morning, crack them on me!"

With the children in the process of developing a private epidemic of measles, our time together was limited as Ruth and I had to move on. As we were to discover all along our route, traditional Chinese courtesy was often neglected. Officious red tape gave an opportunity to assert power where politeness would have sufficed. A few of the individuals who fervently demanded documents could not read. Some spoke sharply. Others ordered us around.

There were threats, veiled and explicit, to delay our departure. We had little status and therefore had no grounds for complaint. Thankfully there were also those, like Comrade Yang in Ya'an and Comrade Wang in Zhaojue, who helped us and facilitated our journey.

Ruth and I were instructed to take the boat down the Yangtze River as far as the city of Hankou[45] and then catch a train south towards the border. We made our way down to the black waters of the quayside around 10pm and queued on the wharf for four hours before the gangway was opened. A tide of Chinese travellers washed over the boards, men and women tumbling along the decks for places. In the wake of the first wave of passengers Ruth gathered herself and plunged into the surge of bodies. 'Push, Joan!' she yelled. 'Don't let humility – or size – get in your way.'

In the crush I inevitably lost her. Swept along in the crowd, I eventually found myself on board the boat. I looked around desperately for Ruth.

'Joan! Here!' Ruth had secured a place above the coal hole where the crew were still shovelling fuel into the bowels of the vessel. 'It will be quite comfy, once they replace the cover,' she reassured me. We spread out our oilcloths and then our *pugai*. There was no telling what colour they would be when we alighted.

It was three days' voyage seated on the cover above the coal hole to Yichang, and, from there, three more to Hankou. Our journey had the appearance of an idle meander as the arcs of the Yangtze uncoiled before our bow. Yet it felt as though we had stumbled into the unravelling of a nightmare. The breathtaking beauty of the

Three Gorges, massive ramparts of rock hemming in the river, cruelly reflected our situation. We sat on our narrow boat, crushed together with exposed humanity. Amongst us, finely dressed prisoners, privileged citizens of the Nationalist regime, were closely shackled to grey guards, unable to move without the attentions of their minders. So few taking in the scenery, so much fear written into faces.

At Yichang we transferred to the more spacious top deck of a second boat, away from the stifling heat of the crowded lower decks. It rained. Ruth and I, with our inadequate umbrellas raised, sheltered beneath torn tarpaulin and directed the rivulets of water off into our washbasins. 'Please...' We smiled as sweetly as English women can. 'Please empty the basin for us over the side... thank you... thank you...' And as hours passed, relationships evolved from our common discomforts. We engaged our travel companions in conversation, listening to their anxieties and the apprehensions they had for their families. We, in turn, told them of our work in Zhaojue and quietly shared our belief in a God who could strengthen them in adversity.

Hankou is the place where river meets railway: a hub of interchange as the native Yangtze intersects with manufactured, pinioned steel ribbons running north and south. A thirty-six hour steam train ride in the discomfort of a hard seat brought us to Guangzhou and close enough to the border with Hong Kong to know that our three-month journey was nearly complete. To our surprise we were directed to a superior hotel in Guangzhou and slept in the welcome comforts of an en suite bedroom. It was an undeniable allowance of luxury to demonstrate that we had been well treated, and a perverse intention that we would leave with a final favourable impression. In stark contrast, we, in our travel-soiled clothes, did not give a particularly favourable impression when we arrived at the hotel reception!

Next morning we travelled by train to the border post. I walked a short distance across a steel bridge suspended over the barbed wire of the border and stood at the threshold that defined the divide between the infant People's Republic and an ageing Empire. A British official checked my passport and authorised my entry to Hong Kong with a simple square stamp, inscribing the date 26 April 1951 across it in black ink. Beyond the barrier I saw members of China Inland Mission staff eager to greet us. I took another step and entered a different world. Behind me a door had shut.

Ruth and I were, of course, just two of hundreds of missionaries and others pouring into Hong Kong. CIM's solution to the need for accommodation had been the acquisition of a derelict camp of eleven Nissen huts, located at the back of a crematorium overlooking the harbour, by a railway siding in Kowloon district. Hurried refurbishment had cleared the site of rubble, repaired broken windows, installed plumbing and electricity. The first group of evacuees had called the site 'Freehaven' and the name had stuck. There was the basic provision of a bed and a chair. As we had done for so long, Ruth and I lived out of our suitcases. When Jim, Janet and the girls arrived, the Mission suggested that we share rooms with them in the better-appointed comfort of an hotel, so we could help care for the children.

As quickly as berths on cargo boats and cruise liners, or seats on aircraft could be secured, missionaries were repatriated to free up space in Hong Kong for new evacuees. The eight of us found our places with twenty-three adults and five other children of the Mission on an airliner chartered by CIM for the substantial sum of £4,000. Forty-eight hours later, 29 May, as darkness fell over west London, we circled above Heathrow Airport, eased down to the edge of the runway and our journey finally came to an end.

'Joan!'

There was my father waiting for me.

Chapter 24

*'As for the Daliangshan, however, they had to be
content with looking at it from afar...'*

That journey was all so long ago. Another age. When China
considered herself under threat from foreign devils
without and fierce demons within. There were still so
many trials for her people to endure before the death of
Mao Zedong in 1976 and the accession of Deng Xiaoping
to supreme authority. In the 1980s there was the slow
recovery of modernisation and, more recently, the
extravagant growth of Chinese industry, dominating world
markets.

With the departure of foreign missions in the early
1950s the Chinese Church did not die. In 1979, after many
years of persecution and closure, churches began to
reopen. Christianity was approved as one of China's

recognised religions. There followed a resurgence of interest in the gospel, first by the elderly who had known the years of religious freedom before 1949, and then amongst the youth. Thriving official churches, associated with the China Christian Council, and unregistered house churches are now to be found across the nation. A church that possibly numbered one million at the beginning of the 1980s has grown fiftyfold, maybe many times more.

For the China Inland Mission there would be no return to China. Expanding ministry into new fields across East Asia brought fresh impetus and new names, the Overseas Missionary Fellowship and, more recently, OMF International. As for me? There was the opportunity to recuperate. I lived with my father in Bournemouth for a short while, eventually relocating to London. My father was as keen as ever that I should marry, but, as always, I resisted his efforts! I began to learn that he admired my 'stubbornness' and that our mutual affection and love were not diminished as I prepared to go back to Asia. He was, I discovered, proud of his daughter. When Jim published a book[46] relating the story of our work amongst the Nosu he bought numerous copies to distribute to our family and friends.

In February 1953 I boarded the SS Canton, a P&O luxury passenger liner heading for Singapore. With me were Janet, Margie and Joy; Jan and Pauline remained in the UK at boarding school. Jim was already in Asia. The Broomhalls were going to work in the Philippines. After a brief stay in Singapore, I moved to central Thailand, embarked on learning a fourth language, and was occupied for thirty years in pioneer evangelism, mainly based in mission hospitals, helping to establish congregations in the surrounding villages. Of the Nosu of Daliangshan and my Chinese 'teenagers' I heard nothing for thirty-seven years.

Ruth went to Malaysia, where I visited her from time to time from Thailand, before she finally retired to the UK after forty-six years of missionary service, aged seventy-three. She died at Mildmay Hospital in London in January 1982, the year before I myself retired.

And God? Well, God had unfinished business...

January 1988

Chapter 25

'Your hair was black; now it is white. You taught me about Jesus.'

NOSU MAN, 11 MARCH 1988

After retiring from OMF International I had settled in Reigate, Surrey, occupying an attic flat close to the centre of town. I had taken on the role of parish worker at St Mary's Church, an opportunity for ministry without the stresses of paid employment. To be honest, by the beginning of 1988 I envisaged myself living out a fulfilled retirement in Britain, growing old gently and gracefully in God.

A phone call put an end to that.

'Joan? Jim here. I'm going back to Zhaojue. Joy is coming with me. Do you want to come?'

I was stunned by the proposal. I had never thought to return to China, let alone Xichang and Zhaojue. 'What about Janet?' I asked, trying to gather my thoughts.

'Janet's not well. Getting a little confused, I'm afraid. It's not advisable for her to travel that distance. She wants you to go.' Sadly, Janet was in the early stages of Alzheimer's disease, an illness that led to her death twelve years later at the age of eighty-seven.

'If money is a consideration, I have some funds: £500. Won't cover everything for you but it will be a start. We're thinking of leaving 28 February. Probably for three weeks.'

'Give me a few days,' I requested. 'I need time to pray about it.' I put the phone back on its cradle. Zhaojue? Was that possible? I knew that tourists were welcome to see the sights of Beijing, Xi'an and other key attractions. A small number of foreigners were studying and working in major cities. But many areas of the country were still closed to travellers and I had thought Zhaojue would be one of them.

It transpired that at Christmas, thirteen months before, Jim and Janet had received a letter from Xichang. The handwritten note on flimsy rice paper was from one of the families in Zhaojue we had befriended. It reminded Jim of his pledge to return to the Great Cold Mountains. Things had changed. Jim could fulfil his promise.

The following Easter, Margie had travelled to Xichang with her husband. It had proved an uncomfortable stay; their visit was viewed with suspicion. They had, however, located the family who had written to Jim and Janet. 'My father is coming next year,' Margie had assured them.

An initial request to see Zhaojue had been politely, but firmly, refused. Margie's obvious anguish and tears at the decision had swayed that verdict and very late in the evening they had been escorted to the Public Security Bureau offices to collect permits for a one-day visit. The officials were adamant that they ride in a black limousine, escorted there and back. A Western woman on a previous visit had, apparently, ridden on a motorbike to Zhaojue and bathed in the river, oblivious to local sensitivities! The four-day journey of the 1940s had been considerably reduced by a more accessible road; Margie's stay lasted just three hours.

Would I go? I said 'Yes', of course. I was thrilled to have the opportunity to see old friends! Suddenly doors began to open everywhere. My church would finance my travel. Jim's offer of £500 would not be needed. Flights were booked, tickets purchased. I retrieved my passport from the drawer and packed my suitcase, bound for Asia once more.

The Kowloon–Canton railway terminus in Hong Kong was an animated bustle of activity as we boarded our train to Guangzhou. It was strange to be travelling with members of the Broomhall family again after so many years, but we had continued to enjoy a close relationship and I certainly took pleasure in their companionship. Jim, Joy and I were joined by Tony Lambert, OMF International's China expert, who, as an excellent Mandarin speaker, could assist us. Our journey brought us to the border station at Lowu and we crossed into China without stopping, through Shenzhen, then no more than a large town, and on towards our destination. The towns were populated by orderly rows of low-rise concrete blocks of flats in walled estates, with strings of small, single-storey shops along dusty highways. In the countryside we saw peasants in tedious, uniform blues and greys hunched over furrows, guiding oxen with rope reins, herding goats and pigs, drawing water into irrigation channels. They laboured under loudspeaker cones perched on poles that stood like guards at the corner of each field and proclaimed the merits of honest citizenship.

Guangzhou was the 'capital' of the Cantonese-speaking world, a gateway to southern China. The city was in the throes of huge changes as a new affluence displaced the relative poverty of previous generations. The traditional roofs and alleyways of the old city were being replaced. Massive billboards and big-character slogans promoted the expediency of the Four Modernisations – agriculture, defence, industry, science/technology. Declarations of the wisdom of late marriage and the one-child policy filled spaces on buildings and decorated walls around pleasant gardens that broke up the acres of coaldust that coated the streets.

A red taxi ferried us from the railway station to 'White Cloud' Airport where we found the plane was delayed. We fended off the cold with cups of exceptionally sweet coffee, laced with spoonfuls of sugar and condensed milk. As we finally sped down the runway I clasped my broken seatbelt to my waist and prayed for an uneventful journey.

It was raining in Chengdu. We were directed to a shed that served as the baggage collection hall and waited beneath the cover of a leaking tarpaulin sheet for our luggage. It was 10.40pm and we had no hotel for the night.

A helpful taxi driver found us a hotel where we filled out forms for the Public Security Bureau's records and paid in advance. Our twin rooms were adequately furnished. Room service arrived with large vacuum flasks of boiling water, paper sachets filled with leaves of green tea, thin tablets of soap and, for each of us, three sheets of toilet paper! So cold was the temperature that I slept in my clothes, my hands sheathed in gloves beneath a bulky duvet.

The railway from Chengdu to Xichang and on to Kunming represents a remarkable feat of engineering persistence. Started in 1958 and completed twelve years later, the 675 miles of track incorporates 450 tunnels and 650 bridges. In places the route passes through such mountainous areas that views of fertile valleys can only be snatched at as the train flits in and out of daylight before the blackness of another tunnel cuts off fleeting glimpses of beauty. As we neared the end of our journey we saw the unmistakable forms of Nosu men and women on the trackside and our excitement grew.

The platform of Xichang station lay several feet below the steps of our carriage. Joy carefully climbed down to the ground. I inspected the drop, watched by a cluster of curious Chinese. There was nothing else to do. I threw my handbag to one of them, arranged my skirt appropriately, and with all the grace I could muster leapt into Joy's arms. There was a collective gasp from the onlookers, which turned into relieved laughter as Joy lowered me to the ground. Such was my arrival in Xichang, our one-time 'base camp', after 37 years!

In the back of our minds lurked questions that had for so long remained unanswered. What would we find? Would we be allowed to go to Zhaojue? Would we find any semblance of a church amongst the Chinese or the Nosu?

And what of Meihua, Baodan and the other young believers I had taught in Zhaojue? How had they fared?

Xichang, like so many other towns and villages, was starting to modernise, but much of the old city remained intact, allowing us to find our bearings without difficulty. Connections with our past emerged from the shadows of time. In the market there was a man from whom Janet had regularly bought vegetables. Jim was delighted to locate a shop where he had purchased a leather binding for a book he had with him. The shopkeeper was moved to tears when Jim pulled it from his bag. He was, however, not keen to be seen talking with us and quickly asked us to move on.

We located Number Two Hospital, an establishment designated for the treatment of Nosu and viewed as a continuation of the work of our clinic in Zhaojue. The hospital was a modern establishment with trained Nosu doctors and nurses working alongside Chinese colleagues. They had Jim's old first-aid kit and showed him medicines and a dental set, complete with amalgam, which he had left behind in 1951. We presented the hospital with a gift of medical equipment.

The Ma family had long since left Komfort Korner, our former abode in Xichang. Jim and I posed at the doorway for a photograph. The buildings were the worse for wear; the unpainted cement rendering was cracked and patched, broken away above the door pillars. The windows had been blanked out with blocks of rough stone. But the occupants were welcoming and surprisingly unfazed at the request of four foreigners to roam through their home.

'We used to live here,' I told them. 'Dr Hai, his wife and daughters. I had a room on that side of the house.'

The old Border Service Department Mission church was still standing down the street from Komfort Korner. We entered the sandy-coloured building with high ecclesiastical windows through a concrete arch bearing a red cross and underneath, also in distinct red, the characters for Protestant Christianity: *Jidu Jiao*. The church had been incorporated into official church structures. There were around thirty-five present at the Sunday morning service, mainly elderly but with five or six younger members. It was gratifying to hear Bible-based messages on John 15 and Psalm 23.

A Chinese man in his late forties came forward and grasped my hands as we entered the church. 'You taught me stories of Jesus,' he told me. Another older believer remembered our names. 'Hai Hengbo. Wei Zhu'an! *Nimen hui lai le!*' Joy was remembered as 'Little Doctor Hai'!

'This afternoon we will collect you from your hotel.' A bank manager and his electrician wife, who approached us after the service, did not seem to have any particular claims on our time but were persistent that they would take us to a local beauty spot. 'There is a nice pagoda. A good view...'

We agreed, somewhat reluctantly, to join them in a walk beyond the outskirts of the town. As we picked our way across a hillside above Xichang that afternoon Jim pointed out two men striding towards us. 'Nosu!' he said. 'Nosu know how to walk down a hill. Good long strides.' The two men approached us and, in a manner that suggested this meeting was not entirely coincidental, stopped in 'surprise'.

'Hai Yisheng! Do you remember us?' They were the

muleteers who had accompanied us from Zhaojue to Xichang on our final journey across the mountains. We were possibly more stunned at this 'chance' encounter than they, but we did remember them.

'Your wife... how is she? And Teacher Di? The children? Did they survive the journey?'

Jim smiled, 'Yes, they all survived.'

'Surely not the baby? She would have been too young to endure that hardship.'

'Yes, even the baby.' Jim pointed at Joy. 'This is Little Hai.'

The appearance of another group of walkers broke up our conversation. Like the Xichang shopkeeper, the Nosu were not eager to be seen with us, unsure as to how welcome we were in the town and still keenly aware of the past. Hurriedly they made their apologies and strode away.

An even greater surprise awaited me at our hotel the following day. Meihua was at my bedroom door, greeting me with a huge smile. She had been the first of my 'teenagers' to believe and now she was the first of them to welcome me back. She was now in her fifties and a grandmother. A friend had informed her of our arrival.

'Of course I am still a Christian,' she reassured me when I asked. 'When you left, they took our Bibles from us. We had to go to propaganda classes where they told us that your stories were all a myth. But we still believed. We never forgot all you taught us. It is easier now. I can go to church.' We prayed together and read from the Bible. It was a very precious moment.

There was also prayer as we approached the Public Security Bureau. We could not go to Zhaojue without permits. Bizarrely, as we entered the offices with a certain amount of trepidation, we found a chiropodist in business at the doorway. We presented our case and waited, but our fears were totally unfounded. The officials told us we could leave for Zhaojue next day.

Clutching precious pieces of purple paper, officially stamped and signed by the PSB, we made our way to the bus station. The road, weaving up into the mountains, was barely adequate in places, the rough surface strewn with rocks or narrowed by landslides. The journey by rickety public bus, however, took no more than four hours. The terrain had been transformed with the seeding of the land to stimulate the growth of trees on the barren landscape. The meagre groups of huts we once knew had now developed into villages. Nosu men and women, clothed in their traditional blue cloaks, appeared by the roadside and watched us grind past. The rifles had gone and there were no checkpoints. It was evident that circumstances had greatly improved but the overriding impression was still of poverty.

Zhaojue fort was gone. As were all the buildings which had been so familiar to us. In their place, lying along a rough road, were the bones of a large village with 200 to 300 dwellings. There was a hospital, wayside restaurants, a few shops – not much more. Our hotel room contained a bunk bed, which commanded half the available space, and was bitterly cold. Once more I was forced to sleep in my clothes to keep warm. The toilets were a hundred metres away down the street; very public facilities, arranged like open cowpens.

Our visit created considerable local interest. We were

encircled by bands of Nosu as we set out the next afternoon for the village which had been the home of Agu, the Nosu chief who had given us his support in establishing our clinic in Zhaojue. Linked on my right arm was Baodan, on my left Shan – my old 'pupils'. The previous evening we had eaten with Baodan and her relatives, chatting about the past and present as the final hideous screeches of the poor pig being slaughtered for supper assailed our ears. Very fresh pork with heavy buckwheat cakes was on the menu.

'Are you still believers?' I asked tentatively.

Baodan and Shan's story was the same as Meihua's. Left without Bibles, they had continued in their faith without contact with other Christians. While Meihua now had the church in Xichang to attend, there was no church in Zhaojue. 'I have even forgotten how to read,' admitted Shan. As we descended out of a copse into Agu's village we saw two columns of Nosu women, dressed in multi-coloured tunics and skirts, walking along the riverbank to welcome us. We were greeted warmly by their headman – a former White Nosu serf. Agu was dead.

The anticipated struggle for supremacy between Han authority and Nosu belligerence had finally been fought in the mid-1950s. In 1955 the new authorities had organised 'democratic reforms'. The degrading caste system was to be abolished and all slaves were to be emancipated. Land would be shared between the landowners and their labourers. Advances in agricultural methods were to be introduced. Black Nosu chiefs, who had refused to accept the changes, rebelled against the reforms, while many of their slaves sided with their liberators. A brief battle for pre-eminence ensued with the forces of the People's Liberation Army. 'Maybe 50,000 Nosu died,' we were told. 'Agu amongst them.' With the conflict at an end the Nosu lost both their independence and their wild repute.

'Agu's wife is alive but very ill.' Jim went to visit her. She was close to death. Jim shared the gospel with her one final time. I met Agu's daughter and spoke with Nosu girls I had taught to read, among them Aji, who still remembered that Jesus loved her.

There were other remarkable moments to remember. We were invited to the home of a Mrs Wang for a meal. Her mother had lived half a day's travel from Zhaojue and we had lodged in her home many years ago. Mrs Wang generously opened precious tins of meat to feed us. 'Hai Yisheng,' she said when we had finished. 'When you left you promised to come back. My mother always said you would.' She went across to a drawer and opened it. 'When she was dying she told me, 'Hai Yisheng hasn't come back, but he will. She handed Joy a small tin ring with cotton wound around it. 'My mother wanted to give you a present. She said that when he came I should give this ring to his daughter. Today I have fulfilled my promise to her, just as Hai Yisheng has fulfilled his promise to return.'

We stayed in Zhaojue for seventy-two hours. On leaving, we headed reluctantly to the bus stop and waited for the bus to take us back down to Xichang. Suddenly, I found myself confronted by an exceptionally tall Nosu man, his arms and cloak spreadeagled. 'I have travelled three days,' he said. 'As soon as I heard you had come, I came.' Three days! To see me! I'm afraid I did not remember him. Perhaps he had been to the clinic. Perhaps he had come to our Christmas celebrations.

'Your hair was black;' he continued, 'now it is white. You taught me about Jesus.' He threw back his head and sang with gusto in Nosu, 'Jesus loves me, this I know...' Musically it was not easy on the ears. But it definitely came from the heart.

Our trip yielded more than we could ever have hoped possible. We had met so many old acquaintances, both Chinese and Nosu, amongst them Meihua, Baodan, Shan and Aji. There was great blessing in finding them still sure in their faith. I had prayed with them and been heartened as we shared Bible passages together. I had seen a desire to communicate their faith to sons, daughters and to grandchildren; they were passing on to succeeding generations the message of the gospel they first heard through the pages of a simple reading aid. But we were aware that no Nosu church existed in Daliangshan.

'You are welcome to come again,' the Nosu hospital administrator had said as we left Zhaojue. We were to take her at her word. In early 1991 Jim rang me again. 'Fancy going back to China?' he said...

Chapter 26

'On behalf of the Nosu people, I say thank you to you and welcome you back.'

NOSU DOCTOR, 1991

Our plans were set for mid-June. Jim and I would be accompanied again by Joy, along with her teenage daughter, Rachel. Jim was now close to eighty but had not lost his love for writing nor for the work of the China Inland Mission. In his retirement he had completed a marathon of research and compiled a comprehensive history of James Hudson Taylor in seven hefty volumes[47]. I was a mere seventy-four-year-old and still parish visitor at St Mary's.

Jim had obtained more medical equipment to take with him. Unfamiliar with the field of laparoscopic surgery, he wanted someone to demonstrate the technique to him. A mutual friend put him in contact with Arthur Wyatt, a consultant general surgeon in London. Arthur was no stranger to China. Nor was he unfamiliar with the Broomhall family. Arthur's father had served alongside Jim's father in a mission hospital in Taiyuan[48] for a number of years in the 1920s. As a young medical student himself, Arthur had read Jim's accounts of the Nosu. Now he and his wife, Margaret, were willing to join us. The three other members of our group were to meet us in Kunming: Dr Jim Taylor, a relative of the Broomhall family and great-grandson of James Hudson Taylor, his wife and son.

Unexpectedly, Jim's health failed. In March he had a major stroke, losing his speech and suffering paralysis down his right side. There was, however, no diminishing of his passion for the Nosu. He made a remarkable recovery, learning to walk again in three months and slowly regaining his speech. It is difficult to know what would have stopped him going on this trip! This was doubtless to be his final opportunity and he had no intention of missing it. He would go to China, even if he needed to travel in a wheelchair.

Difficult as that decision must have been for his family, the tour proved more telling than our first tentative return in 1988. Jim was determined to highlight the needs of the Nosu and see our work continue. His presence initiated a succession of events which I believe would not have otherwise occurred and which have fundamentally shaped the later years of my own life.

If our first return to Xichang had been marked by trepidation as to how we might be received, our second was characterised by unanticipated appreciation. Our train carried us through the night, bringing us to our destination at 6.30 in the morning. A contingent of hospital staff were crowded onto the platform beneath a banner welcoming Hai Yisheng - the founder of medical work in Daliangshan. Our visit was to be marked by a surfeit of splendid banquets, official photographs, the presentations of awards and entertainment performed by troupes of graceful Nosu dancers keeping step with boisterous orchestras.

We were driven to Zhaojue in a minibus provided by the hospital, our paper permits provided without a problem. There was an agreeable irony in our welcome by the officials, who came a mile out from the town to greet us. Forty years before, our Christian friends, with no thought of the consequences to themselves, had walked twice the distance to say their goodbyes to us. While we were pleased that the facilities at the hotel had improved, we were not delighted to discover that the toilets remained down the street!

In the early evening we gathered on the perimeter of a huge bonfire, lit in our honour in the extensive grounds of the hospital. We were entertained by dancers: a flurry of young Nosu women dressed in vibrant felt costumes. Their tunics were adorned with bands of ornate embroidery threaded around their shoulders and prominent Chinese-style buttons, which had the appearance of large daisies. Some wore high-rimmed headdresses, others mob-caps, all elaborately decorated with ribbons of fine needlework. Their ankle-length black cotton skirts were hemmed from the knee in wide concentric circlets, combinations of heavily pleated vivid blue, green, pink, red and yellow, generating extravagant swirls of material with the slightest turn of their bodies.

'Qing... please'

We looked at each other around the table. It was our turn to perform. We contributed to a substantial lowering of the cultural tone with a decision to invite our hosts to share in a round of 'Ring-a-Ring-o'-Roses'. A six-year-old Nosu girl kindly adopted me, concerned that no damage was done when it came to 'all fall down'. We remained 'lowbrow' with a performance of 'Old MacDonald Had a Farm', before we finally redeemed ourselves with a rendition in parts of Psalm 23.

Jim's time in Zhaojue was curtailed. The lack of adequate amenities and the rigours of travel, combined with the inconvenience of his wheelchair, took a debilitating toll on his capacity to cope. He reluctantly returned to Xichang with the Wyatts and Taylors after just one night. Joy, Rachel and I were invited to inspect the 'new' clinic at Zhuhe. The compound, a string of single-storey, yellowing brick outhouses with wooden-framed windows and doors under grey-tiled roofs, was rudimentary but a substantial improvement on the old tavern dispensary we had owned.

The daughter-in-law of the old local chief Vuda, whose marriage I had witnessed amidst distressing scenes in 1949, was living close by. Now a grandmother, she had aged into a short, sturdy woman, her distinctive oval face beleaguered with lines and prominent crow's feet. Her black hair lay hidden beneath the lengthy bindings of an impressively large blue turban. We were invited into her home, a building with an inadequate number of small windows, where we sat in the dark and were entertained by Vuda's grandson. The large number in our party, the staff from the clinic and ourselves, and the dictates of etiquette demanded that another hapless pig was sacrificed. We dined on generous chunks of pork, rice and vegetable soup. Orange juice was substituted for wine out of deference to us.

When Joy, Rachel and I returned to Xichang there was a request to teach English to secondary school English teachers. There seemed little reason to refuse. As we concluded a two-hour lesson, a group gathered around me wanting to know why and how I came to China. I needed little encouragement to share my story. This openness and interest in Christianity was something we had not experienced before. In 1988, apart from contact with our friends from the past, there had been a general reticence to speak with us. Now Chinese and Nosu came to find us of their own volition to hear our story and ask us questions about our faith.

One Nosu doctor deliberately searched us out in our hotel, evening after evening. A well-dressed, professional young man, he had a strong desire to understand the message of the Bible. We sat together in the comfort of the hotel's easy chairs and I pointed out passages to him.

'I would like to have a Bible,' he said.

I had to refuse his request. I didn't have a Chinese Bible to give him. God, however, has a staggering sense of timing. Two days later I met a British teacher and her husband on the streets of Xichang, a 'coincidence' in itself, given the few foreigners likely to visit the town. More amazingly, she was a former colleague, having served with OMF International in Taiwan before her marriage. 'Do you have a Chinese Bible with you?' I asked hopefully, explaining the situation.

She smiled, 'I'll get you a copy.'

One final ceremony at the hospital in honour of Jim brought us to the end of our stay. It was fitting that Jim's vital contribution was at last recognised and with it, a tacit acknowledgment of the work of our Mission. We were escorted to the railway station and into the relative luxury of a 'soft seat' carriage, before the train pulled away, taking us back to Kunming on the first stage of our journey home.

The combination of Jim's vision, Arthur Wyatt's expertise, which he shared in operations at the hospital in Xichang, Dr. Jim Taylor's knowledge of China and a warm welcome from the hospitals visited in Xichang and Zhaojue were key elements in a renewed concern for medical work in Daliangshan. Negotiations with the Sichuan Public Health authorities commenced and were completed. Contracts were drawn up. A new organisation, Medical Services International[49], would work with the approval and valuable support of government authorities to bring foreign medical expertise into the area.

The new NGO would be officially registered in Sichuan Province and composed of a group of Christian medics. 'Coming in the Spirit of Christ', as a senior Beijing consultant expressed it, the new organisation would share the same values as Jim, Janet, Ruth and myself in care for local communities. As well as hospital-based medicine, a community health programme, in keeping with Jim Broomhall's compassion for the poor and meeting the needs of the Nosu people in particular, would be a priority.

'Jim?' In May 1994 David Ellis, OMF UK national director,

stood by Jim's hospital bedside. Jim had been admitted with acute anaemia; leukaemia, the true nature of his illness, had gone undiagnosed. In the hospital he had picked up a chest infection. David had received a message from Hong Kong and driven directly to the hospital to speak to him. 'A memorandum of understanding will be signed in June with the Sichuan Provincial Public Health Bureau and the West China University of Medical Science. It's all been agreed. A long-term commitment to medical work in Chengdu and Daliangshan. Jim Taylor wanted you to know. They're going to continue your work amongst the Nosu.'

There was an awareness of light filling Jim's eyes and expression, transcending his immediate and temporal circumstances, an impression of joy in a final, profound fulfilment that ran deeper than the mere imparting of good news. Just a few hours later Jim Broomhall died, his vision complete.

The formation of Medical Services International was not only significant for the subsequent access of medical professionals to the region. The organisation was soon asked to provide expertise in other disciplines. A requirement for English teachers had resulted from an almost universal aspiration across China to learn English. Short-term programmes lasting just a few weeks could be arranged if MSI would recruit teachers from overseas. By 1993 I had finished my work in Reigate and moved to a bungalow apartment in Kent, living in a complex that catered for retired CIM missionaries. I was keen to return to China. In 1996 I applied to join an international team on a month's English-teaching programme based at the

Public Health School in Xichang. On acceptance I put on the unfamiliar hat of English teacher and booked my tickets. At seventy-nine I was going to be by far the oldest member of a team of three.

My abiding memories are of enduring relationships built with my students, young medics very eager to learn English, of a bullfight at which the bulls, to my relief, refused to fight, of rides on the back of the class monitor's motorbike. And of a student's parting words as we said our formal goodbyes. 'We have sensed love in our classroom. I think it must be because they are Christians.'

Heartened by the experience, I came back determined I would go again. But then my eyesight perceptibly deteriorated and began to fail.

Chapter 27

'More things are wrought by prayer than this world
dreams of.'

ALFRED, LORD TENNYSON

The sudden shadowing of vision, an inability to focus on
small objects, straight-edged surfaces appearing to arch,
was as unexpected as it was disturbing.

'You are suffering with neovascular macular
degeneration. Fluid collects behind the centre of the
retina,' the consultant ophthalmologist informed me. I
waited for his solution. 'There is no cure, I'm afraid. It is a
condition associated with age. As time goes on you may
suffer loss of all but peripheral sight.'

I had never contemplated a serious deterioration in my
sight. Apart from occasional dreadful bouts of dengue
fever and a major operation in Singapore, I had always
been fit and well. Now I was facing a life I had not

envisaged at all. My sight deteriorated rapidly. I could no longer read my regular-print Bible. I could not decipher my own handwriting. Labels in the supermarket defied intelligence. I had to resort to the use of magna-print, magnifying glasses and strong light from angle-poise lamps. I was registered with the local authorities as 'partially sighted'. It was the willing kindness of others, whose faces I failed to recognise, that provided ways for me to function as normal.

Dependence was not a way of life to which I readily acquiesced. My teenage experiences and thirty-eight years on the mission field had forged a confident strength in God, but I was not well prepared for this increasing reliance on friends. 'Why my eyes?' I questioned God time after time. 'If only it had been another part of my body...' I knew people were praying for my healing. But the truth of the matter was that I had become problem-centred rather than Christ-centred. And this was what distressed me most of all.

For two months I struggled with my predicament. I felt like a dying plant – dry, brittle leaves on a withered stem, bearing no flowers. I was no longer bringing joy to God. I wanted to be touched by him. God was not far away. I travelled to Devon to a conference and as we sang in worship I felt him reach out to me.

Like a tree planted by the stream
We've no need to run dry
Held firm and rooted in your love
You will supply the water of life
And all that we need is found in you, Jesus[50].

Suddenly the blessing of God flowed strongly in me. I experienced an overwhelming saturation in his love. I was unreservedly released from my struggle into the relationship I so desired.

There was no healing. But some slight improvement was a genuine gain. In the supermarket I could at least recognise the basic differences between packets holding soapflakes and those containing cornflakes. The settings on my oven came vaguely back into view. The greater joy, however, was my inner healing. I was no longer anxious over the, now peripheral, self-absorbed issue of my illness. I was centred on Jesus. I began to accept that God's plans were simply to praise him in the dusk as I had always praised him at the dawn.

One of my residual pleasures was to babysit the pastor's son, Daniel. 'It's time for our little talk with Jesus,' I reminded Daniel as I tucked him into bed one Sunday evening early in 1999. He put his hands together and screwed his face up in concentration.

'Lord Jesus!' he declared loudly. 'Please bring Auntie Joan's eyes back to normal... Amen.'

I was never sure where Daniel found these words from, but they remained with me. Within a few weeks I began to notice the beginning of recovery of lost sight. The reversal of my condition was slow but the gradual improvements not insignificant. In time I discarded my large-print copy of the Psalms and New Testament. A magnifying glass and good light were again sufficient to help me with the script of ordinary books. I began to see more clearly what I was writing. Shopping, while still stressful, became steadily easier. In church I found the hymns on the overhead screen legible and I was able to read my regular-print Bible. A year after Daniel's prayer I was able to recognise people close at hand and interpret their expressions. The ability to thread a needle confirmed the enormous advances I had made. Within two years my sight had been almost fully restored.

Chapter 28

'And the end... will be to arrive where we started
And know the place for the first time
Through the unknown, unremembered gate...'

T. S. ELIOT

The direction of my life changed once more with the arrival of a neatly packaged digital clock and blank cassette tape from Hong Kong in February 2001. There was a letter. Members of MSI had expressed immense interest in hearing the story of my work with the China Inland Mission. They wanted to understand the heritage they had come into as they entered Xichang and Zhaojue to share their professional skills. Would I record something of God's faithfulness on the enclosed tape? The clock was to show their appreciation. I readily agreed to their request and replied that I was considering joining an English-teaching team to Zhaojue in the summer. I was

310 POINT ME TO THE SKIES

well, believed this could be God's purpose in my healing, had the support of the then MSI UK chairman, Ronald Clements, and was approaching eighty-five.

As I bring my story to an end I have returned from Zhaojue once again, my fifth summer there in six years. God has provided my finances through the kindness of friends. Each year I have taught English to enthusiastic classes of Chinese and Nosu children in a youth centre, run by MSI in partnership with the Chinese authorities, or at the local primary school. My colleagues have been from Britain, Canada, Hong Kong, Singapore and the USA. Some have been students or just starting out on their professions; others have been in mid-career or retired.

Zhaojue is no longer recognisable as the rather depressing village I visited in the late 1980s. Out of step with the more affluent areas of the south Sichuan valleys, development has arrived more slowly. Nevertheless, extensive building and rebuilding and the arrival of a relative wealth of products have brought a radical revision in both its facade and its reputation.

The old regimes of appalling poverty, the abuses of the Nosu caste system and the terrible intertribal warfare have, thankfully, been dispatched to history books. It is encouraging to see young Nosu men and women enrolling on vocational training courses, in agriculture, crafts, computing, construction and home-based skills. Jim Broomhall's desire to see community health and medical programmes initiated has been realised and gradually standards of living are improving.

But there remain vast spiritual needs. Surprisingly, the day of shamans is not over. Atheism did not provide a substitute. In 1951 we left no church of Nosu believers in Zhaojue, nor at Zhuhe. There were isolated Christians, but the possibilities for corporate worship and teaching receded for a time with the arrival of Communism. On our visit in 1991 we found a refreshing interest in Christianity but the revival touching many parts of China was still in its infancy. Ten years later the picture had changed again with the genesis of indigenous growth. There was news of three young male Nosu believers in one of the villages. I heard of one or two female Christians elsewhere. The following year I was privileged to meet some of these new believers.

It is not possible, nor wise, to speculate about the number of Nosu Christians in Daliangshan today. For me, it is sufficient to know that, just as the Chinese Church has grown rapidly, they can now be counted in their tens, not isolated ones and twos. In Xichang they are free to meet at the official church, but in Zhaojue there is not yet a church building. They are beginning to grapple with lifestyle issues raised by following Jesus, emerging from a society with a dark history of immorality, alcohol and drug abuse. They are trying to marry their culture with Christian concepts and create new expressions of worship. They lack resources and training. But, after the prayers of many for so long, they do exist and their numbers are growing.

I have been permitted to see the end from our beginning, the harvest for which Jim, Janet, Ruth, Zhao and Hong laboured alongside Chang, Ming, Tang, Floyd and others. It has been my privilege to be a sower and a reaper across seven decades. I served in the last heartbreaking years of missionary endeavour in China and I have witnessed the great growth of the Chinese Church.

Now I have been blessed to see God nurturing the tender shoots of a Nosu Church in the Great Cold Mountains.

'Will you go to Zhaojue next year?' It is a regular question wherever I talk about my experiences of God. In the mountains of life we walk by faith not by sight, advancing warily around each bend in the path, yet persevering. Often unsure what lies beyond, but always ascending. I have walked God's paths for my life and been grateful to climb to a summit, and glory in the great vista of peaks that point heavenward.

Yes, of course, I will go. For as long as God has unfinished business for me and the Nosu of Daliangshan.

Notes

Chapter 1
1 Xikang Province formed 1939 – 1955, this region now part of Sichuan Province, SW China
2 Qing Dynasty 1644 – 1911
3 George F. Root 1820-1895
4 Jeremiah E. Rankin 1828 – 1904

Chapter 2
5 John 14:1-3 KJV

Chapter 3
6 Matthew 4:21, 22 King James Version (KJV)
7 1 Timothy 5:22 KJV

Chapter 4
8 Young Women's Christian Association
9 Jiangxi Province
10 Hubei Province
11 Formally Sichuan Province, now Chongqing Municipality

Chapter 5
12 Modern Mandarin has four, not five, distinct tones, with a 'neutral' tone which has no inflection.
13 *Vergeltungswaffe* - V1 and V2 missiles
14 Women's Auxiliary Air Force
15 Mumbai
16 KJV
17 Francis Rous 1579-1659

Chapter 6
18 Diary entries adapted from Joan Wales' travel diary, 1945
19 Cantonese and Mandarin used the same script
20 Now the Chattrapati Shivaji Terminus
21 Kolkata
22 Dorothy's letter home records her apparel for this journey – 'one camiknicks, two lightweight vests, three woollen vests, one lightweight knickers, three winter knicks, one petticoat, one costume (skirt and jacket), one other skirt, two woollen jackets, one dress (with pockets for oddments), one suede jacket, one winter coat, one suspender belt, one pair thick stockings, one hat, one topee'. In addition she carried a 'big rug with a blanket sewn on and big mackintosh, handbag, umbrella and hand luggage bag'.
23 Myanmar

Chapter 7
24 Marshall Broomhall CIM 1933
25 1 Peter 1:13 KJV
26 Isaiah 25:8 KJV
27 Chinese dollar
28 Isaiah 25:8,9 KJV, adapted from 1 Corinthians 15:54
29 William Walsham How 1823 – 1897
30 Martin Luther 1483 – 1546, translated Frederick Henry Hodge 1852
31 Matthew 26:8 KJV

Chapter 9
32 *Strong Tower*, CIM 1947
33 13 June 1947
34 23 June 1947
Chapter 10
35 1 *jin* is equivalent to 0.5 kilogrammes

Chapter 11
36 Hai Yisheng translates to 'Dr Hai'; Jim's full Chinese name was Hai Hengbo.

Chapter 12
37 Anna Bartlett Warner 1859

Chapter 15
38 Janet
39 Ruth

Chapter 18
40 Acts 3:6 KJV

Chapter 19
41 Mary D. James 1871
42 Joshua 1:9 KJV
43 'eight-one' – 1 August, reference to the Nanchang Uprising 1927 and designated origin of People's Liberation Army

Chapter 21
44 Romans 10:9 KJV

Chapter 23
45 Part of Wuhan, Hubei Province

Chapter 24
46 *Strong Man's Prey*, Jim Broomhill, CIM 1953

Chapter 26
47 *China's Open Century: The History of the China Inland Mission* Volumes 1-7, Jim Broomhill, OMF 1981 – 1989
48 Shanxi Province
49 Now MSI Professional Services International, a name change in response to the government's request to expand services to cover education, community development and youth work, in addition to providing medical services.

Chapter 27
50 Philip Lawton Johnston, I Q Music/Cloud Music, (c) 2001, used by permission

Source of Chapter Quotations

Chapter 1 Nosu chief quoted by A. James Broomhall in 'Strong Man's Prey', China Inland Mission, 1953

Chapter 2 'Housewife' by Anne Sexton, All My Pretty Ones, Houghton Mifflin,1962

Chapter 3 George Wales quoted by Joan Wales.

Chapter 4 Radio broadcast by Neville Chamberlain, 1938

Chapter 5 'Midnight's Children' by Salman Rushdie, Jonathan Cape, 1981

Chapter 6 Quote and quotes in chapter adapted from Joan Wales' travel diary, 1945

Chapter 7 'Beryl' by H. W. Oldham, China Inland Mission, 1946

Chapter 8 Quoted by Joan Wales, personal communication

Chapter 9 Letter written by A. James Broomhall, January 1948

Chapter 10 'The Explorer' by Rudyard Kipling, 1898

Chapter 11 'A Bridge for Passing' by Pearl Buck, Methuen and Co Ltd, 1961

Chapter 12 'Gold by Moonlight' by Amy Carmichael, Society for Promoting Christian Knowledge, 1935

Chapter 13 'China's Millions', North American edition, Sept 1948, article by Floyd Larsen, China Inland Mission

Chapter 14 'Woman' by Fu Xuan, c. 3rd century AD, quoted in 'The Little Book of Chinese Proverbs', compiled by Jonathan Clements, Parragon, 1999

Chapter 15 'China's Millions' March/April 1949, article by A. James Broomhall, China Inland Mission

Chapter 16 'China's Millions' Sept/Oct 1944, quoted by A. James Broomhall, China Inland Mission

Chapter 17 'Baptist Times' 1946, quoted by Phyllis Thompson, 'Mister Leprosy' Hodder and Stoughton, 1980

Chapter 18 'Emerging from Primitivity – travels in the Liangshan Mountains' by Zhong Xiu, translated by Lily Wu, China Spotlight Series, New World Press, 1984)

Chapter 19 'China's Millions' Jan/Feb 1949, article by Frank Houghton, China Inland Mission

Chapter 20 Letter written by A. James Broomhall, 1950, quoted by Ralph Covell, 'Mission Impossible – The Unreached Nosu on China's Frontier' Hope Publishing House, 1990

Chapter 21 'Parting from Su Wu' by Li Ling (c. 81BC), translated by Arthur Waley, 'Chinese Poems', George Allen and Unwin 1946

Chapter 22 'Gold by Moonlight' by Amy Carmichael, Society for Promoting Christian Knowledge, 1935

Chapter 23 China Inland Mission policy document 1948, quoted by Phyllis Thompson in 'Reluctant Exodus', Hodder and Stoughton, 1979

Chapter 24 'A visit to the Yis in the Great Liangshan Mountains' by Zeng Zhaolun, 1945, quoted by Zhong Xiu in 'Emerging from Primitivity – travels in the Liangshan Mountains', translated by Lily Wu, China Spotlight Series, New World Press, 1984

Chapter 25 Nosu man quoted by Joan Wales, personal communication

Chapter 26 Letter written by Nosu doctor, 1991

Chapter 27 'Idylls of the King –The Passing of Arthur' by Alfred, Lord Tennyson, 1885

Chapter 28 'Four Quartets, no.4 – Little Gidding' by T.S. Eliot, 1944

Other quotations

'Abide with me' by Henry Francis Lyte, 1847

Chapter 1

'Joyful, Joyful will the meeting be' by George F. Root, 1870

'God be with you till we meet again' by Jeremiah Rankin, 1882

Chapter 5

'The Lord's my Shepherd' by Francis Rous, Scottish Psalter, 1650 (also quoted in Chapter 7)

Chapter 27

'Jesus Provider' by Philip Lawson Johnston, I Q Music/Cloud Music 2001. Used by permission

Glossary

Alu Nosu clan occupying territory to north of Zhuhe

Apple-pie bed Arrangement of bed sheets where lower sheet is folded back towards head of bed preventing legs from being extended to bottom of bed

Asu Nosu clan occupying territory to south of Zhaojue

Ba'chie Nosu clan occupying territory around Zhaojue

Cambridge Seven A group of seven young men who joined the China Inland Mission and sailed to China in 1885, all coming from prominent backgrounds in sport, business and the army - Montagu Beaucamp, William Cassels, Dixon Hoste, Arthur Polhill-Turner, Cecil Polhill-Turner, Charles T. Studd and Stanley Smith. All, apart from Hoste, were graduates from Cambridge University; Hoste's brother was at Cambridge.

Communist China's Communist Party was officially founded in 1921. A civil war was waged in the 1930s and 1940s against the ruling Nationalist government from which the Communist forces, under the leadership of Mao Zedong, emerged victorious. The People's Republic of China was established in Beijing on 1 October 1949. The Nationalist government surrendered control of the Chinese mainland shortly afterwards.

Companion-helper Woman paid to live with and provide help to another woman

Coolie Native labourer, often used for carrying baggage

Daliangshan Mountainous region of Sichuan Province, southwest China, home to a number of Nosu clans. In the text also referred to as the 'Great Cold Mountains' and 'Nosuland'. 'Daliangshan' literally means 'big cool mountains'.

DDT bomb White chlorinated hydrocarbon, used as an insecticide

Dragoman Guide or interpreter

Great Cold Mountains See Daliangshan

Han The majority ethnic group in China are the Han Chinese, making up around 92% of the population. China recognises fifty-five Minority Peoples of which the Nosu (Yi) are one group

Hma Nosu clan occupying territory around Zhuhe and to north and west of Zhaojue

Jiaoshi Mandarin for 'teacher' or 'missionary'

Jin Chinese weight; one jin weighs five hundred grams

Kannada Language spoken mainly in the state of

Karnataka, in southwest India

Lisu Minority People in southwest China

M'po Nosu clan occupying territory to northeast of Zhuhe

Mo'm Apu 'God of Heaven' – deity of the Nosu

Nationalist In 1911 when the Qing Dynasty was overthrown, China became a republic. Sun Yat-sen established the National People's Party in 1912, which, after a prolonged period of upheaval, secured control of a 'unified' China under Chiang Kaishek in 1928. The Nationalist forces had to contend with Japanese occupation of large parts of China in the 1930s and 1940s as well as Chinese Communist offences. Japan withdrew from China after the Second World War. The Nationalist forces lost the conflict against the Communist armies and the National People's Party retreated to Taiwan and established a government on the island.

Nosu Name of Minority People in Southwest China, officially called Yi; identified as Tibeto-Burman. The tribes in Daliangshan may have their origin in the Zhou Dynasty, 1122-221 BC. There is reference to a Nosu tribe in the Yuan Dynasty (1279-1368 AD) and records of eleven tribes in the Ming Dynasty (1368-1644 AD). The Qing Dynasty (1644-1911) suppressed the independent Nosu Tribes. After 1727 some Nosu tribes withdrew to the Daliangshan region and established themselves as an independent kingdom there. Other tribes accepted Qing rule but maintained their identity as an ethnic group.

Nosuland See Daliangshan

People's Liberation Army (PLA) Chinese Communist armed forces; formed officially on 1 August 1927

People's Republic of China Formed in 1949 under Communist rule

Public Security Bureau (PSB) Government agency dealing with policing, security and social order and responsible for the travel affairs and residency issues of foreigners

Qing Dynasty China's last dynasty, 1644-1911; founded by Manchu tribesmen

Retainer Servant

Shangdi Mandarin term for God

Yari Nosu term for foreigner

Yi Official name for Nosu people group

Zong Jiao Zi You Mandarin phrase meaning 'religious freedom'

Name List

Name	Description	First chapter mentioned
Agu	Nosu chief, Ba'chie clan	1
Aji	Nosu teenager in Zhaojue	1
Aldis William H.	CIM Home Director	5
Baodan	Chinese teenager in Zhaojue, sister of Baoli	1
Baoli	Chinese teenager in Zhaojue, sister of Baodan	1
Belinda	Jim Broomhall's mule	1
Blackie	Ruth Dix's mule	1
Bond Hilda	CIM women's training warden	3
Broomhall Jan	Daughter of Jim and Janet Broomhall	1
Broomhall Janet	CIM/OMF missionary; member of Nosu team, wife of Jim	1
Broomhall Jim	CIM/OMF missionary; leader of Nosu team, husband of Janet	1
Broomhall Joy	Daughter of Jim and Janet Broomhall	1
Broomhall Margie	Daughter of Jim and Janet Broomhall	1
Broomhall Mrs	Mother of Jim Broomhall	3
Broomhall Pauline	Daughter of Jim and Janet Broomhall	1
Chang	Nosu Christian from Yunnan Province; member of Nosu team	17
Churchill Janet	Maiden name of Janet Broomhall	4
Cork Edith	CIM/OMF missionary	5
Di Lude	Ruth Dix's Chinese name	15
Dix Ruth	CIM/OMF missionary; member of Nosu team	1
Ellis David	OMF UK National Director	26
Feng	Chinese teenager in Zhaojue	14
Hai Hengbo	Jim Broomhall's Chinese name	25
Hai Yisheng	'Dr Hai' - Jim Broomhall	9
Harman Gordon	CIM missionary	5
Harris Annette (Annetta)	CIM/OMF missionary	4
Hong	Chinese businessman; member of Nosu team	10

Jiha	Nosu leprosy patient	17
Jinfeng	Nosu teenager in Zhaojue, married	14
Jones Dorothy	CIM/OMF missionary	5
Lanlan	Nosu teenager in Zhaojue	16
Larsen Floyd	American CIM missionary; member of Nosu team	9
Lili	Daughter of Qiang family in Zhaojue	20
Ling	Nosu prince	18
Lo	Chinese Christian from Chongqing; briefly member of Nosu team	18
Lovegren Levi	American missionary, Conservative Baptist Foreign Mission Society; Major in American Army	7
Madge Ernest	British missionary in Xichang with the Border Service Department of Church of Christ in China	10
Mao Comrade	Head of Communist delegation to liberate Zhaojue	18
Martin family	Joan's employers in Greystones, Ireland; children Neville, Beryl and Heather	3
Meihua	Chinese teenager in Zhaojue	14
Milner Morris Henry	CIM Treasurer, General Director of Fegans Homes	5
Ming	Nosu Christian from Guizhou Province; member of Nosu team	10
Moody Miss	CIM women's training assistant, Aberdeen Park, London	3
Mother Hu	Mother of Songmei and Songan in Zhaojue	18
Polhill May	CIM missionary	5
Qi Furen	Janet Broomhall's Chinese name	15
Qiang Mr	Chinese telegraphist, Zhaojue	9
Qiang Mrs	Chinese wife of telegraphist, Zhaojue	1
Shan	Chinese teenager in Zhaojue, married	16
Songan	Songmei's elder sister, married	14
Songmei	Chinese teenager in Zhaojue	14
Sykes Margery	CIM/OMF missionary	7
Tang	Chinese male nurse; member of Nosu team	10

Vuda	Nosu chief, Hma clan	9
Vuli	Nosu chief, Ba'chie clan	9
Wales Bertha	Joan's Mother, first wife of George Wales	2
Wales Betty (Nelly Watkins)	Second wife of George Wales	2
Wales George	Joan's Father	2
Wales Isabel	Third wife of George Wales	3
Wales Veronica	Joan's stepsister, daughter of Isabel Wales	3
Wang Comrade	Communist official in Zhaojue	1
Wang Mrs	Daughter of innkeeper in Zhaojue	25
Warren Emma	CIM missionary	5
Watkins Nelly (Betty Wales)	Companion-helper for Joan's mother, second wife of George Wales	2
Wei Jiaoshi	'Teacher Wei' - Joan	1
Wei Zhu'an	Joan's Chinese name	7
Weston Beryl	CIM missionary	5
Yang Comrade	Communist official in Ya'an	23
Yang Mrs	Chinese helper; employed by Nosu team in Xichang and Zhaojue	1
Yingying	Chinese teenager in Zhaojue	19
Yu	Nosu Christian from Yunnan Province; member of Nosu team	17
Zhao	Nosu interpreter; member of Nosu team	1
Zitu	Nosu leprosy patient; employed by Nosu team in Zhaojue	1